英语专业实用翻译教材系列

廖益清　主编

English-Chinese Sight Interpreting

英汉视译

廖益清　高平　主编

中山大学出版社
SUN YAT-SEN UNIVERSITY PRESS
· 广州 ·

版权所有　翻印必究

图书在版编目（CIP）数据

英汉视译/廖益清，高平主编. —广州：中山大学出版社，2019.9
（英语专业实用翻译教材系列/廖益清主编）
ISBN 978-7-306-06673-2

Ⅰ.①英…　Ⅱ.①廖…②高…　Ⅲ.①英语—翻译—高等学校—教材　Ⅳ.①H315.9

中国版本图书馆 CIP 数据核字（2019）第 162781 号

Yinghan Shiyi

| 出 版 人：王天琪
| 策划编辑：熊锡源
| 责任编辑：熊锡源
| 封面设计：林绵华
| 责任校对：潘惠虹
| 责任技编：何雅涛
| 出版发行：中山大学出版社
| 电　　话：编辑部 020-84110771，84110283，84111997，84110779
|　　　　　发行部 020-84111998，84111981，84111160
| 地　　址：广州市新港西路 135 号
| 邮　　编：510275　传　真：020-84036565
| 网　　址：http://www.zsup.com.cn　E-mail：zdcbs@mail.sysu.edu.cn
| 印 刷 者：广州一龙印刷有限公司
| 规　　格：787mm×1092mm　1/16　16.25 印张　342 千字
| 版次印次：2019 年 9 月第 1 版　2019 年 9 月第 1 次印刷
| 定　　价：45.00 元

如发现本书因印装质量影响阅读，请与出版社发行部联系调换

编写委员会

主　编：廖益清　高　平
副主编：朱雪娇　陈悦笛　沈美辰
参　编：桂　灵　刘家妠　鲁凯伦　罗彩虹　陈秋丽
　　　　梁昊文　黄越悦　姚　莹　肖岚心　龙　娟
　　　　周雪清

编写说明

随着中国经济持续、快速、健康的发展，中国与世界各国在各个领域的交流也更加密切，对口译的需求也越来越大。对于口译学习者而言，好的口译练习素材是提高口译能力的第一步。《英汉视译》借鉴了同类教材的优点，将视译理论与实践相结合，突出了视译素材的真实性、时代性的特点，旨在为广大口译学习者提供最好的模拟实战体验。

教材特点

1. 科学性。教材吸收了视译最新理论研究成果，以深入浅出的方式讲解理论知识，并将理论与典型材料相结合，具有很强针对性。题材多样，均为真实同传场景中的常见主题。

2. 真实性。当前市面上的英汉视译教材所使用的材料基本上都是经过修改和重新编排的，本教材则是编者在同传实战中的原版口译材料，讲话中会出现口误、模糊、停顿等现象，实操性更强，更能锻炼学生临场应变能力，让学生在使用教材时有身临其境之感。

3. 口音多样化。所使用的音频为同传现场的演讲录音，很多讲者发音并不标准，会有各种英语口音，视译材料的真实感和实操性更强。

4. 时代性。所使用的实战材料均来自近年的同传实战，材料紧跟时代，如虚拟现实和招聘自动化都是当前热门话题，教材实用性较强。

章节介绍

本书共3个部分、12个单元。第一部分为视译简介，共1个单元，包括视译简介、实战练习一和实战练习二。第二部分为视译技巧，共5个单元，每单元都包括视译技巧、实战练习一和实战练习二。第三部分为视译实战，共6个单元，每单元都包括实战练习一和实战练习二。所有的实战练习均为英译中，每篇演讲都由演讲背景、预习词汇、演讲文本三个部分组成。本书练习材料的主题涉及环境保护、文化教育、旅游观光、人力资源、行业介绍、反腐倡廉、会议展览、商事仲裁、时尚潮流、绿色建筑、招商引资和虚拟现实。值得一提的是，本书以段落形式将演讲原文和译文对应起来，方便口译学习者在视译练习之后进行参考。各章节简介如下：

第一单元是视译概论。实战练习一为联合国副秘书长、小岛屿发展中国家第三次国际大会秘书长在"可持续城市及可持续城镇化高级研讨会"上的致辞。实战练习二为荷兰经济事务部能源转型委员会主席在"首届深圳国际低碳城论坛"上的

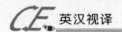

致辞。

第二单元介绍了视译单位。实战练习一为必益教育英国办公室总监在"2017英国伊顿公学前招生官访华教育论坛"上发表的演讲。实战练习二为伊顿公学的前招生官在该论坛上揭秘招生"潜规则"的演讲。

第三单元介绍了视译单位衔接。实战练习一为西澳大利亚黄金内陆区代表在"西澳大利亚州旅游局中国旅游洽谈会"上发表的演讲。实战练习二为来自珀斯铸币厂的代表在该洽谈会上发表的演讲。

第四单元介绍了句子成分转换的技巧。实战练习一为未来人才研究机构的创始人兼主席在"中国（珠海）国际人力资源科技博览会"的研讨会上致辞的第一部分内容。实战练习二为其在该研讨会上致辞的第二部分内容。

第五单元介绍了从句的视译。实战练习一为全球前四大市场研究公司之一捷孚凯公司代表在"广交会英国国际市场论坛"上发表的主旨演讲。实战练习二为国际锰协 IMnI 市场分析师在"电解产品市场高峰论坛"上发表的主旨演讲。

第六单元介绍了长句视译的技巧。实战练习一为英国《2010反腐败法案》立法者在"大成（深圳）法学名家大讲坛暨蓝海法律沙龙"上演讲的第一部分内容。实战练习二为其在该沙龙上演讲的第二部分内容。

在第七单元中，实战练习一为国际大会及会议协会代表在"全球会展（广州）圆桌会"上发表的主旨演讲。实战练习二为博闻集团代表在该圆桌会上发表的主旨演讲。

在第八单元中，实战练习一为英国皇家大律师 Stephen 在"国际商事仲裁交流会"上发表的主旨演讲。实战练习二为瑞士仲裁员协会荣誉主席在该交流会上发表的主旨演讲。

在第九单元中，实战练习一为在线时尚潮流预测公司 Fashion Snoops 的亚太区总监在"广交会设计潮流趋势研讨会"上有关"工匠之旅"主题的演讲。实战练习二为演讲嘉宾在该研讨会上有关"土著领地"主题的演讲。

在第十单元中，实战练习一为英国对华可持续城镇化事务特使在"2016年中英建筑论坛（珠海站）"上的致辞。实战练习二为比利时布鲁塞尔首都大区政府大臣乔茜乐女士 Cécile Jodogne 在"比利时中国绿色建筑经验分享会"上的致辞。

在第十一单元中，实战练习一为美国俄亥俄州托莱多市商务发展组织——区域发展合作组织代表在"创建世界一流高科技园区国际论坛"上发表的主旨演讲。实战练习二为比利时瓦隆大区代表在该论坛上发表的主旨演讲。

在第十二单元中，实战练习一为利物浦大学虚拟工程中心代表在"虚拟现实产业应用国际论坛"上发表的主旨演讲。实战练习二为德国艺术与媒体技术中心的教授在"虚拟现实产业应用国际论坛"上发表的主旨演讲。

使用对象

本书是本科英语专业或翻译专业学生的英汉视译教材，也可作为选修、辅修英语专业或翻译专业学生的英汉视译教材，同时可以作为有志于提高英汉口译实践能力爱好者的自学教材。

结语

本书在理论编写过程中，参考了英汉视译的最新研究成果，均已在教材最后标明出处。如有不当之处，敬请原谅。本书使用的实战练习均为国际会议材料，音频为会议现场录音，非常感谢演讲嘉宾和会议主办方的支持。

由于编写时间有限，本书难免存在纰漏，请各位读者和专家指正。

编　者

2018 年 8 月

目　　录

第一部分　视译简介 … 1
第一单元　环境保护 Environmental Protection … 2
- I. 视译简介 … 2
- II. 实战练习一 … 3
- III. 实战练习二 … 9

第二部分　视译技巧 … 17
第二单元　文化教育 Culture and Education … 18
- I. 视译单位 … 18
- II. 实战练习一 … 19
- III. 实战练习二 … 25

第三单元　观光旅游 Tourism … 46
- I. 视译单位衔接 … 46
- II. 实战练习一 … 47
- III. 实战练习二 … 53

第四单元　人力资源 Human Resources … 58
- I. 句子成分转换 … 58
- II. 实战练习一 … 59
- III. 实战练习二 … 76

第五单元　行业介绍 Introduction to Industries … 91
- I. 从句视译 … 91
- II. 实战练习一 … 92
- III. 实战练习二 … 113

第六单元　反腐倡廉 Anti-corruption … 126
- I. 长句视译 … 126
- II. 实战练习一 … 127
- III. 实战练习二 … 137

第三部分　视译实战 … 147
第七单元　会议展览 Meetings, Incentives, Conferences, Exhibitions and Events … 148

I. 实战练习一 ··· 148
　　　II. 实战练习二 ·· 154
第八单元　商事仲裁 Commercial Arbitration ······················· 165
　　　I. 实战练习一 ··· 165
　　　II. 实战练习二 ·· 173
第九单元　时尚潮流 Fashion Trend ······································ 186
　　　I. 实战练习一 ··· 186
　　　II. 实战练习二 ·· 192
第十单元　绿色建筑 Green Building ······································ 199
　　　I. 实战练习一 ··· 199
　　　II. 实战练习二 ·· 204
第十一单元　招商引资 Investment Promotion ······················· 209
　　　I. 实战练习一 ··· 209
　　　II. 实战练习二 ·· 219
第十二单元　虚拟现实 Virtual Reality ···································· 229
　　　I. 实战练习一 ··· 229
　　　II. 实战练习二 ·· 238

参考文献 ··· 250

第一部分　视译简介

第一单元　环境保护
Environmental Protection

I. 视译简介

1. 什么是视译？

王炎强（2011：5-6）认为翻译实践中有两种形式的视译，一种是广义的视译，另一种则是带稿同传。广义的视译指译员边看文字材料，边进行口译。这种视译比较灵活，译员可以按照自己的节奏将译文译出。另外一种视译就是带稿同传，即"同传译员拿着讲话人的发言稿或者其他相关文字，边听发言、边看原稿、边进行同声传译"（仲伟合、詹成，2009：71）。本教材中所做的视译练习均为有稿同传。

2. 视译语序

汉英两种语言在表达结构上存在较大差异，因此在两种语言之间进行转换时需要根据情况调整语序。在笔译中，译员有充分的时间通读原文、思考译文表达方式，译文语序调整频率较高。在同声传译中，译员一般滞后于发言人几个词或者半句话的差距发言，二者讲话几乎是同步进行。因此译员在做有稿同传时，也就是我们常说的视译时，需要跟上发言人讲话的节奏，尽可能缩短视译与发言人之间的时间差。而"要保持较快的翻译速度，关键还是语序"（秦亚青、何群，2009：1），即译员尽量根据发言人讲话的顺序产出译文。

【例1】The election/which has led to your being chosen to preside over this Assembly—/a very wise choice indeed/—is a tribute to your great country,/which has contributed greatly to the world peace./

译文1：贵国极大地促进了世界和平，因此这次选举您为本届大会的主席，是极为明智的抉择，是对贵国的敬意。

译文1对原文的语序做了调整，使译文更符合中文的语序和表达方式，这在笔译当中较为常见。但如果在视译中进行这样大的语序调整，译员需要等待发言人讲完整个句子才能开始翻译，这样会导致译者跟不上发言人语速，整体表达不流畅。

译文2：这次选举/您为本届大会的主席，/是极为明智的抉择，/是对贵国的敬意，/因为贵国极大地促进了世界和平。/

译文2则是先出来的信息先翻译，后出来的信息后翻译。这说明在不调整语序的情况下,也可以很顺畅地表达出译文,这样有助于译者节省时间。

【例2】There is a variety of ways/to invest in China. /You may establish a joint venture/with a Chinese partner, /or a company solely-funded by yourself, /in which you may manage your business/in whatever way you prefer/within the boundary of the Chinese laws, of course. /

译文1:在中国投资有多种方式。你可以与中方合伙人建立一家合资企业,也可以创建一家由自己经营的独资企业,你可以在中国法律许可的范围内自己决定管理模式。

与原文相比,译文1在语序上做了多处调整,如将原文的一处定语从句提前,将一处介词短语充当的状语提前,这样使译文更加符合中文表达方式。在同传视译中,译员如果做这样的调整,需要等后面的信息出来才能翻译,容易跟不上发言人语速。

译文2:有多种方式/在中国投资。/你可以建立一家合资企业/与中方合伙人合作,/也可以创建一家独资企业,/由自己经营,/管理模式自己决定,/这一切要在中国法律许可的范围内进行。/

由译文2可见,可以在保持原来语序基本不变的情况下,将译文通顺流畅地表达出来。虽然句子切割得较短,但这种表达在口译时是允许的,且充分保证了译员能够跟上发言人的语速。

II. 实战练习一

1. 演讲背景

2013年,在由联合国经济和社会事务部(经社部)与扬州市政府合作举办的"可持续城市及可持续城镇化高级研讨会"上,联合国副秘书长、小岛屿发展中国家第三次国际大会秘书长出席会议开幕式并致辞。他在致辞中谈到了全球城镇化发展的现状、问题、机遇和解决方案。最后还描述了他所憧憬的未来的可持续城市。

2. 预习词汇

Party Secretary of Yangzhou Municipal CPC Committee 扬州市委书记
minister 部长
ambassador 大使
The United Nations 联合国
Yangzhou Municipal People's Government 扬州市人民政府
High-Level Symposium on Sustainable Cities and Sustainable Urbanization 可持续城市及可持续城镇化高级研讨会

urban expansion 城市扩张
slum 贫民窟
energy consumption 能源消耗
carbon emission 碳排放
immune 免疫
prefecture-level city 地级市
traffic congestion 交通拥堵
gross national income 国民总收入
trajectory 轨道
stakeholder 利益相关方
thematic session 主题会议
silo 筒仓；孤岛
piecemeal 零零散散的
social cohesion 社会凝聚力
resilient 有弹性的；有复原力的
environmental regeneration 环境再生

3. 演讲文本

00:00—00:29

Your Excellency Mr. Xie Zhengyi, /Party Secretary of Yangzhou Municipal CPC Committee, /honorable Minister Kasenally, /Ambassador Irene Gener-Reichl, /Ambassador Esala Teleni, /ladies and gentlmen, /

谢正义先生阁下，/扬州市委书记，/尊敬的 Kasenally 部长，/Irene Gener-Reichl 大使，/Esala Teleni 大使，/女士们，先生们，/

00:29—01:34

On behalf of the United Nations, /I would like to join the Party Secretary/and the Yangzhou Municipal People's Government/in welcoming all of you/to this High-Level Symposium on Sustainable Cities and Sustainable Urbanization. /I would also like to extend the United Nations' deep appreciation/to the Yangzhou Municipal People's Government/and its people/for their warm welcome, /hospitality/and support in hosting this Symposium. /

我谨代表联合国，/同市委书记/和扬州市人民政府一道，/欢迎各位/参加可持续城市及可持续城镇化高级研讨会。/我想代表联合国感谢/扬州市政府/和扬州市民/的热烈欢迎/与盛情款待，/以及对本次研讨会的大力支持。/

第一单元 环境保护 Environmental Protection

01:34—02:46

This event is taking place at a time/when the world is witnessing an unprecedented movement of people/from rural areas to cities/and other urban centers. /Already, /more than half of the world's population/lives in cities. /By 2030, /the percentage will increase to 60%. /95% of urban expansion/will take place in the developing world. /In China, /350 million people are expected/to move into cities/in the coming two decades. /

这次会议举行之际/恰逢全球出现了前所未有的人口流动/从农村迁移到城市/以及其他城市中心。/现在,/世界上一半以上的人口/都居住在城市里。/到2030年,/这一比例将增至60%。/95%的城市扩张/将会发生在发展中国家。/在中国,/3.5亿人预计/将迁移到城市,/就在未来的20年里。/

02:46—04:13

Clearly, /such a massive change/will pose social, economic and environmental challenges, /while also creating tremendous opportunities. /Many experts predict/that the battle of the future sustainable development/will be won or lost in cities. /I share that assessment. /It will be critical/to achieve the Post-2015 Development Agenda/and the Sustainable Development Goals, /whether we will be able/to usher in a new era of cities/and a new track of sustainable urbanization. /However, /I would like to put the focus on now, /on today, /the present, /and not 20 or 30 years down the road. /

显然,/如此大规模的变化/将给社会、经济和环境带来挑战,/同时也创造了巨大的机遇。/许多专家预言/未来的可持续发展的战役/成败将取决于城市。/我同意这种看法。/关键是/实现2015年后发展议程/以及可持续发展目标,/也就是我们是否能够/迎来城市发展的新时代、/踏上可持续城镇化的新征程。/然而,/我想聚焦于现在,/今天,/当下,/而不是20年30年之后。/

04:13—05:14

It is our action today, /how to transform old cities, /tackle the social and environmental challenges they created/and how to build new cities, /investing in green, smart, low-carbon, and inclusive urbanization, /it is this action/that will determine the future sustainability/of our cities/and of our planet and society. /That is why this symposium is so timely. /

正是我们今天所采取的行动,/如何改造旧城市,/解决他们带来的社会和环境挑战,/以及如何建设新城市,/投资绿色、智能、低碳和包容的城镇化,/正是这些行动/决定了我们未来的可持续发展,/我们的城市/地球和社会的可持续发展。/这就是为什么本次研讨会的召开正当其时。/

05:14—06:39

Indeed, /cities are ringing the alarm bells/and we ignore the signals/at our own peril. /Worldwide, /828 million people live in slums today/and the number keeps rising. /The world's cities/occupy just 2% of the Earth's land, /but account for 60% to 80% of global energy consumption/and 75% of global carbon emissions. /Rapid urbanization is also putting pressure/on fresh water supplies, /city infrastructure, /social services, /including health/and education/and on jobs. /

事实上，/城市敲响了警钟，/我们忽视了这些信号/将自食其果。/世界上，/有8.28亿人生活在贫民窟里，/而且这个数字在不断上升。/全球的城市，/只占2%的土地，/却占60%至80%的全球能源消耗/以及75%的全球碳排放量。/快速的城镇化也带来了压力，/影响着淡水供应、/城市基础设施、/社会服务，/包括医疗、/教育/以及就业。/

06:39—08:04

China is not immune to this trend. /Take water, for example. /The prefecture-level cities and urban centers/take up 6.5% of China's land, /but they account for 85% of China's total water consumption. /What about transport? /Traffic congestion/has come to dominate the headlines about big cities, /along with alarming reports/on air quality/and the impact on health. /Indeed, /according to some estimate, /economic loss/due to the impact of air pollution/is close to 3% of China's gross national income. /

中国无法置身事外。/以水为例。/地级市和市中心区/占据了6.5%的中国土地，/却占85%的中国总用水量。/交通又如何呢？/交通拥堵/已经占据了大城市的头版头条。/还有令人震惊的报道，/讨论空气质量/及其对健康的影响。/确实，/有预测说，/经济损失，/由空气污染造成的损失/相当于将近3%的中国国民总收入。/

08:04—09:49

In the face of these challenges, /shall we return to the rural economies? /Clearly, /abandoning the cities is not the answer. /From the onset of industrialization, /urbanization has been on an upward trajectory. /For all the problems they create, /cities also create opportunities. /They are the centers of commerce/and engines of economic growth. /In most countries, /cities have become major sites/for education, /culture, /scientific and technological innovations, /enriching our social and cultural fabric. /Cities' role as powerful drivers of economic growth/extends beyond city boundaries. /They create income generation opportunities/for surrounding rural areas, /

helping reduce rural poverty. /

　　面对这些挑战，/我们是否应该回归农村经济？/显然，/放弃城市并不是办法。/从工业化开始，/城镇化一直向前发展。/尽管带来了诸多问题，/城市也创造了机会。/城市是商业中心，/也是经济增长的引擎。/在大多数的国家里，/城市已经成为了主要的场所，/开展教育、/文化、/科技创新活动，/丰富了我们的社会和文化生活。/城市强有力地推动了经济的增长，/惠及了城市以外的地区。/城市创造了创收机会/给周边的农村地区，/有助于减轻农村贫困。/

09:49—10:45

　　Worldwide, /cities generate over 70% of the global GDP. /In Africa, /60% of the region's GDP/is created in cities. /In China, /prefecture-level cities/and other larger urban centers/generate 61% of China's GDP. /Clearly, /the avenue to future sustainability/runs through sustainable cities/and sustainable urbanization. /

　　在世界范围内，/城市创造了超过70%的全球GDP。/在非洲，/60%的地区GDP/是由城市创造的。/在中国，/地级市/和其他更大的城市中心/创造了61%的中国GDP。/显然，/未来可持续发展的出路/在于可持续城市/和可持续城镇化。/

10:45—12:30

　　The common challenge/facing governments, /local authorities, /businesses/and other stakeholders/is one and the same. /How can we work together in partnership/to achieve sustainable urbanization/and create sustainable cities? /What are the measures/that have proven effective? /What are the lessons learned/and successful stories? /It is the purpose of this Symposium/to address these questions. /Through seven thematic sessions, /I hope participants/will share their diverse perspectives/and experiences/on how to advance sustainable cities/and sustainable urbanization. /We hope to gather these lessons/and share them broadly/with all actors/who are actively engaged/in making our cities better, /more productive/and more livable. /

　　共同的挑战/威胁着各国政府，/当地主管部门、/企业/和其他利益相关方，/挑战都是一样的。/我们如何才能携手合作/实现可持续城镇化/和建造可持续的城市？/哪些措施/是行之有效的？/有哪些经验教训/和成功案例？/本次研讨会的目的/就是要解决这些问题。/通过七个专题会议，/我希望与会嘉宾/分享他们不同的观点/和经验，/如何推进可持续城市/和可持续城镇化的发展。/我们希望收集这些经验教训，/并广泛分享/给所有行动者，/他们积极参与/使得我们的城市更美好、/更有生产力、/更宜居。/

12:30—14:50

In this process, /governments, /including local authorities, /will have to take on major responsibilities, /with active participation/by business and civil society. /In doing so, /I invite participants/to think beyond urban planning, /critical as it is. /I hope/participants/will approach cities as a system, /or if you allow, /as a living organism. /We need to think holistically, /cutting across disciplines or sectors. /We need/to put people at the centre of our efforts, /whether it is for housing, /infrastructure, /services, /business/or culture, /and ensure equitable access to public services for all. /We need to approach cities/as an integral part of our sustainable development strategies. /We should avoid/addressing urban challenges in silo. /Our efforts to provide housing, /water, /sanitation, /transport, /health care, /education, /jobs, /disaster relief and others, /ought to be planned, /managed/and implemented/in a balanced, /integrated way, /rather than in a piecemeal fashion. /

在这一过程中，/各国政府，/包括当地主管部门，/必须承担主要责任。/积极参与的/还应包括商界和民间社会。/为此，/我恳请与会嘉宾们/不要只考虑城市规划，/尽管城市规划至关重要。/我希望/与会嘉宾/能把城市当作一个系统，/可以的话，/把它看做一个活的有机体。/我们需要全面思考，/跨越学科或行业的限制。/我们需要/以人为本，/无论是住房、/基础设施、/服务、/商业/还是文化，/确保人人公平享有公共服务。/我们需要把城市看作/可持续发展战略的一个组成部分。/我们应当避免/孤立片面地处理城市挑战。/我们努力提供住房、/供水、/卫生、/交通、/医疗、/教育、/就业、/救灾等等，/规划、/管理、/和实施的时候/应当采取平衡、/综合的方式，/而不是零零散散的方式。/

14:50—16:43

For me, /a sustainable city/will be a place of economic dynamism, /an engine of inclusive, /balanced, /smart, /green/and low-carbon economic growth, /a place for social progress/with social cohesion, /socially-balanced housing, /as well as public services for all, /including health care/and education. /A city like this/will be a resilient city, /capable of dealing with disasters/and fighting climate change. /A sustainable city/will also be a place for youth, /for cultural dialogue/and diversity. /A sustainable city/will be a place of green space/and environmental regeneration. /In short, /a sustainable city/is a city we all want, /not only for us/but for our children. /I look forward to your presentations/and discussions. /Thank you very much! /

对我而言，/一个可持续发展的城市/将充满经济活力，/推动包容、/平衡、/智能、/绿色/和低碳的经济增长，/推动社会进步，/增强社会凝聚力，/提供公平的住房，/以及面向所有人的公共服务，/包括医疗/和教育。/这样的城市/将充满弹性，/有能力应对灾害/和气候变化。/可持续发展的城市/也将成为年轻人的场所，/促进文化交流/和多样性。/可持续发展的城市/将是绿意盎然的，/有利于环境再生。/简而言之，/可持续发展的城市/是我们都梦寐以求的城市，/不仅仅是为了我们，/也是为了我们的子孙后代。/我期待你们的发言/和讨论。/谢谢大家！/

III. 实战练习二

1. 演讲背景

为促进绿色发展、循环发展、低碳发展，2013年深圳市政府在龙岗区坪地创建了深圳国际低碳城，其中采用了许多荷兰与其他发达国家的先进绿色环保技术。下文摘自"首届深圳国际低碳城论坛"，演讲嘉宾为荷兰经济事务部能源转型委员会主席。他在演讲中介绍了荷兰与深圳在环保方面的密切合作，详细阐述了荷兰打造智慧城市阿姆斯特丹、新城阿尔梅勒和智慧港埃因霍温市的方法和经验。

2. 预习词汇

Excellency 阁下
Vice Mayor 副市长
strategic vision 战略愿景
low-carbon summit 低碳峰会
memorandum of understanding/MOU 谅解备忘录
front-runner 领跑者
prime time 黄金时段
documentary 纪录片
urbanization 城镇化
mobility 交通；出行方式
Almere 阿尔梅勒
Amsterdam 阿姆斯特丹
Rotterdam 鹿特丹
energy-efficient building 节能建筑
energy-efficient heating 节能供热
biogas 沼气
electric vehicle 电动车
smart city 智慧城市
multidisciplinary approach 跨学科的方法
Eindhoven 埃因霍温

Philips 飞利浦公司
cluster 集群
ZTE 中兴公司
Build Your Dreams/BYD 比亚迪公司
Mindray 迈瑞
industrialization 工业化
eco-city 生态城
brain port 智慧港
water-to-energy 水力发电
waste-to-energy 垃圾发电
topnotch 最高品质的；一流的
horticultural exposition 园艺博览会
low-carbon city 低碳城

3. 演讲文本

00:00—00:28

Your Excellency Vice Mayor Chen, /ladies and gentlemen, /First of all, /congratulations towards this new building, /this example of ecological construction. /It has been built in six months, /I heard. /This would be a world record in the Netherlands. /Congratulations with it. /

陈副市长阁下，/女士们，先生们，/首先，/祝贺大楼落成！/这是生态建筑的典范。/六个月就竣工了，/听说。/在荷兰这也算是一个世界记录。/祝贺你们！/

00:28—01:18

It is my pleasure today/to tell you/about the cooperation between the Netherlands and Shenzhen. /The seeds of this partnership/were sowed already four years ago/when parties from the Netherlands/including the Dutch universities, /designed its strategic vision/for the development of Pingdi into a sustainable urban zone. /Two years ago, /we started our government to government collaboration. /Today is a special occasion, /because, /at this low-carbon summit, /no less than four memorandums of understanding/will be signed/between Dutch and Chinese parties. /This shows/that our joint efforts/are really bearing fruits. /

今天非常高兴/能跟大家谈谈/荷兰与深圳的合作。/合作的种子/四年前就播下了。/当时，荷兰各方，/包括荷兰的大学，/制定了战略愿景，/要把坪地建设为可持续发展的城区。/两年前，/我们启动了政府间合作。/今天是个特别的日子，/因为，/在本届低碳峰会上，/至少四份谅解备忘录/将被签署，/由荷兰和中国双方签

第一单元　环境保护 Environmental Protection

署。/这证明了/我们的合作/硕果累累。/

01:18—01:52

Shenzhen wants/to be a front-runner both in China and worldwide/in reducing CO_2 emissions/and in improving the living environment. /Last week/when I was on Saturday evening, /watching television, /I noticed Shenzhen/even reached prime time on the Dutch television/in a documentary/that showed the city full of energy/carried forward by a clear vision on the future, /an example to other cities in the world. /

深圳希望/引领全国甚至全球,/减少二氧化碳排放,/改善人居环境。/上星期,/我在上星期六晚上,/看电视的时候,/注意到深圳/出现在荷兰电视节目的黄金时段,/以纪录片的方式/展示这座城市的活力/和未来清晰的愿景,/为世界树立了典范。/

01:52—02:59

My country, the Netherlands, /can take part in this development. /We have a long history/and our struggle with water/as you will probably know. /For centuries, /we have been battling/the rising waters of the sea and the rivers. /As a saying goes, /God created the world, /but the Dutch created the Netherlands. /In this way, /we have gained a lot of knowledge/about how to protect ourselves/against the water, /but also how to make use of the water for transport/or knowledge about how to upgrade the quality of the water/or even use it as pure drinking water. /Water is not just as an enemy, /but also as a friend. /This water knowledge has become/one of our major export products today. /The reason I am telling this to you is/because it shows/how a disadvantage can be turned into an advantage. /

我的祖国荷兰/可以助力深圳的发展。/我国历史悠久,/长期与水患抗争,/这个大家可能都了解。/数个世纪以来,/我们一直对抗/不断上升的河海平面。/俗话说,/上帝创造了世界,/而荷兰人创造了荷兰。/因此,/我们积累了丰富的经验,/知道如何保护自己/免受水灾,/也知道如何运用水力运输,/知道如何改善水质/甚至获取纯净的饮用水。/水亦敌,/亦友。/水资源的专业知识已成为/荷兰主要的出口产品之一。/我分享这个例子/是因为这个证明/我们可以把劣势转化为优势。/

02:59—03:24

This kind of development/has also taken place in other areas. /After water, /we have to battle air pollution/and to deal with waste. /We have to take on challenges/ related to (include) urbanization and mobility, /all issues/we had to solve in the past

11

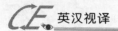

40 years/in order to keep our societies not only wealthy, /but also healthy. /

此类发展的情况/其他领域也有。/除了水资源,/我们还得治理空气污染/和处理废弃物。/我们需要应对挑战,/解决城镇化和交通问题。/所有问题/我们过去40年都得解决,/就是为了确保社会不但繁荣昌盛/而且健康发展。/

03:24—04:03

Forty years ago, /many people/lived out of our cities in the Netherlands. /They wanted space/which was not available in the old cities. /Our Government built new towns, /like Almere, /to deal with the population pressure. /However, /today, /people want to move back to the cities. /As we have managed to renovate the old neighborhoods, /the former port areas of Amsterdam and Rotterdam, for example, /have become hot spots. /Many people want to live there, /areas where living and working is integrated. /

40年前,/许多人/生活在荷兰城市以外。/他们想要空间,/旧城所没有的空间。/荷兰政府建设了新城,/如阿尔梅勒,/来应对人口压力。/然而,/如今,/人们想回归城市。/我们已经翻新了旧城区,/比如如阿姆斯特丹和鹿特丹的旧港口区域/已成为了热门地点。/很多人都想住在那里,/那里生活和工作完整融合。/

04:03—04:44

I mentioned environmental issues. /I mentioned population pressure. /In the 90s/came the issues of CO_2 emissions/together with the challenges of sustainable energy. /All these separate issues of/water, /waste, /require integrated solutions. /Effective solutions/in the field of energy-efficient buildings, /energy-efficient heatings, /winds, /biogas, /electric vehicles, /all things together, /all things concentrated and integrated. /It is about creating smart cities, /offering a perfect combination of living, working and mobility. /

我提到了环境问题,/也提到了人口压力。/90年代/出现了二氧化碳排放问题/以及可持续性能源的挑战。/这些独立的问题,/包括水资源/和废弃物,/都需要采取综合的解决方案。/行之有效的解决方案,/如节能建筑、/节能供热、/风能、/沼气、/电动车,/综合这一切,/形成综合的解决方案。/也就是建设智慧城市,/提供一体化的生活、工作和交通解决方案。/

04:44—05:24

This requires/a multidisciplinary approach by universities/and a strong link between science and market. /An excellent example in this is/the region of Eindhoven, /the hometown of Philips. /In this region, /they made a deliberate choice for a number of

12

第一单元　环境保护 Environmental Protection

technologies, /which to a number of open innovation/resulted in a world-class cluster. /Recently, /Eindhoven was chosen/as the world's smartest region. /Later this morning, /Vice Mayor Schreurs/will tell you how they want to share their experience/with Shenzhen. /

这需要/大学运用跨学科的方法,/科学界与市场紧密结合。/典型的例子就是/埃因霍温市,/飞利浦公司的总部所在地。/在那里,/他们精心挑选了许多技术,/取得大量开放式创新成果,/促成了世界级集群的诞生。/最近,/埃因霍温被选为/世界上最智慧的地区。/今天上午晚些时候,/副市长Schreurs/将与你们分享他们的经验,/与深圳交流。/

05:24—05:52

And just like Philips did in Eindhoven, /Shenzhen-based companies like Huawei, /ZTE, /Build Your Dreams/and Mindray, /can lead your city/to the next smartest region in the world, /I am sure. /This is important, however, /to realize that/success can only be achieved/if one is willing to face the challenges of industrialization/in an open and innovative way. /

与埃因霍温市的飞利浦公司一样,/深圳的公司如华为、/中兴、比亚迪、迈瑞,/将引领深圳/成为下一个世界最智慧的社区,/对此我深信无疑。/然而重要的是/要意识到,/想要成功,/就必须直面工业化的挑战,/解放思想,注重创新。/

05:52—06:33

This is what we are trying to do in our country. /Through this approach, /we want to create a new industry, /which is able to compete/in a global emerging markets, /like China. /In the coming years, /Shenzhen wants to move ahead as an eco-city. /This requires a joint effort/with international partners/in order to get access to the appropriate knowledge, /experience/and technology. /The Netherlands wants to be one of Shenzhen's partners. /We do have the knowledge/and we do have the capacity to contribute this knowledge/to help Shenzhen fulfill its ambition. /

这是荷兰的做法。/通过这样的方法,/我们希望创建新的行业,/有竞争力/参与全球新兴市场竞争,/比如在中国参与竞争。/未来几年,/深圳希望建成生态城市。/这需要共同努力/与国际合作,/才能获取相关知识、经验/和技术。/荷兰期待与深圳合作。/我们有专业知识,/也有能力分享知识,/帮助深圳实现愿望。/

06:33—07:24

By the way, /Shenzhen is also contributing to the Dutch society. /Many people in the Netherlands/are using the network equipment/of Huawei and ZTE. /Shortly, /

13

electric buses/powered by the technologies of Build Your Dreams/will be driving in the Netherlands. /The Netherlands also has something else to offer. /We have learned that/local government cooperation/is key to success. /This involves collaboration/between those who know all about planning and construction of cities, /those who have to take care of mobility, /those who must maintain a healthy living environment/and those who are responsible for sufficient clean energy and clean water. /

同时，/深圳也助力荷兰的发展。/许多荷兰人/在使用的网络设备/是由华为和中兴提供的。/很快，/电动巴士，/采用比亚迪的技术，/将在荷兰投入使用。/荷兰还有别的优势。/我们知道，/当地政府的合作/是成功的关键。/这需要通力合作，/联合城市规划建设人员、/交通管理人员、/健康人居环境管理人员/以及清洁能源和洁净水供应方。/

07:24—07:44

In the Netherlands, /we have gained a lot of experience/in this type of joint approach/to serve the needs of the society. /This is how we created the smart city Amsterdam, /new town Almere/and brain port Eindhoven, /all areas of excellence with its own and unique identity. /

荷兰/积累了丰富的经验，/采取联合的方法，/满足社会需求。/我们就是这样打造了智慧城市阿姆斯特丹、/新城阿尔梅勒/和智慧港埃因霍温。/这些优秀的地区都有自身鲜明的特征。/

07:44—08:43

Let me show you some pictures/to illustrate my story. /First, /the smart city Amsterdam, /is a very old city, /750 years old, /that has some of the smartest facilities in the world. /In particular, /their water-to-energy/and waste-to-energy facilities are topnotch. /They are about to share this technology with Shenzhen. /An MOU in this point/will be signed during this summit. /Secondly, /close to Amsterdam, /Almere, a new town, /is the fastest growing city in the Netherlands. /On 20th to 22nd, /they will hold the largest horticultural exposition/in the world. /And this will turn Almere from a new town/into a green city/like Shenzhen is today. /In a few days, /Almere will sign/an MOU with Shenzhen/to make Shenzhen its partner/in becoming a green city. /

我给大家看看一些照片，/作进一步阐述。/首先，/智慧城市阿姆斯特丹，/历史悠久，/有750年的历史，/拥有世界上最先进的设备。/尤其是/水力发电/和垃圾发电设施世界一流。/他们将与深圳分享这方面的技术。/相关的谅解备忘录/将在本届峰会上签署。/第二，/靠近阿姆斯特丹的/阿尔梅勒新城，/是发展最快的荷兰城市。/20号到22号，/那里将举办最大规模的园艺展，/乃世界之最。/这将推动阿尔梅勒由一座新城/转变为绿色城市，/就像如今的深圳一样。/几天之后，/阿尔梅勒将签署/与深圳的谅解备忘录，/与深圳合作，/建成绿色城市。/

08:43—09:06

Finally, Eindhoven, /which I mentioned before, /has managed to realize a real brain port. /With one of the highest concentrations of high-tech companies/in the world, /they will offer Shenzhen/the recipe for this brain-port/through an MOU to be signed today by Vice Mayor Schreurs. /

最后是埃因霍温，/我之前也有提到过，/已经建成了真正的智慧港。/那里聚集了大量高科技公司，/密度名列世界前茅。/他们将与深圳分享/建设智慧港的经验，/谅解备忘录今天将由副市长Schreurs签署。/

09:06—10:01

The Dutch Government/fully supports this cooperation/between the cities of Amsterdam, /Almere, /Eindhoven/and Shenzhen. /We believe/we can bear success/on strong relationships/between the Netherlands, these three cities/and Shenzhen. /We want to offer you our best practices, /best practices that are the results of intensive cooperation at the local level/between local authorities, /local companies/and local institutions. /At the same time, /we are very open to the best practices of Shenzhen. /We can learn a lot from your ambitions, /your open attitude to the challenges of today. /We can only admire your courage/to take on the challenges/of becoming a world-class low-carbon city. /Thank you for your attention！/

荷兰政府/全力支持合作，/支持阿姆斯特丹、阿尔梅勒、埃因霍温和深圳之间的合作。/我们相信，/我们能够成功/建立紧密关系，/加强荷兰这三个城市/与深圳之间的联系。/我们希望与你们分享最佳实践方案，/这些方案源于紧密的地方合作，/当地的主管部门、/公司/和机构的密切合作。/同时，/我们欢迎深圳分享实践经验。/我们受益良多，比如你们远大的抱负、/开放的态度和应对当今挑战的精神。/我们钦佩你们的勇气，/应对挑战，/打造世界级低碳城。/感谢大家的聆听！/

第二部分 视译技巧

第二单元 文化教育
Culture and Education

I. 视译单位

在视译中，译员要根据发言人讲话的顺序产出译文，尽量使译文与原文语序一致。合理断句在视译中是实现顺译的重要手段。断句的基本方法是划分类意群，"我们可以将类意群作为视译单位"（秦亚青、何群，2009：26）。类意群包含以下三个特征：

（1）相对独立的意义概念：指一个具有相对独立意义的词组或者短语，可以独立翻译出来，不会产生意义上的误会或不完整。如例1所示，每两个斜线之间都是一个相对独立的概念。

【例1】In this process, /national governments, /including local authorities, /will have to take on major responsibilities. /

译文：在这一过程中，/各国政府，/包括当地主管部门，/必须承担主要责任。/

（2）在一目可及的范围内：有时一个独立概念很长，难以迅速看完，只能再度切分。

【例2】The moment <u>when all the people in the organization became angry and began to argue with one another as to who should take the responsibility</u> was exactly the time when an even more serious event took place.

如果moment单独作为一个主语名词，其独立意义并不明确，因此一般不将其作为单独的意群。但是例2中moment后面跟了很长的定语从句，不在一目可及的范围之内，这种情况下可在moment后开始断句，如下所示：

The moment/when all the people in the organization/became angry/and began to argue with one another/as to who should take the responsibility/was exactly the time/when an even more serious event took place. /

译文：当时，/组织的所有成员/都很愤怒，/他们争执不休，/试图辨明谁要对此负责任。/恰恰在这个时候，/一个更加严重的事件发生了。/

（3）能通过连接语较灵活地与前后视译单位结合：由于中英两种语言在表达方式上存在较大差异，尤其在英语视译中，断句之后容易使句子显得支离破碎。在这种情况下可增加连接词，使译文表达完整顺畅。

第二单元 文化教育 Culture and Education

【例3】In 2015,/the British Consulate General/and UK Trade and Investment Promotion Association/held/a number of international workshops/in Beijing and Shanghai./

译文：2015年，/英国总领事馆/和英国投资贸易促进会/举办了/许多国际研讨会，/地点在北京和上海。/

中文的表达习惯是将时间、地点等状语放在句首，而在英语中可放在句首也可放在句末。在例3的视译中，译员坚持顺译原则，可增加"地点"，这样译文就不会显得支离破碎。

II. 实战练习一

1. 演讲背景

在2017英国伊顿公学前招生官访华教育论坛上，必益教育英国办公室总监应邀发表演讲，他在演讲中强调了伊顿公学为学生们提供各种各样参加课外活动的机会，老师们和舍监们都期待学生把握机会，学习独立生活。他还介绍了他在伊顿体验过的一些非同寻常的课外活动，如：划船、墙手球、携猎兔犬打猎、击剑。最后演讲结束前呼吁计划到英国留学的中国学生在面试中要展现自己与众不同的一面。

2. 预习词汇

UK Director for BE Education 必益教育英国办公室总监
Eton College 伊顿公学
scholarship 奖学金
orchestra 管弦乐队
saxophone 萨克斯管
rehearsal 排练
instill 逐渐灌输
Prince Harry 哈里王子
housemaster 舍监
ensemble 合唱队
art department 艺术部
Head of Art 艺术部长
rowing 划船
fives 墙手球
squash 壁球
beagling 携猎兔犬打猎

19

fencing 击剑
extra curricular activity 课外活动
Head of Admissions 招生官

3. 演讲文本

00:00—00:34

Good afternoon, /ladies and gentlemen, /boys and girls. /My name's Raff Flackett/and I am UK Director for BE Education. /I studied at Eton College/from 1990 to 1995. /Things were very different then, /of course, /no mobile phones, /no Internet, /but also very few international students. /But things have certainly changed at Eton, /as they have at most independent schools in the UK. /And schools are very welcoming/of international students, /particularly for their work ethic/and for all the other talents they bring with them. /

下午好, /女士们, 先生们, /同学们。/我叫 Raff Flackett, /我是必益教育英国办公室总监。/我在伊顿公学求学的时候/是 1990 到 1995 年。/那个时候情况很不一样, /当然了, /没有手机, /没有网络, /也几乎没有国际学生。/如今伊顿公学的情况肯定已经改变了, /就像英国大多数私立学校一样。/我们非常欢迎/国际学生, /特别欣赏他们的学习态度/和与生俱来的天赋。/

00:34—01:44

Now I'm not going to talk about, /very deliberately/not going to talk about academics today. /We all know that/Eton is very academic. /I just want/to talk generally/and briefly/about what I consider to be/the most important thing about Eton, /which is opportunity. /Now this was me/in my final year at Eton. /It was 1995. /So I'm afraid that/this was the preferred haircut at the time! /Now, /I'm not going to pretend that/I was the best student at Eton, /but I like to think that/I got involved/and I took advantage of all the great opportunities/that Eton offered. /Opportunity is a word/you hear very often/when people are talking about/independent schools in the UK/and what I take it to mean/is the chance to try pretty well anything, /whether it is sport, /music, /art, /design/or even learning a new language. /Despite what many international families think, /Eton isn't just about pushing children/to get top grades. /What the school cares about is that/you are going to use the abundant free time you have/as constructively as possible/and you will take advantage of all the great facilities on offer. /This is what I mean by opportunity. /

我今天不谈, /故意/不谈学术。/众所周知, /伊顿公学很注重学术。/我只想/大概谈谈、/简要说说/我认为什么是/伊顿最大的优势, /那就是机会。/这是我/在

第二单元 文化教育 Culture and Education

伊顿的最后一年。/当时是1995年。/恐怕/这就是当时流行的发型了。/现在,/我不会假装/自己是伊顿最优秀的学生,/但我认为/我积极参与/并充分把握了所有宝贵的机会,/那是伊顿所提供的。/机会这个词/大家常有耳闻,/比如当人们谈到/英国的私立学校的时候。/而我所说的机会/是指努力尝试任何事情的机会,/无论是运动、音乐、艺术、设计、或是学习一门新的语言。/与许多国际学生的家庭想的不一样,/伊顿并不会一昧逼迫学生/去追求高分。/学校看重的是/学生会利用宽裕的个人时间/尽量做些有建设性的事情,/并利用学校提供的所有资源。/这就是我所说的机会。/

01:44—02:31

Now I was awarded a music exhibition at Eton/which is essentially a half scholarship. /With this came great commitment/and responsibility. /As I played the violin in the school orchestra/and the saxophone in the school band, /I had to spend around 4 hours of every week/doing rehearsals. /All of this on top of my music practice, /my lessons, /my homework, /sports and other activities. /And this time commitment has to be organized/by the boy. /Although your lessons will be scheduled to a timetable/and you are allocated a certain amount of time each day/for your homework, /you are expected to fit all your other activities around this. /Nobody will tell you/how to do this/so you need to learn to be very independent/from the start. /

我曾获得伊顿公学的新生音乐奖,/这基本上相当于获得了一半的奖学金。/我也因此承担很大的义务/和责任。/我在学校管弦乐队拉小提琴,/在学校乐队吹萨克斯管,/所以我每周需要花4个小时/去排练。/除此之外还要练习乐器、/上课、做作业、做运动和其他活动。/时间安排/完全靠我自己。/尽管上课的时间是课表决定的,/而且您每天都有一定的时间/来完成作业,/但您需要据此来安排其他的活动。/没有人会告诉您/要怎么做,/所以您需要学会非常自立,/从一开始就得学会。/

02:31—02:59

Independence is something/that is instilled in boys at Eton/from the very first start. /Every boy/has his own bedroom/from day one/which is unique in Eton/among independent schools. /So every boy/has his own personal space/in which they have to organize their lives/and complete their homework etc. /Here is a very famous Etonian, /Prince Harry, /in his bedroom. /But there is nothing a housemaster hates/more than finding a boy/sitting in his room/in the afternoon doing nothing. /

自立是/学生在伊顿被灌输的理念,/从一开始就灌输。/每个学生/都有自己的卧室/从第一天起就自己住,/这是伊顿的特色,/和其他私立学校不同。/所以每个学生/都有自己的私人空间，/可以安排自己的生活、/做作业等等。/这是一位非常著名的伊顿公学校友，/哈里王子，/当时他正在他的卧室中。/但是舍监最不想看到的就是/发现学生/躲在自己的房间里/一整个下午都无所事事。/

02:59—03:18

To explain, /Eton runs a house system/where there are 25 houses, /each with about 50 boys. /Each house will have a housemaster, /as Mr. Reese was, /who acts as a sort of parent to the boys. /The housemaster/will know all the boys/intimately/and will take an interest/in their lives and progress. /

解释一下，/伊顿公学有一个宿舍体系，/包含25栋宿舍楼，/每一栋有50名学生。/每一栋楼安排有一个舍监，/Reese先生曾经就是舍监，/他们相当于学生的父母。/舍监/会认识所有学生，/与学生很亲近，/会关注/他们的生活和进步。/

03:18—03:41

So as I said, /each house has about 50 boys, /10 in each year. /You will spend 5 years/living with these boys/and you will become very close/and very loyal. /This is a picture/of my final day at Eton. /Although we've all gone a different direction career-wise, /I am very proud to say that/I am still in touch with every boy in this photo. /Just in case you're wondering, /I'm on the third row up on the right. /

我刚才已经提到过了，/每一栋宿舍有50名学生，/每个年级10名。/您有5年时间/都会和这些学生住在一起，/所以你们会十分亲密/和忠实。/这张照片/是我在伊顿公学最后一天拍的。/尽管我们现在从事不同的职业，/但我可以很自豪地说，/我与照片中的每一个同学仍保持联系。/您可能找不到我，/我在右边的第3排。/

03:41—04:00

Although as I mentioned, /boys are very independent, /they do at least have the housemaster/should their academic performance start to drop/or (since) in case they need disciplining, /which even I had to be once in a while. /It is also the housemaster's responsibility/to ensure that/the boys are using their time properly, /which takes me back to opportunity. /

虽然我说/学生都十分独立，/但舍监还是会帮助他们，/比如成绩退步了/或者需要管纪律的时候，/哪怕是我，/偶尔也需要别人来管管我。/舍监也负责/确保/学生能够合理利用时间，/这又让我想起了机会这个话题。/

04:00—04:37

At Eton, /you are expected to get involved/in all kinds of activities, /even if you are not particularly talented. /I, for example, /was terrible at sports, /but I still had to play nearly every day. /Those boys/who were very talent at sports/got to represent the school/and play against other sports schools. /Boys like me, /who weren't particularly talented, /got to represent their house/and play against other houses. /Similarly, /if you weren't particularly talented at music/but you still want to participate, /there were so many bands/and so many orchestras/and groups/and ensembles/that anybody at any standard/can take part/if they want to take the opportunity. /

伊顿公学/希望您参加/各种各样的活动,/哪怕您并非天资聪颖。/以我为例,/我体育很糟糕,/但仍须每天做运动。/学生/如果很有体育天分,/就会代表学校/与其他体育学校比赛。/像我一样的学生,/体育不怎么好的,/就会代表所在的宿舍楼/与其他楼的学生比赛。/同样,/如果您不是很有音乐天分,/但仍想参与,/那么有许多的乐队、/管弦乐队、/社团、/合唱队,/不管您是什么水平/都可以参加,/只要您想把握住机会。/

04:37—05:06

Now, /the art department as well/was not just for those/who were great artists. /I was not particularly good at art/and rarely visited the building. /However, /one day, /I remember, /I was very curious/to discover more about the works of Andy Warhol. /I still remember/how the Head of Art/spent the entire afternoon with me, /showing me how he worked/and helping me create my own version. /This despite him not knowing who I was/and the fact that/I hadn't visited the art department/for years. /

还有,/艺术部/也不仅仅是为/有艺术天分的学生设立的。/我不是很擅长艺术,/也很少去艺术部的大楼。/但是/有一天,/我记得,/我十分好奇,/想要了解更多 Andy Warhol 的作品。/我仍记得/艺术部部长/整个下午都和我在一起,/向我展示他是如何创作的,/也帮助我创作了自己的作品,/尽管他不知道我是谁,/也不知道其实/我没去过艺术部/有好些年了。/

05:06—05:32

So why am I telling you this? /Because I think/it exemplifies/the commitment of each teacher at Eton/to help you take the opportunity/if you want to do it. /If you take an interest/and show a passion, /then teachers/and excellent housemasters/like Mr Reese, /will ensure that/you get to experience anything you want. /There are clubs and societies at Eton/covering almost anything you can think of. /And if there isn't, /then you can start the club or society yourself! /

我为什么要告诉你们这件事情呢？/因为我想/这件事情证明了/伊顿公学每位老师的责任，/即帮助您把握机会，/只要您想去做。/如果您感兴趣、/有热情，/那么老师/和优秀的舍监，/像 Reese 先生，/会确保/您可以尝试任何您想做的事情。/伊顿有很多的社团，/包罗万象，应有尽有。/如果没有的话，/您还可以自己创立一个社团！/

05:32—05:55

Some of the more unusual things/I got to experience:/Rowing,/which is a very big sport at Eton,/fives,/which is another very important sport at Eton/which is a bit like squash/but you play with your hands,/and beagling,/which is a form of hunting with dogs/but on foot,/and fencing,/which I did enjoy very much./

有一些更特别的活动/是我体验过的：/划船，/这是伊顿一项很重要的体育运动。/墙手球，/这在伊顿也很重要，/有点像壁球，/但是是用手来打的。/携猎兔犬打猎，/就是猎犬狩猎的一种，/不过是徒步进行的。/还有击剑，/我非常喜欢的项目。/

05:55—06:23

So my message to anyone/who wants to come and study in the UK is:/if you just want to come to the UK/and sit in your room studying/then consider very carefully/whether a UK private education/is right for you./The emphasis on extra curricular activities/is not unique to Eton/and all schools will expect you/to get involved./Take advantage of what the schools have to offer,/because you will never in your life/have the time and the opportunity/to try so many different things again./

所以我想告诉那些/想来英国上学的学生：/如果您来英国/仅仅是待在房间里学习的话，/那么您需要认真考虑/英国私立学校/是否适合您。/注重课外活动/并非伊顿公学所特有，/所有学校都希望您/能够参与。/充分把握学校提供的机会，/因为您永远不会在人生中/找到时间和机会/再次尝试这么多不同的事情了。/

06:23—06:59

Think about what your talents are/but also think about what you interest in/and what want to try./As another former head of admissions at Eton,/not Mr. Reese,/once said to me,/"When I meet a Chinese boy,/I know/he'll be good at math,/I know/he'll be good at badminton/and I know/he'll play the piano a bit./Show me something different!"/So think about what makes you unique/and be ready/to demonstrate this at interview./There's no room for modesty./Be ready/to sell yourself!/Thank you very much!/

想想您有什么天赋，/也想想您有什么兴趣、/想尝试什么。/另一位伊顿的前招生官，/不是 Reese 先生，/曾经对我说：/"当我见到中国男孩的时候，/我知道/他会很擅长数学，/我知道/他羽毛球打得很好，/我也知道/他还会弹一点钢琴。/向我展示你们不同的一面吧！"/所以想想您的与众不同之处，/准备好/在面试中展示出来，/不要谦虚。/做好准备/展示自己的优点吧！/谢谢大家！/

III. 实战练习二

1. 演讲背景

在 2017 英国伊顿公学前招生官访华教育论坛上，主讲嘉宾伊顿公学的前招生官揭秘招生"潜规则"，详细介绍了英国私立学校的教育特点、招生年龄、测试系统、面试要求，并给在场的中国家长提出了诸多忠告。最后还分享了他自己的"院校排名"。

2. 预习词汇

BE Education 必益教育
Head of Admissions 招生官
education consultant 教育顾问
independent school 私立学校
curriculum 课程
soft skill 软技能
pastoral（教师对学生）生活辅导的
Eton 伊顿公学
Harrow 哈罗公学
Winchester 温切斯特公学
Wycombe Abbey 威雅公学
Cheltenham Ladies' College 切尔滕纳姆女子学院
day school 走读学校
entry 入学
senior boys' school 男子高中
co-educational boarding school 寄宿制男女混合学校
girls' boarding school 寄宿女校
prep school/preparatory school 预备学校
A-level/General Certificate of Education Advanced Level 英国中学高级水平考试
league table 院校排名

Radley 拉德利学院
Heathrow Airport 希思罗机场
single sex school 男校/女校
ISC/Independent Schools Council 英国私立学校委员会
BSA/Boarding Schools' Association 寄宿学校协会
ISYB/Independent Schools Yearbook 私立学校年鉴
Good School Guide 优秀学校指南
rugby 橄榄球
soccer 足球
burn-out 筋疲力尽
disillusionment 幻想破灭
Taunton 陶顿
Sherborne 谢伯恩
Tonbridge 汤布里奇公学
single assessment system 统一的入学考试系统
UKiset/The UK Independent Schools Entry Test 译赛/英国私立学校入学测试
common entrance 英国的小升初考试
scholarship application 奖学金申请
waiting list 候补名单
Charterhouse 切特豪斯公学
IB/International Baccalaureate 国际文凭组织
ALIS/Association of Leading Independent Schools 全球精英寄宿制学校联盟
Roedean 布莱顿罗丁
St. Mary's Ascot 圣玛丽学校·阿斯科特
Headington 海丁顿
Queenswood 昆斯伍德学校
Wellington College 惠灵顿公学
Wellington School 惠灵顿学校
King's Canterbury 坎特伯雷国王学院
Caterham 凯特汉姆中学
Cranleigh 克雷格学校
Bryanston 布莱恩斯顿
Wells Cathedral 威尔士教堂学校
Millfield 米尔菲尔德学校
Milton Abbey 米尔顿阿贝学校
Shiplake 船湖学院

Lord Wandsworth 万斯沃斯勋爵学院

3. 演讲文本

00:00—01:02

Good afternoon/and it's a great pleasure/to be here today/and to be associated with BE. /Firstly, /as head of admissions at Eton/and since leaving Eton/as an education consultant, /I have been observing BE's operation/of the growth of the company/for the last 13 years. /Since William Vanbergan/brought his first student/to me at Eton/which I remembered very well, /I am convinced that/BE provides a highly professional, /personal/and complete educational service/to families, /and this is a field/where there are some bad agents/who would take your money/and not do an honest job for you, /would not work in the interest of your child. /Above all, /BE will always do that. /

下午好! /我很高兴/今天可以来到这里/参加必益教育主办的活动。/首先, /作为伊顿的前招生官, /我离开伊顿之后/就一直当教育顾问, /我一直在关注必益教育的运作/和公司发展, /已经有13年了。/自从 William Vanbergan/将他的第一个学生/带到伊顿交给我时, /我印象深刻, /我就相信/必益教育提供非常专业、/个性化/和全面的教育服务/给每个家庭。/在这个领域, /有一些滥竽充数的中介, /他们收了钱/但不办实事, /从不为孩子的利益着想, /最重要的是, /必益教育永远用心做事。/

01:02—01:49

Now, /thousands of people around the world/are sending their children, /as you've heard, /to UK schools, /independent schools in the UK. /What is an independent school? /Independent schools/are private fee-paying schools, /not controlled by the state, /though they are subject to inspections, /which ensure excellent teaching quality/and the welfare of children. /The quality of their leadership today/is highly professional/and visionary. /They are not profit-making companies. /They do not have shareholders. /Any surplus is reinvested/in facilities/and staff. /

如今, /世界上成千上万的家长/都把孩子送去, /众所周知, /送进英国的学校、/英国的私立学校。/什么是私立学校呢? /私立学校/就是需要自费的学校, /不受国家管控, /但会受到监督, /这也确保了优秀的教学质量/和学生的福利。/私立学校的领导层如今/也相当专业, /富有远见卓识。/他们并不是以盈利为目的的企业, /而且也没有股东, /任何盈余都会重新投入/到教学设备/和教职员工身上。/

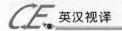

01:49—03:05

Independent schools/go well beyond the state curriculum/in what they teach, /and then the opportunities they provide/for the all-round sporting, /cultural/and personal development of every individual student. /They build all the "soft skills":/confidence, /resilience, /emotional intelligence, /good listening, /friendly competitiveness, /teamwork, /loyalty/and social skills, /and they encourage individual initiative, /leadership/and responsibility. /Within a community/that gives strong pastoral support/and a shared sense of purpose/that Eton College probably achieves/this complex and creative balance in education/best of all. /A friend of mine/who is a leadership and management trainer/said to me recently, / "The young men produced by Eton/are wild ducks/who know how to fly in formation". /Wild ducks/who know how to fly in formation. /

私立学校的课程/不限于国家的标准课程, /教授更多内容, /还会提供机会/像是各种体育运动、/文化/和个人发展的活动给每一位学生。/他们培养所有"软技能", /例如自信、/适应力、/情商、/良好的倾听能力、/友好竞争意识、/团队精神、/忠诚/和社交技能, /并鼓励学生积极主动, /培养领导力/和责任感。/在这个群体里, /学生会得到无微不至的照顾, /有共同使命感。/伊顿公学实现了/这种复杂又有创意的教育平衡, /在同类学校中首屈一指。/我的一位朋友, /一个领导力和管理培训师, /最近告诉我, /"伊顿教育出来的年轻人/就像野鸭子一样, /懂得如何列队飞行。"/野鸭子/知道如何列队有序飞翔。/

03:05—04:36

Within a framework/which preserves/the best of British tradition, /the teaching programs/at British independent schools/are at the cutting edge of modern education, /with a creative interaction/between teacher and student/at the heart of it. /These schools also provide/a smooth transition to the best universities in the UK and the USA, /and expert support/in that application process. /Now, /a few of these schools, /Eton, /Harrow, /Winchester for boys, /Wycombe Abbey, /Cheltenham Ladies' College for girls/are world-famous/and they are very difficult to get into, /not because their admission process/is mysterious, /these days/it is very transparent/and meritocratic, /but because of the intense competition for places. /I can assure you that/there are many other fine schools in the UK/where the pressure for places is not quite so acute, /and which may offer just the right environment/for a Chinese child. /So have an open mind, /don't over-focus/on the famous schools. /

我们的框架体系/保留了/英式传统的精髓。/教学课程/在英国私立学校里/都处于现代教育的前沿, /创造性的互动/在师生之间开展, /这是其核心。/这些学校

28

也提供/顺畅的升学机会考取英美顶尖学府,/提供专业支持/帮助学生申请大学。/其中,/有几所此类学校,/例如伊顿公学、哈罗公学、温切斯特男子学校、威雅公学、切尔滕纳姆女子学院/都举世闻名,/但极难录取。/这并不是因为招生过程/有多么神秘,/如今/所有程序都是透明的,/择优录取,/而是因为学位竞争非常激烈。/我向各位保证,/还有很多其他好的英国学校,/学位没有那么紧张,/足以提供良好的环境/给中国的孩子。/因此,/大家应该持开放态度,/不要过度关注/名校。/

04:36—05:43

How is the system structured? /Well, a lot of independent schools/and they are all independent. /They all do things/in their own way. /But it is possible to identify features/or something we could call a system. /Now this talk/isn't about London day schools. /There are excellent senior day schools/in London. /Briefly, /their main entry/is at age 11/with a few at 13. /I'll just say a brief word/about these schools,/because/mainly I want to talk/about boarding schools. /And a kind of warning for you in a way, /admission to top day schools in London/is extremely competitive. /Children/are under intense pressure/in a market with more demand than supply. /But if you are relocated to London/and you do prefer/a day school option, /then BE can advise you. /

这个体系的结构是怎样的呢?/很多私立学校/它们都是独立的,/处事/也各有风格,/但还是可以找出它们的特征,/或者我们称之为体系。/我今天的演讲/主题不是伦敦的走读学校。/有优秀的走读高中/是位于伦敦的。/简而言之,/他们的入学年龄/是11岁,/少数是13岁。/我只稍微提一下/这些学校,/因为/我主要想介绍/寄宿学校。/我想给各位一个忠告,/入读伦敦顶尖的走读学校/竞争是非常激烈的。/孩子/压力巨大,/市场也供不应求。/但如果各位移民伦敦/而且更喜欢/走读学校的话,/那么必益教育可以给您建议。/

05:43—06:14

But I want to concentrate mainly/on boarding schools. /Outside London, /most senior boys'/and co-educational boarding schools/have their main entry at 13, /with a few at age 11. /Conversely, /senior girls' boarding schools/outside London/mostly have their main entry at age 11, /with a few at 13. /

我主要想讲讲/寄宿学校。/在伦敦以外,/大多数男子高中/和寄宿制男女混合学校/入学年龄多在13岁,/少数是11岁。/与此相反,/女子寄宿高中/在伦敦以外/多数是11岁入学,/少数是13岁。/

06:14—06:49

There are many preparatory schools. /You have seen/some examples earlier/and preparatory schools/educate children up to the age of 13. /They play an important role/in preparing children/for entry to senior school. /Overseas candidates, /such as candidates from China, /have to compete with British children/coming from British preparatory schools, /and I'll return to that theme later. /

还有很多预备学校。/你们已经看了/前面一些例子,/预备学校/的学生年龄最大是13岁,/这些学校很重要,/帮助孩子做好准备/上中学。/海外申请人,/例如中国的申请人,/需要与英国学生竞争,/与英国预备学校的学生竞争,/这个我稍后再说一下。/

06:49—07:40

Many schools/also have an entry at age 16/and this can be a good option/for Chinese families/if their children/are not ready/to go at 11 or 13. /Maybe their English/is not strong enough yet/at 11 or 13/and sometimes this can be a very good option/to go at 16/for the two years to A-level/or equivalent pre-university exam. /Certainly, /we are thinking about it. /Entry for this stage of education at 16/needs to be planned/at least a year in advance, /so it needs to be planned/really before the child is 15/to get into that market successfully at 16. /My talk today/is aimed mainly at parents with younger children. /

很多学校/也有入学年龄是16岁的,/这是个不错的选择,/中国家庭可以考虑,/因为他们的孩子/可能还没准备好/11岁或13岁就去留学。/可能他们的英语/还不够熟练,/毕竟才11岁或13岁,/所以有时候这是个很好的选择,/16岁留学,/准备两年再参加高中课程/或者同等水平的大学入学考试。/当然,/我们也在考虑这一点。/入学年龄定在16岁的话,/需要规划,/至少提前一年,/所以是需要规划的,/真的要在孩子15岁前规划好,/这样才可以在16岁时成功入学。/我今天的演讲/针对的主要是孩子比较小的父母的。/

07:40—09:03

So when should you start planning? /Simply, /the earlier, the better. /The higher the academic level of the senior school, /the earlier you need to register/and pay a small registration fee/for assessment/at age 11 for senior boys and co-educational schools/and assessment at age 10 for girls-only schools. /At the top schools, /if you leave it until a boy is approaching 11/and a girl approaching 10, /you will almost certainly be too late. /The later you leave it, /the fewer options you will have/at the top end of the market. /There are plenty of schools/in the middle and lower levels of the market/

where you may find a place reasonably comfortably/at the later stage. /But for the top schools, /don't leave it too late. /Some of the schools/in the middle and lower areas of the market/are not so selective academically, /and you may well find a place there/at the later age. /But if you are ambitious for the top schools, /act early. /

那么你们应该什么时候开始规划呢?/简而言之,/越早越好。/学校的学业水平越高,/就需要越早注册,/还要交一点注册费/用于入学评估,/11岁是男子高级中学和男女混合学校的注册年龄,/女校则是10岁。/如果是顶尖学校,/等到男孩子快11岁、女孩子快10岁时才申请/肯定太晚了。/越晚申请,/选择就越少,/顶尖学校的选择就越少。/有很多学校/是属于中低端的,/你们可以比较容易申请到学位,/哪怕申请得比较晚。/但如果想要申请顶尖学校,/一定不要拖到太晚。/一些学校,/中低端的,/对成绩要求没那么高,/你们还是可以申请到学位的,/晚一点也可以。/但如果你们有志申请顶尖学校,/一定要趁早行动。/

09:03—10:09

And I am talking about top schools, /middle level schools, /lower level schools. /How do you identify/the academic status of a senior school? /Given the all-round nature of British education, /this should not be your only criterion. /But of course, /examination results/are important/in judging the right targets for your child, /but examination results/are only part of the picture. /There is a bewildering range of information. /The worst sources of information/are the so-called league tables/published in British newspapers. /They are rubbish. /Ignore them. /They give a very misleading view of the truth. /I haven't got time/to explain that in detail. /It would take a long time, /but take my word for it, /take my experience for it, /league tables in newspapers, /not the right source of information. /

我提到了顶尖学校、/中端学校、/和低端学校。/那么你要如何辨别/一所学校的学业排名情况呢?/鉴于英国教育全面发展的本质,/这不应该成为你们唯一的标准。/当然,/考试成绩/是很重要的/判断标准来为孩子选择好的学校,/但是考试成绩/只是其中一部分而已。/现在信息多得令人眼花缭乱。/最不靠谱的信息来源/就是所谓的院校排名,/刊登在英国各种报纸上。/这些排名毫无价值。/不要去看。/这些只会误导你们。/我没时间/详细解释了。/因为要花很长时间。/但请相信我的话/和我的经验,/报纸上的院校排名/不是正确的信息来源。/

10:09—11:30

I would give you a simple, /objective/comparative measure. /Go to a school's website/and look for A-level results, /the exam taken at age 18. /If you can't find them on the school's website, /try an Internet search. /It should be there. /Identify the cumulative percentage/of students scoring A+, /A/and B grades/at A-level. /The grades/would get the students into a top or a good university. /Don't just consider the 2016, 2017 results. /Look at the last five years/to see what the trend is at that school, /but you should be able to do all of that online. /The figures vary a little bit from year to year, /but as a rough guide, /the top London day schools will probably score about 98% on that measure, /Winchester and Eton about 95%, /top London day schools/and the top girls' schools, /such as Wycombe Abbey, /even better, /probably 97%, /Radley and Harrow about 93%, /and so on. /

我想给大家一个简单、/客观的/比较方法。/登录学校官网,/查询高中课程的分数,/这是学生在18岁时进行的测试。/如果你们在学校官网上找不到,/那就在网上搜索,/应该都会有的。/找到累积百分比,/看学生成绩为A+,/A/和B等级的/占高中课程考试各多少。/这个分数/可以帮助学生进入顶尖大学。/不要只看2016和2017年的数据,/看看过去五年的分数,/了解学校的分数趋势,/这些你们都得在网上完成。/数据每年都有一点不同,/但还是可以大概地参考一下,/顶尖的伦敦走读学校得分约为98%,/温彻斯特公学和伊顿公学约95%,/顶尖的伦敦走读学校/和顶尖女子学校,/例如威雅公学,/得分更高,/大约是97%,/拉德利中学和哈罗公学约93%,/等等。/

11:30—12:33
You can make your own league table/by doing this. /Any school scoring 80 to 90%/is academically good to very good. /A school in the 70% range/is quite good academically, /may be improving, /and it's likely/to have other strong qualities/as a community that may suit your child exactly. /It may not be highly selective at the point of entry, /but it will get the best/out of a student of average ability/and give them a terrific all-round education. /There are schools scoring 60%-65%/not strong academically, /but they have other great qualities/as warm, nurturing communities/which are just the right places for certain kinds of children/who are not going to be academic high fliers/but who will flourish in other ways, /whose needs are a bit different. /

大家可以制作自己的院系排名表,/按我说的去做。/任何学校分数能达到80%到90%的,/学业水平都是优秀或者十分优秀的。/学校分数在70%左右的,/学业水平相对不错,/但还有提升空间,/也可能/有其他优势,/这种学校可能正好适合您的孩子。/这些学校可能没有很高的入学门槛,/但仍会挑选最优秀的/中等生,/提供优质的全面教育。/而分数介于60%和65%的学校,/学业成绩就没那么好了,/但有其他优点,/比如温馨的成才环境,/这非常适合某些孩子,/比如不是学霸/但有其他突出才能的,/他们的需求略有不同。/

第二单元　文化教育 Culture and Education

12:33—13:05

So how do you form a long list/and work it to a short list? /There is a lot of work to be done here, /but it is worth it. /Establish the geographical area/you consider in the UK. /There are good independent schools/all over the UK. /You may want/to focus/relatively close to London/but don't be inflexible about that. /There are excellent schools/within two hours, /three hours most/of Capital or Heathrow Airport. /

那么该如何列出一长串名单/再精简筛选呢？/工作量很大，/但都是值得的。/选定地理位置，/您想去英国哪个地方。/优秀的私立学校/遍布英国。/您可能想要/关注/相对靠近伦敦的学校，/但也不要太死板。/也有优秀的学校/两个小时以内的车程，/顶多三个小时，/就可以到达首都或希思罗机场。/

13:05—13:29

Do you want single sex/or co-education? /The more open-minded you are about this, /the more flexibility of choice you will have. /On the whole, /academic selection is more intense/at the top single sex schools/than it is at co-educational schools. /

你们想上男校女校/还是男女混合学校呢？/你们态度越开放，/选择就越灵活。/总的来说，/分数要求更高/的是顶尖的男校女校，/而男女混合学校要求低一点。/

13:29—14:43

There are sources/which will give you/basic information/by area, /type of school, /some identifying features. /Independent Schools Council（ISC）, /Boarding Schools Association（BSA）, /the Independent Schools Year Book（ISYB）/all contain basic information/about schools in different categories. /There are commercial advisory companies, /the largest being the Good Schools Guide. /Some schools/provide link on their website/to the Good Schools Guide, /especially if their review is favorable. /If there is no link, /maybe the review is not so favorable. /If you use the Good Schools Guide, /remember that you are getting one opinion/that should never substitute for your own personal visit to a school. /And of course, /BE has built up a great range of contacts/and depth of experience and expertise/in connecting UK schools/with potential entrants from China, /and in advising parents/on appropriate schooling for their children. /

有些来源/可以给你们/一些基本信息，/包括地区信息、/学校类型/和一些突出特征。/英国私立学校委员会、/寄宿学校协会、/私立学校年鉴，/都提供了一些基本信息，/介绍不同类型的学校。/也有商业咨询公司，/其中最大的是优秀学校指南。/一些学校/会在官网提供/优秀学校指南的链接,/尤其是口碑很好的学校。/如果没有提供链接,可能是评价不是很好。/如果您使用优秀学校指南,/别忘了这仅供您参考而已,/还不如您亲自去学校参观。/当然,/必益教育人脉甚广,/经验丰富,非常专业,/擅长连结英国学校/和中国学生,/为家长提供咨询服务,/选择适合孩子的学校。/

14:43—15:01

You can explore/individual schools' websites, /most of which are now very good. /Some school websites/have a special section/for overseas students. /So you can get from some schools/a Chinese version of the website. /

您可以浏览/私立学校官网,/大部分都做得很好。/有些官网/有专门的板块/面向海外学生,/所以您可以在一些学校的官网找到/中文版的网页。/

15:01—15:49

Choose potential schools in a range/that is appropriate to your child's abilities, /personality, /sporting and cultural interests. /At the simplest level, /don't choose a school/which specializes in rugby/if your son/is passionate about soccer. /I have seen it happen many times. /At the most basic level, /parents simply not identifying the school/that suits their children/and their children's passions and talents. /And you need schools/that are appropriate/to your child's likely level of fluency in English/by the time of assessment/at the age approximately 11. /

您选择的学校/要符合孩子的能力、/个性、/运动和兴趣。/最简单的,/不要选一所学校/是专门训练橄榄球的,/如果您的儿子/热衷的是足球。/这种情况我看过很多次了。/很简单,/家长们就是没有找到那所学校,/适合他们的孩子、/符合他们孩子的爱好和天赋的学校。/您需要的学校/要适合/您孩子的英语水平,/能应对入学测试,/也就是他们11岁左右的时候。/

15:49—16:51

Now in the course of this talk, /I need/to say a couple of things to you, /give you a couple of massages/that are a bit difficult, a bit challenging for you/but I think very necessary things/for you to hear. /And I'll speak/very much from experience. /Your child needs/to be comfortable and happy/at a school/in order to flourish. /Your child/will not benefit/from being pushed and driven/to meet unrealistic parental aspirations. /I have witnessed in my career/many problems caused by that:/burn-out, /disillusionment, /conflict, /unhappiness. /Nobody wants that for children. /Choose a school/appropriate to your child's ability/and personality. /Don't push your child to a school/that's beyond their natural capacities. /

在这次演讲中，/我需要/告诉你们一些事，/给你们一些信息，/有点难以接受，/但我认为很有必要/说给你们听。/我会讲/很多经验之谈。/您的孩子需要/舒服快乐/度过校园时光/才能茁壮成长。/您的孩子/不会受益，/如果他们被迫/去实现家长不切实际的期待。/我在职业生涯中目睹过/很多由此导致的问题：/筋疲力尽、/幻想破灭、/矛盾冲突、/郁郁寡欢。/大家都不希望孩子这样。/选择学校/要符合孩子的能力/和个性。/不要逼迫孩子去就读/他们力所不能及的学校。/

16:51—17:09

There are incidentally two British schools/which have international sections/that specialize in the progressive integration of children/whose English is not strong at the beginning. /They called Taunton and Sherborne. /You will see their names/at the end. /

顺便提一下，有两所英国学校/设有国际部，/专门帮助学生逐渐融入，/这些学生的英语水平一开始不是很好。/这两所学校是陶顿和谢伯恩男校。/您会看到它们的名字，/就在后面。/

17:09—18:37

Taking advice from BE, /move from a long list/to a short list/of potential senior schools. /Then ideally come to the UK/when your child is age nine or ten/to visit those schools/and you can do it on a Group Open Day/or by individual arrangement. /Tour the school, /meet academic and boarding leaders, /teachers and students. /Meeting the head of the school in person/is more likely/at a small, less selective school/than it is at a large school/with high demand for places. /Then make your formal application for assessment/at several schools, /at least three, /perhaps four maybe even five. /And it is most sensible/if your group of schools are not all at the same academic level. /So for example, /don't apply to Eton, /Winchester, /Harrow, /Tonbridge/and Radley/and nothing else. /Because those are all very close to being at the top level. /You need to aim high of course, /but have an insurance policy, /or several insurance policies/in case your child doesn't make it to your first choice. /

向必益教育咨询，/从一长串学校/精简名单/选择合适的学校。/然后最好来到英国，/在孩子9岁或10岁时，/去参观学校，/可以在开放日去，/或自选时间。/参观学校，/见一见学业和寄宿负责人，/见见老师和同学。/见到校长本人/更有可能/是在规模较小、门槛较低的学校，/不太可能是在规模较大的学校，/因为学位竞争激烈。/然后正式申请入学评估测试，/多申请几所学校，/至少3所，/可能4所甚至5所。/最明智的做法是/您申请的学校的分数段是不一样的。/例如，/不要

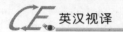

只申请伊顿、/温切斯特、/哈罗、/汤布里奇、/拉德利/然后其他的就都不申请了,/因为这些都属于顶尖学校。/当然要高瞻远瞩,/但也要有保险措施,/留几所学校保底,/以防孩子被首选学校拒绝。/

18:37—18:58

So I've talked about assessment, /assessment happening at age approximately 11. /Ten for the single sex girls' schools/with an entry at 11, /11 for boys' schools/ and co-ed schools with an entry at 13. /They assess children two to three years in advance. /

我之前谈到了入学评估,/测试时的年龄约为11岁。/女校则是10岁考试,/11岁入学,/男校11岁,/男女混合学校13岁入学。/学生需要提早两三年参加测试。/

18:58—19:34

There is no single assessment (schools) system. /Independent schools/are independent. /They can make their own decisions/how they do these things. /There are broad similarities though. /Within that, /every school/has its own registration deadline. /You need to be very careful/about registration deadlines. /I have met a lot of Chinese families/who want their children/to go to Eton or Winchester, /but they are too late. /They missed the deadline. /You need advice. /You need to be very careful about that. /

没有统一的入学评估系统。/私立学校/是独立的,/可以自行决定/如何测试。/但也有很多相似之处。/例如,/每个学校/都有各自的注册截止日期。/您需要特别留意/截止日期。/我见过很多中国家长,/他们想要孩子/上伊顿公学或温切斯特公学,/但太晚注册,/错过了截止日期。/您需要我们的建议。/您需要特别留心。/

19:34—20:30

The forms of assessment vary, /but there is broad pattern/which tends to involve tests, /reasoning skills, /English and math, /and interviews. /And the interview/will gauge the all-round personality/and potential of the child/as well as intellectual engagement/and curiosity, /not test scores. /Test scores are measured/in a different way. /The interview measures intellectual curiosity, /engagement with ideas. /That's what, /how it's happening in an interview. /Reasoning tests/are mainly done on a computer. /They can't be directly practiced, /but there are similar tests/available online. /And a report will be required/from the candidate's current school, /and if necessary, /BE can translate that for you. /

评估形式多种多样,/但总的来说/会有考试、/推理能力、/英语、数学/和面试。/面试/会全面考察孩子的个性、/潜能、/智力/和好奇心,/而不是看考试分数。/考试分数的衡量/有其他方式。/面试则考察求知欲/和学生是否有想法。/这就是/面试的形式。/推理能力测试/主要通过电脑完成。/测试题无法直接提供给你们练习,/但是有类似的测试/在网上可以找到。/还需要成绩单,/由考生现读学校提供,/需要的话/必益教育可以为您翻译。/

20:30—21:55

Probably 250 schools in the UK/are now using a new test/called UKiset, /U-K-I-S-E-T. /This is for students/whose first language is not English. /This is a very good thing in everyone's interests. /Some schools are using this UKiset test/as a direct entrance test. /Other schools/with large numbers of applicants/are using it as a pre-test/ to manage numbers/before their main assessment. /The results of this UKiset test/can be sent to five schools. /In fact, /you can pay extra/and have it sent to more than five schools, /so that reduces the need for a lot of journeys to the UK. /This test can be taken/as an indicative assessment, /even before applying to schools. /That can be very helpful/in targeting the right academic level of school for your child/and comparing performance with UK children of the same age. /So you can look it up online, / UKiset, /to find out more about it, /and of course/BE is familiar with it, /has contacts with its administrators/and can process it here in China. /

大概有250所英国学校/在用一个新的考试,/叫做译赛,/英文拼写是U-K-I-S-E-T。/这是面向/母语非英语的考生的,/对每位学生都有利。/有些学校用译赛/作为直接的入学考试。/其他学校,/申请人数多的,/则用作预先测试/去控制人数,/通过后才能参加主要测试。/译赛成绩/可以发给五所学校。/事实上,/您付额外费用/就可以发给五所以上的学校,/这样就可以减少去英国的次数。/这个测试可以/作为指示性评估,/即使您还没有开始申请学校。/这个测试很有用,/可以选出分数水平符合您孩子的学校,/还可以对比英国同龄学生的成绩。/所以您可以上网查阅/译赛的信息,/深入了解,/当然,/必益教育对译赛非常熟悉,/考官中也有熟人,/可以在中国考试。/

21:55—23:19

Let's come back to the interview. /The interview may well be/the student's first experience/of the teacher-student relationship/in UK schools. /There is another important message for you. /This can be a culture shock/for children from Asia. / Some can't deal with it. /It's completely different experience/of relating one to one with a teacher. /And I've seen in my life/a lot of Asian children/become very nervous/and talk far too much, /so it's not an interview at all. /Or they become completely silent. /They don't know what to do, /because they are being asked/to offer opinions, /insights. /They are being invited/to argue and disagree with the teacher, /as well as expressing their enthusiasms/and their interests. /Practice interview experience/is really important. /Children who turn up for an interview/without having any experience/of what is going on/are very unlikely to do well. /BE can help/with interview experience. /

让我们回到面试这个话题。/面试很可能是/学生初次体验到/师生关系/在英国学校里是怎样的。/还有另外重要的一点。/这可能是文化冲击, /对于亚洲学生而言。/有些人无法应对。/这是完全不同的体验, /学生要与老师一对一交流。/我曾经见过/许多亚洲学生/太过紧张, /说话没完没了, /这根本不是一场面试。/也有沉默寡言的, /不知所措, /因为他们被要求/发表观点、见解, /被要求/与考官辩论, /展现激情, /谈论兴趣。/锻炼面试技巧/真的十分重要。/孩子去参加面试, /没有任何经验, /一头雾水, /是不可能表现好的。/必益教育可以帮助您/提升面试经验。/

23:19—23:58
What are UK boarding schools looking for/in potential entrants? /This is probably/one of the most important questions/in your mind. /The answer lies in my description of UK schools/at the beginning of the talk. /They are not looking simply for candidates/who are very good at math/and computing, /but have little else to offer. /Schools are motivated/only partly by academic results. /And this is absolutely vital/and understanding of this. /

英国寄宿学校想要招/什么样的学生呢? /这可能是/最重要的问题之一, /是您想问的。/答案就在我对英国学校的描述中/开场就讲到了这一点。/这些学校不是招收/擅长数学/和计算机/却没有其他特长的学生。/学校关注的/不仅仅是学习成绩。/这一点至关重要, /要了解这一点。/

23:58—27:07
And here is the second really quite difficult challenging message for you, /but I need to say it. /I have met many candidates/from Asian countries/whose parents want/to send their children/to the UK/but who have not understood/this important distinction, /and they have deprived their children/of a broad sporting and cultural life, /indeed deprived them of opportunities/just to play in an imaginative undirected way, /in favor of an intense over-focus on academic work, /tests and exams. /This

第二单元 文化教育 Culture and Education

isn't/what British schools are looking for. /It's sad. /When these candidates come up/against boys and girls from UK preparatory schools, /they can't compete/in breadth of activity and personality. /They are less interesting. /UK boarding schools/are looking also for international students/who will integrate socially, /not just stay within their own national and ethnic group, /students/who will contribute to the life of the community/and participate actively/in everything that is going on, /team and individual sports. /I'm gonna give you a list now/of everything that happens in a UK school, /in addition to academic work. /Team and individual sports, /music, /theatre, /art and design, /debating, /journalism, /army cadets, /adventure training, /community service, /clubs and societies of every kind, /all to be enjoyed. /Very important point is/all these activities/to be enjoyed for their own sake/and not for certificates. /We are looking for students/who are going to put a lot in/and get a lot out, /developing all their potential/as human beings. /(Just asking for the door to be shut. /It's quite a lot of noise out here. /Thank you. /Noise was distracting. /Thank you.) /No child can do all of it, /and sometimes the job of a housemaster, /I have experience of being a housemaster, /is to stop a student/trying to do much, /and help the student/to make choices. /That's a problem sometimes, /because there are so much opportunity available. /But if the child is not willing/to come to the UK/and engage in at least some of these activities, /and frankly/there is no point in coming, /no purpose. /If the interests are purely academic, /there is no point. /

第二条忠告也有点逆耳，/但我必须说出来。/我见过许多考生/来自亚洲，/他们的父母想要/送他们/去英国留学，/但他们并不理解/这个重要的特点，/他们剥夺了孩子/广泛参加运动和文化生活的权利，/不给他们的机会/去天马行空、自由自在地玩耍，/而是过度关注学习/和考试。/这并不是/英国学校想要的。/很遗憾。/当这些考生面对/英国预备学校的学生时，/没有竞争优势，/他们在活跃度和个性上都要逊色些。/他们没那么吸引人。/英国寄宿学校/要招的国际学生/是能够融入社会的，/而不是只会呆在自己的同胞社交圈里；/招的学生/是能够投入学校生活的，/并积极参加/一切活动，/不管是团体还是个人运动。/我给你们展示一份清单，/看看英国学校的所有活动，/学习以外的活动。/有团体和个人体育运动、/音乐、/戏剧、/艺术设计、/辩论、/新闻、/军训、/冒险训练、/社区服务、/各种各样的社团。/这些内容都非常有趣。/非常重要的一点是/这些活动/都是他们自己喜欢而参与的，/而不是为了考取证书。/我们希望学生/积极参与、受益良多，/开发他们的潜能，/把他们当作真正的人。/（请关一下门，/外面有点吵。/谢谢！/噪音有点干扰。/谢谢！）/学生无法做到面面俱到，/有时舍监的工作，/我做过舍监，/就是阻止学生/参与过多活动，/协助他们/做决定。/有时候这也是个问题，/因为有太多机会可以选了。/但如果学生不愿意/来英国/或参加这些活动的

话，/坦白说，/没必要来，/没意义。/如果学生的兴趣仅仅是学习，/来英国读书就没意义了。/

27:07—27:56

What happens after assessment? /Unless your child is a girl/entering a senior school directly at age 11, /many places at the top schools are offered at 11/for entry at 13, /subject to a final qualification/called Common Entrance, /which is what most schools do. /Some schools will offer an alternative examination/at 13 for children from overseas/who have not been able/to prepare Common Entrance. /But these examinations/need to be prepared/and practiced. /The strongest candidates academically/may try for a scholarship, /and there are music, /art, /sport/and other kinds of scholarships/in addition to the academic ones. /

测试完了下一步是什么呢？/除非您的小孩是女生/需要11岁直接入学，/不然的话许多顶尖学校是11岁录取，/13岁入学，/他们要参加最终资格考试，/叫小升初考试，/在大多学校都会举行。/有些学校会举行其他的资格考试，/面向13岁的海外学生，/因为学生无法/准备小升初考试。/但这些考试/需要做好准备/和练习。/成绩拔尖的学生/可以尝试申请奖学金，/有音乐、/艺术、/体育/及其他类型的奖学金，/也有学业奖学金。/

27:56—28:33

There are many schools/also operate a waiting list, /which is necessary for them/but the uncertainty/is very difficult for overseas parents. /So if you're offered a firm place of one school/and you like it, /then a waiting list place of another school, /unless the child/is going to a preparatory school in the UK, /it's best to take the firm offer/rather than hope/for an offer from a waiting list. /That's a difficult place to be for overseas students. /

许多学校/有招生候补名单，/对他们来说是必要的，/但这种不确定性/会让海外家长难受。/所以如果您确定被录取了，/您也喜欢这所学校，/然后又在另一所学校的候补名单上，/除非您的孩子/准备去上英国预备学校，/否则最好去录取他的学校就读，/而不是期待/候补学校来录取他。/这对海外学生来说是个两难处境。/

28:33—29:54

Once the place is offered/and accepted, /the school will then help you/if necessary/to secure an education visa for your child. /As an alternative to planning for entry at 13/or indeed at 16, /if your child is ready for it/in social and emotional terms, /consider the value/of moving your child/to one of the excellent UK preparatory schools, /you heard a bit about those earlier. /You could move your child to a preparatory school/at age 11/but best of all at 10, /before the senior school assessment. /Cause a prep-school will help the child/to prepare for the senior school assessment/or get the child into the mainstream of the educational style/and content/and ethos of British education, /and provides a smooth transition/at age 13. /Going to a prep school, a preparatory school, /it is particularly advisable/for those aspiring to the top senior boys' schools, /such as Eton, /Winchester, /Harrow, /Radley, /Tonbridge. /And again, /BE is very well-placed/to give advice/and has very good contacts here. /

一旦收到了录取通知,/您也接受了的话,/学校就会帮助你们/在必要的情况下/获得教育签证。/除了计划在13岁时入学,/或实际上16岁才入学,/如果您的孩子准备好了,/在社交和情感上比较成熟,/那么可以考虑/让您的孩子去/上英国顶尖的预备学校,/你们之前也有所了解了。/您可以让孩子读预备学校,/11岁可以去,/但最好10岁时去读,/之后再参加中学考试。/因为预备学校会帮助学生/准备好应对中学入学测试,/让学生适应主流的教育风格、/教育内容/和英国教育理念,/帮助学生顺利升学,/13岁时能被录取。/读预备学校/是非常明智的选择/尤其是那些立志上顶尖男校的学生,/例如伊顿公学、/温切斯特公学、/哈罗公学、/拉德利学院、/汤布里奇公学。/再说一下,/必益教育很有资格/提供建议,/人脉也非常广。/

29:54—31:14

You will see from my final slide/where I'm gonna put up some lists of schools. /There are a few senior schools/have their own preparatory schools, /so you can put your child through one institution/through its preparatory section/and then its senior section. /This is a big decision, /a lifelong decision. /There is a lot of hard work involved in it. /It needs a lot of thought/and discussion within the family. /Is it the right decision for your child? /When to go? /Which is the right point of entry/for your child? /Is it at 10? /Is it at 11? /Is it at 13? /Is it at 16? /What's right for your child? /But British schools/offer all those options. /Is it worth all these hard work and thinking/if you want to secure this world-class education/for your child? /And at every stage, /advice is available from BE. /Now what you are going to see now are/my own league tables. /My personal league tables, /recommended schools. /And I put them in categories. /

在最后的幻灯片上/有学校名单。/有些学校/有自己的预备学校,/所以您可以让您的孩子选择同一所学校的,/先读它的预备学校,/再就读它的中学。/这是个重大的决定，/是一生的决定。/会有很多困难。/需要深思熟虑，/一家人一起讨论。/这个决定是否适合孩子？/什么时候留学？/最佳入学时间点/对您孩子来说是什么时候？/10岁？/11岁？/13岁？/还是16岁？/几岁比较合适您的孩子？/英国学校/能提供所有这些选择。/但值得去努力和考虑/将世界顶尖教育/带给您的孩子吗？/各个阶段，/必益教育都可以提供建议。/现在你们看到的是/我自己的院校排名。/这是我自己做的院校排名，/我推荐的学校。/我都分好类了。/

31:14—32:19

And each category, /I put them in an academic order, /so you can see the top boy boarding schools/in purely academic terms/is Winchester. /Winchester is smaller than Eton. /Winchester is more academically focused than Eton. /Eton offers boys/a broader range of possibilities and choices/than Winchester. /Eton is just behind Winchester. /And purely academic terms/are the great schools Tonbridge, /Radley. /And I'm very pleased that/in the last couple of years, /largely through the efforts of BE, /Radley has become more open to Chinese students. /Until a few years ago, /Radley used to be very English, /quite close to international candidates. /And BE has now created a good relationship with Radley. /And Radley is now more open to Chinese students/and it's a great school. /

每一类/我都是按分数排名的，/所以你们可以看到顶尖男子寄宿学校/只看分数的话/是温切斯特公学。/它的规模比伊顿公学小，/但更专注学业。/伊顿公学则给学生提供了/更大的可能性和更多选择，/比温切斯特要多。/伊顿公学仅次于温切斯特公学。/只看成绩的话，/优秀的学校有汤布里奇公学/和拉德利学院。/我非常高兴看到，/过去几年间，/主要由于必益教育的努力，/拉德利开始招收更多的中国学生。/几年前/拉德利只招收英国学生，/不招国际学生。/必益教育现在和拉德利的关系非常好，/拉德利也在招更多的中国学生，/这也是一所顶级学校。/

32:19—33:01

Harrow, /Abingdon, /Charterhouse. /Charterhouse goes co-education at age 16. /Girls arrive at 16. /I've also mentioned us with Charterhouse/where a school offers the IB, /the International Baccalaureate/as an alternative to A-level at age 18. /And students can choose at those schools/whether they prefer to do A-level/or IB. /I've also added a boy school/at a slightly lower level, /Sherborne. /And Sherborne/will be coming to the ALIS Conference/in September. /

哈罗公学、/阿宾登、/切特豪斯公学。/切特豪斯公学是16岁入学的男女混合学校，/女生16岁入学。/我也提到过切特豪斯公学/提供IB课程，/也就是国际文凭组织课程，/用来替代18岁时参加的高中毕业考试。/学生也可以选择那些学校，/就看他们是喜欢高中课程/还是 IB 课程。/我还加了一所男校，/略微逊色一点的，/叫做谢伯恩。/谢伯恩/会参加精英寄宿学校联盟会议，/会议在九月份召开。/

33:01—33:40

Top girls' schools. /The top girls' school/is Wycombe Abbey, /follow by Roedean, /where I've added, /very international. /A very high proportion/of students of Roedean/are not British. /If you want a British school, /visit Roedean, /have to look at it, /have to think about it. /Of course, /it's a very good school academically, /but it isn't particularly British. /And then Cheltenham Ladies' College, /St. Mary's Ascot. /St. Mary's Ascot/may be a particular interest/to family who are Roman Catholic, /a very good school/and a Catholic school. /

顶尖的女子学校。/顶尖的女子学校/有威雅公学，/接着是布莱顿罗丁女子学校，/我也列举了这所学校，/非常国际化的学校。/很大一部分的/布莱顿罗丁学生/不是英国人。/如果孩子想读英国学校，/去参观布莱顿罗丁吧，/一定要去看看，/好好考虑一下。/当然，/这所学校成绩很好，/但不是特别英式。/接着有切尔滕纳姆女子学院，/圣玛丽学校·阿斯科特。/圣玛丽学校·阿斯科特可能很热门，/很受罗马天主教家庭欢迎，/是一所很好的学校，/也是一所天主教学校。/

33:40—34:04

You'll see some other schools, /such as Headington, /where you will see a plus sign. /And on this list/a plus sign means/this is a school/with its own preparatory school/where the child can join at an early age/and go right through the preparatory/and senior departments/on the same place. /

你们还会看到其他学校，/例如海丁顿，/标有加号的学校。/在这张清单上/加号意味着/这些学校/有自己的预备学校，/学生可以很小就入学，/先读预备学校/再读中学，/都在同一个地方。/

34:04—35:20

And as with Sherborne Boys on the boys' side, /I've added this school/at a slightly lower level academically, /Queenswood, /which is also coming/to ALIS in September. /And then co-educational schools. /Best co-educational school/at the moment/is Wellington, Wellington College. /Be very careful! /There are two schools/called Wellington. /There are Wellington College/and Wellington School. /This one is Wellington College. /Wellington/is the most improved school in Britain/in last 10 to 50. /King's Canterbury, /a great school, /an old school, /very good at sports, /very good at music/and good academically. /And others there, /you can see a number of examples of schools/with their own preparatory schools, /such as Caterham, /Cranleigh, /and Cheltenham College/and others. /There are some schools there/that you have probably never heard of, /but they are all good/and they are all worth considering. /

在谢伯恩男校这一边，/我添加了这所学校，/成绩排名稍微低一点，/就是昆斯伍德学校，/该校也会来/参加九月份的精英寄宿学校联盟会议。/然后是男女混合学校。/最好的男女混合学校/目前/是惠灵顿公学。/请注意，/有两所学校/都叫惠灵顿，/一所叫惠灵顿公学，/一所叫惠灵顿学校。/我说的这所是惠灵顿公学。/惠灵顿公学/是进步最大的英国学校，/在过去10到50年间突飞猛进。/坎特伯雷国王学院，/非常优秀，/历史悠久，/擅长体育、音乐，/成绩优异。/还有其他的学校，/你们可以看到许多学校/有自己的预备学校，/如凯特汉姆中学、/克雷格学校、/切尔滕纳姆女子学院/等等。/有些学校/你们很可能从未听过，/但都很优秀，/值得考虑。/

35:20—36:31

At the bottom of the list, /I've put some schools/that are not strongly academic/but have other great qualities. /Bryanston/where the arts are very strong/and where the students are encouraged very much/to be individuals. /I mean, /I said that/the Eton boys were wild ducks/who know to fly in formation. /Bryanston students/are wild ducks. /Then there is Wells Cathedral school, /very strong music, /may be not as strong academically. /But if your child, if your child/is best talented in music, /that kind of school/is worth considering. /Millfield/also has strong music. /But above all, /Millfield is famous/for being very powerful in sport. /And Millfield School/produces more former students/who are in the Olympic Games/than any other schools. /So if your child's main talent/is in sport/rather than academics, /and Millfield would be one to think about. /

在清单的底部，/我列了一些学校，/成绩不突出，/但有其他优势。/布莱恩斯顿，/艺术是其强项，/非常鼓励学生/发展个性。/我的意思是，/我说过/伊顿公学的学生是野鸭子，/会列队飞行，/布莱恩斯顿的学生/也是野鸭子。/这是威尔士教堂学校/音乐很厉害，/可能成绩逊色一点。/但如果您的孩子/最擅长音乐，/那么这类学校/值得考虑。/米尔菲尔德学校/音乐也很好，/但是，/这所学校最出名的/是强大的体育实力。/而且米尔菲尔德学校/培养出了很多学生/参加了奥运会，/人数超过了其他学校。/所以如果您的孩子擅长/体育/而不是学习，/那么米尔菲尔德学校可以考虑。/

36:31—36:53

Then there are prep-schools/I mentioned earlier/with international sections/for the progressive integration/for students with weak English. /They are both in the southwest of England. /And they are called Taunton/and Sherborne. /

这是预备学校,/我之前提到过的,/它们有国际部,/可以逐渐融入环境,/适合英语薄弱的学生。/学校都在英格兰西南部,/名字叫汤顿/和谢伯恩。/

36:53—38:11

I have also added three schools, /which are very good at looking after/and developing students/who are not really academic at all, /but who have other needs/and other interests, /and these schools will nurture/and develop those children/and look after them/in the best possible way. /I mentioned three, /they are called Milton Abbey, /Shiplake/and Lord Wandsworth. /Milton Abbey is very interesting. /At Milton Abbey at the moment, /students who have some flair/for entrepreneurship for business, /but who are not very good at, /are being encouraged/to take a very business approach to education. /And a lot of businessmen/and engineers/and creative developers/and entrepreneurs/are going into Milton Abbey School. /These are children/who will not go to university, /who will go straight into industry/or into design/or into some other creative practical field. /So different schools/offer different opportunities/for children. /Two others, /they're called Shiplake/and Lord Wandsworth. /

我还加了三所学校,/非常擅长照顾/和培养学生,/那些成绩不太好的学生,/这些学生有其他需要/和兴趣,/这些学校会培养/和开发他们的潜能,/照顾他们,/尽可能给他们最好的照顾。/我说的这三所学校/分别叫米尔顿阿贝学校、/船湖学院/和万斯沃斯勋爵学院。/米尔顿阿贝学校非常有趣,/现在在米尔顿阿贝学校/学生如果有天赋/创业,/但不是很擅长,/学校就会鼓励他们/选择商业课程。/许多商人、/工程师、/创意开发人员、/企业家/都选择了米尔顿阿贝学校。/这些孩子/不打算上大学,/而是直接进入行业工作、/从事设计/或其他创意实用领域。/因此,不同学校/会提供不同的机会/给学生。/另外两所学校/分别是船湖学院/和万斯沃斯勋爵学院。/

38:11—38:23

And there will be an opportunity/I think/during the panel discussion later/to follow up with questions, /but I will stop there for the moment. /Thank you for listening! /

会有机会,/我想,/在接下来的小组讨论中/回答大家的问题。/我就暂时先说到这了。/感谢大家的聆听!/

第三单元　观光旅游
Tourism

I. 视译单位衔接

顺译是视译最基本的原则，要实现顺译，就需要划分类意群，进行合理断句。在一些情况下，依照类意群的顺序进行翻译，不需要添加任何连接词，译文语句表达也比较清楚、流畅。但由于中英文在表达方式上存在较大差异，有时依照类意群断句之后，译文语句会显得支离破碎，在这种情况下，可使用一定的衔接手段来连接类意群，使译文表达完整顺畅（秦亚青、何群，2009：59）。主要有如下两种情况需要使用衔接手段。

1. 需要增加名词或代词作连接成分的句子

英语句子会频繁地使用复合句，在视译中要对其进行拆分顺译，往往拆分后的中文句子不够通顺、连贯，在这种情况下，可以相应增加名词或代词。

【例1】The international and regional financial institutions/saw a drastic reduction/in resources/allocated to the agriculture. /
译文1：国际和区域金融机构急剧减少资源投入，在农业活动。
译文2：国际和区域金融机构/急剧减少/资源投入，/这些资源是投向农业活动的。/
例1中resources一词后面的分词短语充当定语，而在中文表达中，定语基本都是放在修饰的名词之前。在顺译的情况下，原文拆分之后则会出现译文1，句子后半部分语义不完整。译文2增加了"这些资源是投向"，使得译文表达相对比较顺畅。

【例2】An old friend came to our university/to visit us/last night. /
译文1：一个老朋友到学校来看望我们，在昨晚。
译文2：一个老朋友到学校/来看望我们，/这是昨晚的事。/
英文的时间状语可以根据情况放在句首，也可以放在句中或句末，而中文基本上没有时间状语放在句末的情况。例2在顺译的情况下译成译文1，则时间表达较为突兀。译文2根据情况增加了"这是"和"的事"，译文听起来就通顺许多。

2. 介词引导的句子成分

按照中文的表达习惯，很多英语介词短语在翻译中都需要调整语序。而在视译中，可以将介词短语转换成其他连接成分，使译文表达通顺。

【例3】 The villagers spent a lot of human and material resources/on a 10-year drive/to make such a glorious achievement. /

译文1：村民们在10年中花费了大量人力物力，才取得了如此辉煌的成就。

译文2：村民们花费了大量人力物力，/经历了10年的奋斗，/才取得了如此辉煌的成就。/

例3可以划分为3个类意群，如果在笔译中，通常会对第二个介词短语进行语序调整。而在视译中，可以在不调整语序的情况下，增加"经历了"和"奋斗"这两个连接部分，译文就比较流畅。

【例4】 The construction team finished the project/in 2 years. /

译文1：施工队完成了这项工程，在两年时间里。

译文2：施工队完成了这项工程，/花了两年时间。/

英语中很多介词引导的句子成分作状语出现在句子的后半部分，而中文多将状语放在句子前半部分。在笔译中，则需要调整例4中的时间状语在句中的位置；而在视译中，可以将介词转换成动词"花了"，这样译文就比较通顺。

II. 实战练习一

1. 演讲背景

2012年，西澳大利亚州旅游局在广州举办"西澳大利亚州旅游局中国旅游洽谈会"，来自西澳大利亚州的20家当地旅游运营商和多家中国旅行社深入交流，积极探讨如何进一步开展合作，共同推广西澳大利亚州丰富的旅游资源。下文为来自黄金内陆区代表的演讲，介绍了当地的特色景点，包括波浪岩、种类繁多的野花，还为听众推荐了两个必去的地方，分别是埃斯佩兰斯和嘉哥利。

2. 预习词汇

Australia Golden Outback 澳大利亚黄金内陆区
Tourism Western Australia 西澳旅游局
Wave Rock 波浪岩
a day trip 一日游

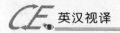

Australian Pinnacle Tours 澳大利亚尖峰旅行社
self-drive 自驾游
Margaret River 玛格丽特河
Pemberton 潘伯顿
Walpole 沃波尔
Albany 奥尔巴尼
Hyden 海登
Perth 珀斯
Esperance 埃斯佩兰斯
SkyWest 澳洲天西航空公司
Lucky Bay Beach 幸运湾海滩
aboriginal 土著的
B&B stay 家庭旅馆的住宿
Kalgoorlie 嘉哥利
Qantas 澳洲航空公司
gold nugget 金块
gold bullion 金条
golf course 高尔夫球场
Rydges Hotel 雷吉斯酒店
Nullarbor Links Golf Course 诺拉波林克斯高尔夫球场
Ceduna 塞杜纳

3. 演讲文本

00:00—00:28

Hi! 你好!/I am Gabby/from Australia Golden Outback./It is a real thrill/to be with you this afternoon,/to introduce the Golden Outback to you./Who are we?/Australian Golden Outback,/we are one of the five tourism regions/funded by Tourism Western Australia./And we are that big region in the middle/that you can see,/the gold region./So this afternoon,/I am going to share with you/some of the key features/and attractions from the Golden Outback./

嗨,你好!/我是加比,/来自澳大利亚黄金内陆区。/非常激动/今天下午和你们在一起,/向你们介绍黄金内陆区。/我们是谁?/澳大利亚黄金内陆区,/我们是五大旅游区之一/得到了西澳旅游局的资助。/我们是中间的那个大区域,/你们可以看到,/黄金区域。/所以今天下午,/我将和你们分享/我们的主要特点/和黄金内陆区的景点。/

00:29—00:45

So the first one being Wave Rock. /Wave Rock is very famous/in Western Australia. /It is called Wave Rock/because it looks like a wave/that crashes over the surrounding bush. /Most people who visit Wave Rock/will do it as a day trip/with Australian Pinnacle Tours. /

第一个是波浪岩。/波浪岩非常有名,/享誉西澳大利亚。/它被称为波浪岩/是因为它看起来就像一个波浪/撞上了周围的灌木丛。/大多数要去波浪岩的游客/都会选择一日游,/参加尖峰旅行社的旅行团。/

00:46—01:29

But many also undertake it/as a self-drive experience. /Particularly, /after, /if you are going to see/Jasmine's region of Australia Southwest/after you've visited Margaret River, /the beautiful trees in Pemberton, /and Walpole/and then onto Albany. /This is normally a five, /four-to-five-day itinerary. /But we suggest/get your clients to extend their trip/just by one night. /They can drive/from Albany/to Hyden, /explore Wave Rock. /In the following day, /they can drive back to Perth/ and it would take them four hours/from Hyden. /I will show you/your clients will have a lot of fun/in Wave Rock. /

但也有很多游客/会选择自驾游。/特别是,/之后,/如果您准备游览/Jasmine 小姐介绍的澳大利亚西南部,/在游览玛格丽特河之后,/然后您可以观赏潘伯顿美丽的树木,/再去沃波尔,/然后是奥尔巴尼。/这通常需要 5 天/或 4 到 5 天的行程。/但我们建议/让你们的顾客延长他们的行程,/延长一晚即可。/他们可以开车/从奥尔巴尼/到海登,/探索波浪岩。/在接下来的一天,/他们可以开车回珀斯,/要开四个小时/如果从海登出发。/我保证/你们的顾客会玩得很开心,/享受在波浪岩的时光。/

01:30—02:04

Western Australia, /we are renowned for our beautiful species of wildflowers. /We have 12,000 in the state. /In the Golden Outback, /our flowers, /actually, /start to bloom/from July to October. /And these are the wonderful, /everlasting/and these bloom as far as I can see. /We also have many other species of wildflowers as well/that bloom a little bit later in the year. /But typically/our wildflower season/is anywhere from late July to October, November. /

西澳大利亚州,/以美丽的野花而闻名。/我们州有 12,000 个品种。/在黄金内陆区,/我们的鲜花,/实际上,/开始开花,/从七月一直持续到十月。/这些盛开的花朵非常迷人、/美妙永恒、/灿烂热烈。/我们也有许多其他种类的野花,/在今

年晚些时候开花。/但通常/我们的野花花季，/大概是七月末到十月、十一月。/

02:05—02:59

Now, /this is Esperance. /Esperance is renowned/for its spectacular coastal scenery, /beautiful national parks. /We've got seven national parks nearby. /Getting to Esperance, /you can undertake a self drive. /Our recommendation is/minimum two-night stay in Esperance/or you have got multiple daily flight/with SkyWest/from Perth. /Now Esperance is very famous/for having the whitest beach in Australia. /And this is Lucky Bay Beach, /where even the friendly kangaroos/will come down to the water's edge/and say "你好" to you. /

这个/是埃斯佩兰斯。/埃斯佩兰斯非常有名，/以其壮观的沿海风光/和美丽的国家公园著称。/我们有七个国家公园在附近。/到埃斯佩兰斯，/您可以自驾游。/我们的建议是/至少要有两晚停留在埃斯佩兰斯，/或者您可以乘坐每天的多趟航班，/选择澳洲天西航空公司/从珀斯飞过来。/现在埃斯佩兰斯很有名，/因为它拥有澳大利亚最洁白的海滩。/这就是幸运湾海滩，/这里甚至会有友好的袋鼠/来到水边，/对您说"你好"。/

02:59—03:12

There are a number of tours/that you can actually do/while you are in Esperance. /Very popular tour/is an Aboriginal cultural experience. /And this is with Kepa Kurl. /And it is run by a local, /Aboriginal elder/called Doc Reynolds. /But everyone calls him Uncle Doc. /So if you have your clients/wanting to come to Esperance, /book them on a Kepa Kurl Tour. /And Doc will show you/how the Aboriginal lived/prior to European settlement of Australia. /

有很多旅行团/您都可以参加/去游览埃斯佩兰斯。/非常流行的旅行团/是土著文化体验。/这就是 Kepa Kurl 旅行社。/它的老板是一个当地人，/一个土著老人，/名字叫多克雷诺兹。/但大家都叫他多克叔叔。/所以如果您有顾客/想去埃斯佩兰斯，/给他预定 Kepa Kurl 的旅行团。/多克会向你们展示/土著人的生活，/在欧洲人定居澳大利亚之前的生活方式。/

03:13—03:39

You will be spoilt for choice/with the accommodation in Esperance. /You have got hotels, /motels. /But one of our recommendations is/get your clients/to stay with an Australian family/and undertake a B&B stay. /You will really be spoilt for choice. /You can actually wake up/to the sound of the ocean and birds/and clear, sunny, blue skies. /You will see funny dolphins/and also whales in season. /

第三单元　观光旅游 Tourism

您将有很多种选择，/挑选在埃斯佩兰斯的住宿。/您可以选择酒店，/汽车旅馆。/但我们的建议是/让你们的顾客/住在澳大利亚家庭中，/享受家庭旅馆的住宿。/您真的有很多种选择。/您醒来时/会听到海洋和鸟类的声音，/看到清澈、晴朗、湛蓝的天空。/您还会看到有趣的海豚/和当季的鲸鱼。/

03:40—04:07

We are now onto Kalgoorlie. /Kalgoorlie is actually/the Gold Capital of Australia/ and it is Australia's largest outback city. /There are multiple daily flights/with SkyWest and also Qantas. /So getting around to Kalgoorlie/is not a problem. /Or you can simply undertake it/as part of a self-drive experience. /Now our recommendation is/ minimum one-night stay in Kalgoorlie. /

我们现在来看看嘉哥利。/嘉哥利实际上/是澳大利亚的"黄金之都"，/也是澳大利亚最大的内陆城市。/每天有多趟航班，/是由澳洲天西航空公司和澳洲航空公司提供的。/所以去嘉哥利/交通非常便利。/或者您可以简单地把它/作为自驾游的一部分。/我们的建议是/在嘉哥利至少停留一晚。/

04:08—04:45

Kalgoorlie is also obviously/being the gold producing capital of Australia. /It is famous for its gold. /While there, /your clients can actually undertake a tour, /a gold prospecting tour. /One such tour/is put together by company/called Finders Keepers. / It is called Finders Keepers/because/if your clients find the gold nugget, /they get to bring it home, /but in the off chance. /They are not lucky/in finding their gold nugget. /They can actually purchase their own gold, /Western Australian nugget or bullion/from a specialty store/around Kalgoorlie. /

嘉哥利显然/是澳大利亚的"黄金之都"。/它以黄金而闻名。/在那里，/你们的顾客实际上可以参加旅行团，/开始一次黄金勘探之旅。/这样的旅行/是由一家公司组织的，/叫"捡到归我"公司。/它叫做"捡到归我"/是因为/如果你们的顾客找到了金块，/他们可以把它带回家。/但这种可能性很小。/他们并没有那么幸运/能找到金块，/不过他们可以购买金块，/西澳大利亚的金块或金条，/在专卖店可以买到，/嘉哥利附近就有。/

05:01—05:17

In Kalgoorlie, /we are also renowned/for having a golf course. /Excuse me. / This is the Kalgoorlie Golf Course, /designed by Graham Marsh. /Most people going to Kalgoorlie/will undertake, /they will fly in the morning, /play a bit of golf, /and maybe come back in the afternoon/or on evening flight. /18 holes fully reticulated, /

51

and you can see/it is really contrasted, /you know, /with this rich wet earth/of the Western Australian Outback. /

嘉哥利/之所以也有名/因为我们拥有高尔夫球场。/不好意思。/这是嘉哥利高尔夫球场, /由格拉罕·马斯设计的。/大多数人去嘉哥利/都会/在早上坐飞机去, /在那里打一会儿高尔夫球, /也许会下午回来, /或乘坐晚上的航班返回。/18个高尔夫球洞连成网。/您可以看到/这是一种强烈的对比, /您知道的, /这是一片肥沃湿润的土地, /就在西澳大利亚内陆区。/

05:18—05:35

In Kalgoorlie, /you will be spoilt for choice in accommodation. /The best accommodation/is the Rydges Hotel. /There are also lots of dinning options. /You've got Chinese restaurants/and many other restaurants. /So your clients will be spoilt for choice. /

在嘉哥利/您也有多种住宿选择。/最好的住处/是雷吉斯酒店。/那里也有很多用餐选择, /有中餐馆/和许多其他餐馆。/这样你们的顾客就有多种选择了。/

05:36—06:18

And speaking of golf, /Australian Golden Outback, /we are also part of the Nullarbor Links Golf Course. /It is the world's longest golf course. /It starts in Western Australia, /finishes in Ceduna, /or the other way, /extends 1,400 kilometers. /So the idea is/every hundred kilometers or so, /your clients will actually drive, /play a bit of golf, /and they will be on their way. /And at completion, /they will actually get a certificate/to say they have completed the world's longest golf course. /This is just a few more pictures/of the Nullarbor Links. /They recently won a Gold Medal/at the Western Australian Tourism Award/only last week, /hence the best attraction. /So we are really thrilled with that. /

说到高尔夫球, /澳大利亚的黄金内陆区, /也是诺拉波林克斯高尔夫球场的一部分。/它是世界上最长的高尔夫球场。/从西澳大利亚州开始, /直到塞杜纳结束, /或者这么说吧, /它绵延1,400公里。/所以就是说/每一百公里左右, /你们的顾客会开车, /打一会儿高尔夫球, /然后他们就上路了。/一路打完高尔夫球后, /他们将获得一份证书, /证明他们在世界上最长的高尔夫球场上打完球。/还有几张图片/是关于诺拉波林克斯高尔夫球场的。/他们最近获得了一枚金牌, /荣获西澳大利亚旅游奖, /就在上星期, /因此这是最好的旅游景点。/所以我们对此非常兴奋。/

第三单元 观光旅游 Tourism

06:19—07:13

We do have a website, /australiasgoldenoutback. com. /If you visit us, /there is actually a Google translate button. /So you can click/on Chinese language simplified, /it will actually convert our website/back into Chinese for you. /Some of you may also have taken an opportunity/during our tea time/to actually pick up one of our brochures. /But I am here to help you/if you have got any questions. /If you need help/with self-drive itineraries, /please get in touch with me. /And we look forward/to seeing yourself/and your clients/in the Golden Outback very soon. /Thank you! /

我们有一个网站,/australiasgoldenoutback. com。/如果您访问我们的网页,/上面有一个谷歌翻译按钮。/您可以点击/选择简体中文,/它会把我们的网站/翻译成中文。/你们也需抓住机会了,/在茶歇的时候/拿到了一份宣传册。/我也可以帮助您/解答问题。/如果您需要帮助/规划自驾游路线,/请和我联系。/我们期待/见到您/和你们的顾客/马上来到黄金内陆区游玩。/谢谢!/

III. 实战练习二

1. 演讲背景

下文同样摘自"2012西澳大利亚州旅游局中国旅游洽谈会"。演讲嘉宾是来自珀斯铸币厂的代表。她介绍了到珀斯铸币厂的交通路线,展览区的主要展品,黄金浇铸秀,销售的产品包括纪念徽章、硬币、珠宝首饰等。

2. 预习词汇

Perth Mint 珀斯铸币厂
gold nugget 金块
gold bar 金条
gold bullion 金条
12 Chinese Lunar Series 十二生肖系列
Argyle pink diamond 阿尔盖粉钻
Kailis pearl 卡利斯珍珠

3. 演讲文本

00:00—00:15

大家好!/Hello!/我的名字叫Samantha。/And I will be talking about the Perth Mint for you today. /Thank you! /

大家好!/你们好!/我的名字叫萨曼莎。/我今天将会和大家谈一下珀斯铸币

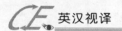

厂。/谢谢!/

00:19—00:22
Can you please put your hand up/if you've been to the Perth Mint? /
请举手/我看看有谁去过珀斯铸币厂?/

00:26—00:34
No one? /Yes? /No? OK! /I can hear some responses. /Thank you. /
没人去过吗?/有吗?/没有? 好的。/我能听见一些回应了。/谢谢你们。/

00:36—00:42
So the Perth Mint. /We are actually a tourist attraction/as well as a shopping venue/combined in one. /
来说说珀斯铸币厂。/我们实际上是一个旅游景点/也是一个购物点,/二合一。/

00:43—01:07
And the Perth Mint/is located/just on the east side of the Perth City Mall. /And you can actually walk from the city. /It is about a 15-minute walk. /Or if you want/and you are a little bit more lazy/like me, /you can actually take the free Red Cat Bus. /And that takes about maybe five minutes/from the town. /
珀斯铸币厂/就坐落在/珀斯城购物中心的东边。/其实您可以从城市里走过去。/差不多要走15分钟。/或者如果您愿意的话,/您可能有点懒,/像我一样,/您可以坐免费的红色猫巴。/这差不多要花五分钟/从市中心过去。/

01:08—01:19
And just around the Perth Mint, /I have actually put some different, other tourist sites. /So the Perth Mint isn't isolated. /There are other things to do/while you are in Perth City, too. /
就在珀斯铸币厂周围,/我其实也放了一些不同的、其他的旅游景点上去。/所以,珀斯铸币厂并不是孤立的。/还是有其他地方可以参观的,/您来珀斯都可以参观。/

01:20—01:42
So when you visit the Perth Mint, /do you actually can join the tour? /We do have three Chinese tour guides now available/to help those that only speak Mandarin. /And

we can start off with the front of the building/and our tour guide actually talks/about the history of the Perth Mint, /what the Perth Mint is, /what we do there, /and what we are doing now. /

所以你们参观珀斯铸币厂时, /能不能参团呢? /我们现在这里有三名说中文的导游/可以帮助只讲普通话的游客参观。/我们的旅程从这座建筑前开始, /导游会介绍/珀斯铸币厂的历史, /珀斯铸币厂是怎样的, /我们在这里主要做什么/以及正在做的事情。/

01:46—02:11

And later on/you can actually continue into the exhibition area. /And we have a tour guide talking about/how gold nugget was done in the past. /At the Perth Mint, /you actually can see/the second world's largest gold nugget/that is still in existence. /This is called/the Newmont's Normandy Nugget. /And it weighs approximately 25.5 kilograms. /

之后/你们就真正进入展览区了。/我们有导游讲解/金块过去是如何铸造的。/在珀斯铸币厂, /您可以目睹/世界第二大的金块, /现存至今的金块。/它被称为/纽蒙特公司的诺曼底金块, /重量约25.5公斤。/

02:12—02:33

At the Perth Mint, /there are not just things you can see, /but things you can actually do as well, /so experience such as touching gold. /And the value of this gold bar/currently today/is approximately 700,000 dollars. /A lot of us wouldn't have touched gold/in our lives. /

在珀斯铸币厂, /您不仅可以参观, /还有一些可以参与的事情, /比如触摸黄金这样的体验。/这个金条的市值/目前/约为七十万美元。/我们很多人都没有摸过黄金, /一辈子都没机会。/

02:34—02:46

And we also have just lastly created, /the world's largest gold coin. /So this coin weighs one ton of pure gold, /and it is valued/at more than 50 million Australian dollars. /

而且我们最近才铸造了/世界上最大的金币。/这枚硬币重量是一吨的纯金, /价值/超过5千万澳元。/

02:47—03:46

So, /what's the best thing to do at the Perth Mint? /Well, /the best thing that/I would probably suggest would be/to actually go and experience and see/what a gold pouring show is actually like. /Our theater for this gold pour/sits 100 seats. /So basically/if you only have a few days/with the tours booked out, /but normally/anyone can just come to the Perth Mint/and there will be lots of seats available to jump on the tour. /

那么/在珀斯铸币厂最好做什么呢？/其实, /最好/我建议/去体验并看一下/黄金浇铸秀是怎样的。/我们这种浇铸表演的影院/有100个座位。/所以基本上/如果您只有几天的行程/且票都被订完了, /但通常情况下/只要您来了珀斯铸币厂/总会有很多空位的。/

03:46—03:55

And one of the nice little gifts/you can take home for your family, /your friends, /your boyfriend, /your girlfriend, /your husband/or your wife, /it's actually a little souvenir medallion. /Just this year/we create the last 12 Chinese lunar series. /And this is made with pure silver, /so that is 99.99% pure silver. /And with the designs, /you can put/any words, /any pictures/that we have in the computer/and it only takes about five minutes, /which is very very convenient. /So you can take home straight away. /

有一些不错的小礼物/您可以带给您的家人, /朋友, /男朋友, /女朋友, /您的丈夫/或是妻子, /其实就是一枚小小的纪念徽章。/就在今年, /我们铸造了最新的十二生肖系列。/这些都是纯银打造的, /所以含银量为99.99%。/徽章也会有一些设计, /您可以加一些/文字、/图片, /从我们的电脑里选, /只需要5分钟, /非常方便。/您可以直接带回家。/

03:56—04:21

And the main thing that we sell at the Perth Mint/is obviously our coins. /We make coins/in the factory at the Perth Mint. /And this year/we have sold out a lot of the Year of the Dragon 2012 lunar series. /And next year/we will be creating the Year of the Snake, /bullion, /silver, /gold/and platinum as well. /

我们珀斯铸币厂主打的产品/当然是硬币了。/我们制造硬币/是在珀斯铸币厂的工厂里。/今年/我们已经售罄了2012龙年十二生肖系列。/明年/我们会铸造蛇年的产品, /金条, /白银, /黄金/和铂金的。/

04:22—04:47

This is our beautiful jewelry room. /In the jewelry room/we try to feature, /and we try to sell Western Australian products, /such as the Argyle pink diamonds, /which you can see here. /The pink diamonds are the most rare diamond in the world. /They are the least available out of all the diamonds. /And that is why/they are so expensive/ and very, very sought-after. /

  这是我们美丽的珠宝室。/在珠宝室,/我们的特色是/销售西澳大利亚的产品,/例如阿尔盖粉钻,/您在这里可以看到。/粉钻是世界上最稀有的钻石。/是所有钻石中最少见的。/因此/它们价格高昂,/备受追捧。/

04:47—05:07

The other thing we sell in this particularly room/is actually the Kailis pearls, / pearls in Australia, /in particular, /Western Australia by Kailis. /They only have one shell, /and there is only one pearl in the shell. /So it takes, /it is a very good quality; /it is white. /There is no chemicals/or dye in it, /so naturally made. /

  我们在这间房子里卖的另外一种产品/就是卡利斯珍珠,/这是澳大利亚的珍珠,/尤其是/西澳产的卡利斯。/他们只有一个贝壳,/里面只有一颗珍珠。/所以/它的质量上乘,/洁白无瑕。/不含化学物质/或染料,/是天然形成的。/

05:08—05:35

And of course, /we do have our Australian gold nuggets/that been made into jewelry pieces, /such as rings, /earrings, /necklace pieces, /for your loved ones. / And it is OK for people that have smaller budget. /So not all of us have a lot of money. /But, /of course, /if you would like to buy something, /take it home for a friend, /a pen, /a key ring, /a little gold model. /We have other items/in this Gift Room/available for you, too. /

  当然,/我们也有澳大利亚的金块/做成的各种珠宝,/比如说戒指,/耳环,/项链,/这些都可以送给您的挚爱。/这些对于预算较少的人也是可以负担得起的。/所以并不是所有人都很有钱。/但是,/当然了,/如果您想买一些礼物/带回家给朋友的话,/可以是一支笔,/一个钥匙环,/一个小的黄金模型。/我们还有其他物品/在这个礼物店里/供您选择。/

05:38—05:46

And that is just the picture of the evening, /a night shot of the Perth Mint. /And we look forward to seeing you hopefully soon. /Thank you very much! /大家谢谢! /

  这是一张晚上的照片,/珀斯铸币厂的夜景图。/我们希望很快可以和大家见面。/谢谢! /谢谢大家! /

第四单元　人力资源
Human Resources

I. 句子成分转换

英语是一种静态的语言，动作意义经常借用同源名词或者其他词类来表达；汉语则是动态的语言，多用动词表达动作意义。英语中介词使用较多而汉语介词匮乏。因此在视译中可考虑将英语中的名词、动名词和介词与汉语中的动词进行相互转换。

1. 名词或动名词转换为动词

英语中许多包含动作意义的名词可以在译文中转换成动词，转换之后译文可以按照顺译的语序流畅表达出来。

【例1】As you know, /this outbreak of flu/is yet another <u>reminder</u>/that the world is an interconnected one. /

译文1：正如各位所了解的，这次流感爆发是对世界是相互连结的再次<u>提醒</u>。

译文2：正如各位所了解的，/这次流感爆发/再次<u>提醒</u>我们/世界是相互连结的。/

"Reminder" 如果在译文中以名词的形式出现，则需要等从句的内容译完才能翻译出"提醒"一词，需要颠倒语序。但如果将其处理成动词，就不需要大幅度调整语序，且译文更符合中文表达习惯。

【例2】The international food shortage/had a direct <u>impact</u>/on Kuwait and other barren desert countries. /

译文1：国际粮食的缺乏对科威特和其他贫瘠的沙漠国家产生了一种<u>直接的影响</u>。

译文2：全球性粮食短缺现象/<u>直接影响了</u>/科威特和其他贫瘠的沙漠国家。/

例2中 had a direct impact on sth. 是包含动宾关系的名词词组，"impact"形式上是名词，实际上表达的是动作，译文2处理成动词更有利于顺译。

2. 介词短语转化为动词结构

在英译汉中，可以将介词短语转换成动词结构，这样转换后的动词结构可以独立成小句。

【例3】Just last month, /I was in Changsha/at a highly-successful seminar/<u>on international education</u>. /

译文1：就在上个月，我在长沙，参加一个非常成功的国际教育研讨会。

译文2：就在上个月，/我在长沙，/参加一个非常成功的研讨会，/<u>讨论国际教育问题</u>。/

例3可以划分为4个类意群，如果在笔译中，通常会对最后一个介词短语类意群进行语序调整。而在视译中，可在不调整语序的情况下，将英文介词"on"转换成中文动词"讨论"。

II. 实战练习一

1. 演讲背景

未来人才研究机构的创始人和主席应邀参加"中国（珠海）国际人力资源科技博览会"并在研讨会上发表主题为"如何通过自动化实现人才评估与参与"的演讲。他在演讲的第一部分阐述了自动化将完全改变工作场所，尤其是人力资源领域。由于我们没有数据，也没有证据，目前人力资源部门做选择都是基于感觉或想法。但现在自动化可以帮助我们搜索求职者，筛选或评估人的技能及文化适应性。即将面世的自动化工具有预测分析、物联网技术、机器人技术、虚拟现实、增强现实、聊天机器人等。

2. 预习词汇

recruit 招聘
The Future of Talent Institute 未来人才研究机构
think tank 智囊团
McKinsey 麦肯锡
automation 自动化
kiosk 售货机；售货亭
flip 抛
recruiting process 招聘流程
cultural fit 文化适应性
screen 筛选
shovel 铲
Predictive Analytics 预测分析（一个预测分析工具）

VR/Virtual Reality 虚拟现实
AR/Augmented Reality 增强现实
Chatbot 聊天机器人
customer support 客户支持

3. 演讲文本

00:00—01:06

Good Morning. /Thank you for coming today. /We are gonna talk about the future. /We are gonna talk about what's happening/in the space of recruiting, /particularly recruiting, /and the future of technology in that space. /I will tell you a little bit first of all/about the Future of Talent Institute. /We are a think tank. /We do research into the future of work, /into the future of employment, /the future of learning. /And we try to do the research/by talking to a lot of people around the world, /by seeing what's happening in the technology space, /what is emerging, /what's starting to become popular. /And we also work with many companies/to help them/use technology better, /to do recruiting particularly/and to do human resources more effectively. /

早上好。/感谢大家的参与。/我们会讲讲未来, /讲讲有什么事情会发生/在招聘领域, /尤其是招聘过程, /以及该领域未来的技术。/我会首先跟大家谈谈/未来人才研究机构。/我们是智囊团, /研究未来的工作, /未来的就业, /未来的学习。/我们试着进行研究, /主要方式是与世界各地的人们进行交流, /观察技术领域的变化, /观察新兴事物, /和流行事物。/我们还与许多公司合作, /帮助他们/更好地利用技术, /尤其是做好招聘工作, /提高人力资源效率。/

01:07—01:32

So it's really fascinating for me/because I travel all over the world. /I work in many many different countries/from South America, /Africa, /Asia, /Europe/and America. /And in each of these countries, /I try to see/what's happening in the technology space, /what's different, /what's new, /what's emerging/and what's the future look like. /So that's what we are gonna talk about today. /

这对我来说真的很棒, /因为我往返于世界各地。/我在许多不同的国家工作, /包括南美洲、非洲、亚洲、欧洲和美国等。/在各个国家, /我都试着了解/技术领域发生了什么, /有什么不同, /有什么新事物, /什么正在兴起, /未来是什么样子。/这些就是我们今天要谈论的话题。/

第四单元　人力资源 Human Resources

01:33—02:07
So/I think the first thing to remember/is that the world is changing really quickly. /I'm sure that many of you/have seen incredible change in China/in the last 10 years/and the last 5 years. /Yesterday/I toured Zhuhai, /and they told me/just a few years ago/there was nothing here almost. /And I look at it today/and I see a beautiful, beautiful city/that's been created very quickly and very rapidly. /And this is happening everywhere in the world. /

所以，/我认为首先要记住的/是世界瞬息万变。/我相信你们很多人/已经目睹了中国惊人的变化，/就在过去十年、/五年之中的变化。/昨天/我参观了珠海，/他们告诉我/就在几年前，/这里几乎什么都没有。/今天看看这儿，/我看到了一个非常美丽的城市，/建设速度非常之快。/世界各地都是这样的情况。/

02:08—02:57
But it's not just with cities. /It's with technology；/it's with how we recruit people；/it's how we do human resources. /And I think/in human resources, /we're behind；/we're slow；/we haven't gone as fast as the rest of the world has gone. /And we need to do more to get there. /But the consulting firm, /McKinsey, /a few years ago, /two or three years ago, /they did a study of/what's happening with the world of automation and robotics. /And they predicted/that about 19 million people globally around the world, /we just don't need them at all to work. /They can stay home/and sleep/if they want/because we don't need them to work, /because the robots/or automation/can do their job. /

不仅城市是这样，/科技如此，/人才招聘如此，/人力资源也是如此。/我认为/在人力资源方面，/我们落后了，/进展缓慢，/我们的速度落后于世界其他地方。/我们要努力追赶。/但咨询公司/麦肯锡/在几年前，/两三年前，/就研究了/自动化和机器人技术领域的发展。/他们预测/全球大约有1,900万人，/根本不需要去工作。/他们可以呆在家里/睡觉，/如果他们愿意的话，/因为我们不需要他们去工作，/因为机器人/或自动化/可以代替他们工作。/

02:58—03:47
So one of the examples of this/is McDonald's. /And if you go to a McDonald's in Australia, /and if you go to some of the McDonald's in the US, /you will find no people. /You walk into the McDonald's, /and there is a kiosk, /like a bank machine/with pictures of hamburger, /French fry, /cola, /and you just push the button, /use your credit card to pay, /and there's one person in the back/who will bring you food. /And in a year or two, /that person in the back/will be a robot. /So pretty soon, /there

61

will be nobody in the McDonald's. /And if you think how many people/work in McDonald's today, /it's a lot of people that work in the McDonald's. /OK? /So we won't need them anymore. /

其中一个例子/是麦当劳。/如果您去澳大利亚的麦当劳,/去美国的麦当劳,/您会发现都没有人。/走进麦当劳,/有一个售货机,/就像银行的机器,/上面的图片有汉堡包、/薯条、/可乐,/您只需按一下按钮,/用信用卡支付,/后台就会有工作人员/把食物送给您。/一两年后,/后台工作人员/就会是机器人了。/因此很快,/麦当劳就不需要人了。/您想想有多少人/现在在麦当劳工作,/人非常多,/对吧?/我们以后就不需要他们了。/

03:48—04:07
So/the question then for human resources is:/what happens to those people? /And that means/we have to educate them better, /we have to give them new skills to learn, /new things to do. And this is a big job/for every person and HR. /This is what we have to think about in the future. /

因此,/人力资源的问题是:/那些人会怎么样?/这意味着/我们要为他们提供更好的教育,/让他们学习新的技能,/从事新工作。/这是一项巨大工程,/对每个人和人力资源都是如此。/这是我们未来需要思考问题。/

04:08—04:34
But more things are gonna be automated/than we can imagine. /Many jobs/that today we think of as OK jobs, /good jobs/may not be here tomorrow. /We soon will have automatic cars/that drive by themselves, /so we won't need taxi drivers, /alright? /Pretty soon/we are going to have all kinds of automation/that's gonna change the workplace totally, OK? /

但更多的东西将被自动化,/多得超出我们的想象。/许多工作,/今天我们认为是还可以的工作、/好工作,/可能明天就没有了。/我们很快就会有自动驾驶汽车,/可自动驾驶,/我们就不再需要出租车司机了,/对吧?/很快/我们将有各种各样的自动化,/这将彻底改变工作场所。/

04:35—05:30
So what do we mean/when we use the word "automation"? /What do we mean? /What is automation? /And the simple definition/is either it removes the need for a person, /or we help people/do more than they used to be able to do. /We've already have a lot of automation/in our life. /For example, /a hundred years ago, /if you wanted to build a highway, /you had a lot of people/digging the dirt, /right? /You

had hundreds of people. /Today we have a machine/that does the digging for us. /That's automation. /So we already have automation/in physical work. /Now we are getting automation/in mental work. /

那么，我们是什么意思呢？/当我们使用"自动化"一词时，指什么呢？/我们想说明什么？/什么是自动化？/简单来说，/它消除了对人力的需求，/或者我们帮人们/做更多他们能做的事。/我们已经有很多自动化/应用于生活中。/例如，/一百年前，/如果想修建公路，/就需要很多人/去挖土，/对吧？/需要成百上千个人。/今天有机器/帮我们挖土，/这就是自动化。/所以我们已经有自动化/应用于体力劳动，/现在我们要把自动化/用于脑力劳动。/

05:31—06:18

So/now we can begin to automate/what we do with our head/not just with our hands and our body. /And this is a big big change/from just five years ago/or ten years ago. /And so this is your future. /It's going to be what is the machinery/that will change the future of our minds/and what kind of thinking is happening. /So today/we think about things like recruiting/or talking with people/as important skills. /But what if/those could be automated? /What if/you can hire people/without any of your work? /And what if/you could just find good people? /Or maybe that would not happen, /but I think it can happen. /And that's what we will talk about here, OK? /It's possible. /And it can happen. /

因此，/现在我们可以开始自动化/脑力劳动，/而不仅是体力劳动。/这是巨大的变化，/也就开始于从五年前/或十年前。/这就是你们的未来。/什么样的机器/会改变我们将来的想法？/未来又会有什么样的想法？/现在，/我们考虑招聘/或人际交流/并将这些当做重要的技能，/但如果/这些都能被自动化了呢？/如果/你们能招到人/且不需要你们参与呢？/如果/你们很容易就能招到合适的人呢？/或许这还不会发生，/但我认为这是有可能的事。/这就是我们要讲的事，对吧？/这是有可能的，/是会发生的事。/

06:18—07:20

We've already have a lot of automation. /We've already have many things/that are automated. /You can automatically apply for a job/on the computer. /You can fill everything in, /and push the button/and you apply for the job. /Ten or fifteen years ago, /you had to write on paper, /and then you had to turn the paper in/to the employment office, /and they had to maybe read that/or put that into a computer. /Now you don't have to do that anymore. /So that's automation. /That's easy automation. /But now we are getting more and more sophisticated in our automation skills. /Now we have things/that help us to find people. /You have things like Weibo/ and Renren, /and many other products in China/that can help you/to find people to work for you/if you can use those products. /So/we've got many things/that are coming to make our jobs easier and better/to help us become good at recruiting. /

　　我们已经有很多自动化。/我们已经有很多东西/是自动化的。/您可以自动申请一份工作，/就在电脑上操作。/您填好所有资料，/然后按下按钮，/就申请这份工作了。/十年或十五年前，/申请要写在纸上，/然后递交纸质材料/给招聘办公室，/他们可能需要查看/或把它输入电脑里。/现在您不再需要这么做了。/这就是自动化，/这是非常简单的自动化。/但是现在我们有越来越复杂的自动化技术。/现在我们有工具/帮我们找人，/比如像微博/和人人网，/及中国许多其他的工具/都能帮您/找潜在员工，/您能使用这些工具的话就可以。/因此，/很多工具/会让我们工作更轻松、做得更好，/帮我们做好招聘工作。/

　　07:21—07:59

I think/it's already a lot of automation/that we do. /We already have many of these things happening already in the tools/and products/you can buy today. /If you go over to the expo hall, /and you look at the technology over there, /you will find many things/that are already automated. /Many of the things I'm gonna talk about/already exist over there in the expo hall. /So you should go and have a look/and talk to those vendors/about what can they do/that automates or helps you to do your job better than you do today, /right? /

　　我认为/很多自动化/我们都实现了。/我们已经有很多自动化的工具/和产品，/大家现在都可以买到。/如果你们去展厅，/看看那里展览的技术，/您会发现有很多东西/都已经自动化，/很多我将要谈论到的东西/已经出现在展厅里。/所以你们应该去看看，/跟参展商聊聊，/看这些产品能做什么？/是不是能让您的工作更自动化、更高效？/对吧？/

　　08:00—09:06

So/a lot of reasons for why we automate the job, /why would you want to automate this work, /why automate it, /why not just use people. /China has a lot of people, /so why not use the people, /right? /So why would you do this? /And there are many reasons for why you would do this. /Number one, /it's better than interviewing. /You know, /actually, /interviewing/is a very bad way to choose people. /If you look at the evidence, /the research on an interview, /it is about the same accuracy/as if you take a coin/and you flip it in the air, /and you pick the person from that. /Or if I just say, / "You and you and you/will come to work for me", /

第四单元　人力资源 Human Resources

and I've never even talked to you. /That's about the same success rate/as if you do the interview today. /So interviewing is not a very good way/to choose people. /That's one good reason/to use automation, /because automation is gonna be more accurate than that. /

　　因此，/工作自动化的原因有很多，/为什么要工作自动化/而不用人呢？/中国人口众多，/为什么不用人呢？/对吧？/为什么要自动化？/原因很多。/第一，/它比面试更好。/您知道，/事实上，/面试/是一种非常糟糕的选人方式。/如果您看了证据，/看了有关面试的研究的话，/面试的准确性/就像您拿一枚硬币/抛向空中，/根据抛掷结果来选人。/或者例如我说/"你、你还有你/来上班"，/但我甚至从来没有和你们说过话。/这是相同的成功率，/跟今天面试的成功率一样。/所以面试并不是一个很好的方式/来挑人，/这就是一个很好的理由/去使用自动化，/因为自动化更精确。/

09:07—10:20
The second one is we often say, /"Oh, if we interview good people, /they will stay longer in our company, /and they will not leave our company."/But we have no proof of that. /We have no research/that says that's true. /We think it's true, /but we don't know/that it's true. /So in HR, /we do many things in HR/that we think are true. /But if I ask you to prove it to me, /you couldn't. /You couldn't prove it to me. /You couldn't give me data. /You couldn't show me numbers. /If you ask an engineer, /"Will this building fall down?" /And he says, /"I don't think so". /You would not come in this building, /OK? /This engineer has done a lot of calculations/and mathematics/and research, /and they know/this building/will not fall down. /But we don't have that data in HR, /so if the CEO says to you, /"Is this person better than that person?" /How do we answer that question? /We have no data. /This is the problem with HR. /We have no data. /OK? /

　　第二个是我们经常说：/"哦，如果我们面试合适的应聘者，/他们会在公司呆得更久，/不会离开公司。"/但是我们没有证据。/没有研究/表明这是真的。/我们认为这是真的，/但我们并不知道/是不是真的。/所以在人力资源领域，/我们做很多事情/都是自己认为是正确的事。/但是如果我要求你们证明给我看，/你们却做不到，/你们无法证明。/你们无法给我数据，/你们给不了具体数字。/如果你们问一位工程师/"这幢楼会倒吗？"/他说：/"我认为不会。"/你们不会来这幢楼，/对吗？/这位工程师做了大量的计算、数学运算/和研究，/他们知道/这幢楼/不会倒。/但是我们人力资源没有这样的数据，/所以如果CEO问你们/"这个人比那个人优秀吗？"/我们怎么回答这个问题呢？/我们没有数据，/这就是人力资源的问题。/我们没有数据，/对吧？/

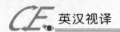

10:20—10:47

And the third thing/is you know/the hiring managers/and recruiters/have all your own beliefs, /like we might say, / "I think people that went to this university/are better than people who went to that university". /But can you prove it? /I say, / "I think people who smile a lot/are better than people who don't smile", /but can I prove it? /OK? /

第三件事是,/您知道,/招聘经理/和招聘人员/都有自己的信念,/就像我们可能会说:/"我认为这所大学的学生/优于那所大学的学生。"/但你们能证明吗?/我说:/"我认为经常笑的人/优于不笑的人。"/但我能证明吗?/对吧?/

10:48—11:16

So/this is what we make choices/in human resources all the time/that are just based on/what we feel/or what we think, /but we have no data, /we have no proof of that. /And so/if we want to make HR/a really respected profession, /then I think/we have to have data, /we have to start to be able to prove to people. /This is important. /

因此,/这就是我们的选择,/人力资源一直都是如此,/做选择都是基于/感觉/或想法,/但是我们没有数据,/没有证据。/因此,/如果我们想让人力资源/成为一个真正受人尊敬的职业,/我认为/我们必须有数据,/要能证明我们的选择。/这个很重要。/

11:17—12:06

And you look at certain companies in the US. /They are starting to do this now. /And they began to really research/and measure/what makes a person successful in our company. /And when they learn what it was, /it was very different/than what they thought it was. /They used to have a requirement/that you must have a certain score/in school. /If you don't have a certain score, /they would not hire you. /But then they did research, /and they found out/it has no meaning at all. /If you have low score/or high score, /the performance was exactly the same. /So this is the thing we have to think about in HR. /So that's one reason. /And these are some reasons/to automate the recruiting process, OK? /

你们看看美国的一些公司,/他们现在开始这么做了,/开始真正研究/和衡量/一个人在公司成功的原因。/当他们得知原因时,/发现完全不同/与他们之前所想的不同。/他们过去要求/你们必须考到一定的分数,/在校期间要这样,/如果您没有考到这个分数,/他们不会聘用您。/但后来他们做了研究,/发现/分数根本没有意义。/不管您是低分/还是高分,/您的表现都完全一样。/所以这是我们人力资源

第四单元　人力资源 Human Resources

必须考虑的问题。/这是其中一个原因。/这些就是为什么/要自动化整个招聘流程的原因。/

12:07—13:01

So it's many benefits to doing it. /You have a lot less of your personal opinion, /less bias/in what we are doing. /That's a huge positive thing for assessment. /You can actually get more good candidates, /because right now/you say four people/come to your company, /they want to work for your company. /You interview the four people, /and you hire one. /But you actually need many people, /but from the four/you pick one. /What if you could pick three from the four? /But today we don't do that. /And we don't do that/because we just don't do that. /We have no reason for that. /We have no good proof for that. /We could probably hire all of them, OK? /We can make sure/the candidate/is going to really fit our company well. /

所以这样做有很多好处。/会少了很多个人观点,/少了个人偏见/来影响我们处事。/这样非常有利于评估求职者。/您实际上能招到更多优秀的人,/因为现在,/比如说有四个人/来您的公司应聘,/他们想在您的公司工作。/您面试了这四个人,/只要了一个。/但实际上您需要很多人,/但是从四个人中/您挑了一个人。/要是您从四个人中挑三个人呢?/但现在我们不会这样做。/我们不这么做/仅仅是因为我们不这么做。/没有理由这样做,/没有证据证明要这样做。/我们可能四个人都录用,/我们可以确保/求职者/真的符合公司的要求。/

13:02—13:44

By doing assessment, /we can determine/is this person gonna work happily in this company? /Are they going to be happy/working in our company? /That's pretty important, OK? /You can find out/if people are not telling you the truth. /You can find out/if they are lying to you, /or if they are telling you things/that are only a little bit true/but they make it sound like it's a lot true. /So there is a lot of things you can do/by testing, /by using automated tools, /you can improve tremendously/being out of bad people that you hire. /You can have many fewer bad hires. /

通过评估,/我们可以确定/这个人是否会在公司里愉快地工作。/他们会愉快地/在我们公司工作吗?/这个相当重要,对吧?/您能知道/别人是不是讲了真话,/您能知道/他们是不是在撒谎,/或者他们告诉您的事情/是不是不太可信/但他们却言之凿凿。/所以您可以做很多事情,/方法就是做测试、/使用自动化工具,/您可以大大提高效率,/淘汰不合格的员工。/这样您就可以减少不合格员工。/

67

13:45—14:46

So/I think in the 21st century, /we are gonna see recruiters/and everybody else/that are automated by automation. /Automating just means/help you do your job. /That's what automating means. /That's a very simple thing. /You have software/and tools/that help you do your job/just like when they build the highway, /they have tools/to help them build the highway, OK? /You are gonna have tools/that help you to do a better job, /to be able to prove things/that you couldn't prove before. /And I think/it's very exciting/to be an HR right now today, /because you will actually see/you will be part of the future. /You will see/what's going on in this space, OK? /So remember the word "automate" /or "help you do your job". /Not so much to replace you, /but to help you do your job. /

因此，/我认为在21世纪，/我们会看到招聘人员/和其他所有人/都被自动化给自动化了。/自动化只是指/帮您完成工作，/这就是自动化的含义，/很简单。/您有软件/和工具/来帮您完成工作，/就像建公路一样，/他们有工具/帮他们修路。/您也会有工具/帮您把工作做得更好，/能够证明一些事，/以前证明不了的事。/我认为/非常令人兴奋的是/现在能去做人力资源，/因为您会看到/您将参与未来。/您会看到/这个领域发生了什么。/所以请记住"自动化"这个词/或"帮您完成工作"这个表述。/不是完全取代您，/而是帮您完成工作。/

14:47—15:23

So where are we heading? /What's the future look like for this space? /I think you are gonna find out/that we are going to use automation/to replace people/in helping you/to find good candidates. /The software/can search through the Internet. /It can search through all the places/where people are. /And it can help you/to find people who might be good people/to work in your company, /for that's the first thing you can have. /

那么我们将前往何方？/这个领域的未来是什么样的？/我想您会发现/我们将用自动化/取代人，/帮您/找到优秀的求职者。/软件/可以搜索互联网，/可以搜索任何地方/找到求职者，/也能够帮您/找到可能适合的人选/到您的公司工作。/这就是您能做的第一件事。/

15:23—15:54

The second thing/is screening/or assessing people for their skills, /their cultural fit. /Their personality/will be completely automated. /You will not have to interview anybody, OK? /And you will be able to provide to each person/a personal message. /You can give them a message/that is important for them/one by one/instead of one message/for many people. /

第二件事/是筛选/或评估人的技能/及文化适应性。/他们的个性/将完全自动化解读。/您不必面试任何人。/您可以给每个人/发送一条私人信息,/您可以给他们发送信息,/一条对他们来说很重要的信息,/一个个单独发,/而不是同一个信息/群发给很多人。/

15:55—16:47

So right now today, /all of our communication/is called "one to many", /meaning that I put something on the Internet, /I say, /"Come and work for our company. /It's a great company". /And everybody sees the same thing. /But what if the message you got/was different from the message that you got? /Everybody gets a different message/based on your own personality, /based on your own interest. /So/if you're interested in recruiting, /you might get a message/saying, "You want to work in our company, /because we have a great recruiting department/and you are gonna love to work here." /And if you are an engineer, /you will get a message/that says, "Come and work for our company, /because we have the best engineering group/in the world." /So everybody gets a message/that's good for what they have interest in, OK? /

所以如今,/我们所有的交流/都被称作"一对多",/意思是我把某些信息放到互联网上,/我说:/"来我们公司上班吧,/这是一家非常好的公司。"/每个人都看到同样的信息。/但是如果您收到的信息/不同于别人收到的信息呢?/每个人都收到不同的信息,/基于您的个性、/和兴趣爱好而定制。/因此,/如果您对招聘感兴趣,/您可能会收到一条信息/说:"您会想来我们公司工作的,/因为我们有很好的招聘部门,/您会喜欢这儿的。"/如果您是工程师,/您会收到一条信息,/说:"来我们公司工作吧,/因为我们有最优秀的工程团队,/世界一流。"/所以每个人都收到一条信息,/内容跟他们的兴趣相关。/

16:48—17:06

This is what we can do with automation. /You can't do it by yourself/because you have to work too hard. /You couldn't do it. /You will be doing nothing but that. /But with automation, /you can do this very easily. /And everybody can have a personal message. /So that's a really positive thing/in terms of attracting people/to your company. /

这是我们利用自动化能做的事。/单靠您自己无法完成,/因为一个人太辛苦,/您做不到。/您也只能忙于这一件事。/但有了自动化,/您可以很容易完成任务。/每个人都能收到一条个人信息。/所以这确实是一件好事,/能够吸引人才/到

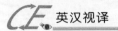

您的公司工作。/

17:08—17:19
And you can schedule anything automatically. /Someone can say, /on the computer/they can look at a calendar/and say "OK, this is one I can come, /this is one I can talk to you." /It's automatic. /

您可以自动安排任何事情。/有人可以说，/在电脑上，/他们可以看着日历/说："好，这天我能来，/这天我有空跟您谈话。"/这都是自动的。/

17:20—18:01
So these are things that we will replace you. /You don't have to do these things anymore at all. /These things will help you to do/and I think it will help you/to send the candidates really good information/because you can control that. /You can spend more time now/communicating with candidates/individually, /because you are not spending so much time/interviewing/and screening/and looking for the candidates. /Now you can spend time actually/talking to the candidates, /and learning about them/and convincing them/to come work in your company. /It will help you/to answer any questions that they have. /

所以这些是您将被取代的工作，/您不必再做这些事情。/自动化工具会帮助您完成，/我认为自动化工具会帮您/发送给求职者真正有价值的信息，/因为这都在您控制的范围之内。/您可以花更多的时间/与求职者交流，/一对一沟通。/因为您不必花费太多时间/去面试、/筛选/和寻找求职者。/现在您可以花时间/与求职者交流、/了解他们、/说服他们/加入贵公司，/这有助于您/解答任何求职者的问题。/

18:02—18:48
So right now we are often very busy, /we can't really have time/to do a personal conversation/with every candidate. /But if you let the tools/help you do the screening/and assessment, /again you will have more time/to do the assessment, /right? /When they come to work for your company, /then you can help them/to become used to working in your company. /You can tell them/about what it's like to work here, /you can spend time with them. /It's important and useful. /It's probably not that important/to spend time in the assessment, /because we can do that with automated tools. /But it is important to spend time/when they come to work for your company, /and when they have an issue with you. /

所以现在我们通常很忙，/我们没有时间/进行一次私人对话/去了解每个候选

第四单元 人力资源 Human Resources

人。/但是如果您利用工具/帮您筛选/和评估,/您会有更多的时间/来做评估,/对吧?/当员工新入职时,/您可以帮助他们/适应工作环境。/您可以告诉他们/在贵公司工作是什么样的,/您可以陪他们。/这很重要,也很有用。/没那么重要的就是/把时间花在了评估上,/因为我们可以使用自动化工具。/但需要花时间的是/新员工入职的时候/以及他们跟您有分歧的时候。/

18:48—19:19

So/these are the way/you can use the technology/to help you do a better job/by letting other machines/do what you do now. /So/you let them do/what you're doing now/and then you have more time/to do the other things. /And again, /just like building the road, /I don't have to have a hundred people shoveling. /Now I can have more people/who are driving the equipment/or doing other things/that are more useful for me/than digging in the dirt. /

因此,/就是这些方式,/您可以利用技术/帮您更好地完成工作,/您可以让其他机器/做您现在的工作。/所以,/让他们做/您现在所做的事,/然后您就有更多的时间/做其他事情。/而且,/就像修路,/不需要有一百个人去挖土,/现在我可以有更多的人/来操作设备/或做其他事情,/为我做更有用的事情,/而不是挖土。/

19:20—20:19

The computers can also do something/that is often difficult for us. /They can analyze/the entire job market, /and recommend how much to pay somebody. /They can recommend some kind of things/to give to an employee. /Because they can research a lot of information/and make a recommendation for you/about how much they should make for money/or what things you should offer to them/to get them to come and work for you. /So automation is a very good thing/for our profession. /There is a lot of exciting things/going on out there. /And this is just some of the technologies that are going on out here. /But all of these here, /all of these technologies/have been around for a long long time. /This is the Internet, /social networking, /your mobile phone. /I'm sorry/this pie is not good here, /it doesn't look good. /

计算机也可以做一些/对我们来说很困难的事。/计算机能分析/整个就业市场,/给出薪酬建议,/可以推荐一些东西/作为给员工的福利。/因为计算机可以调查大量信息,/建议您/支付员工多少薪水,/您应为员工提供什么待遇/来吸引他们入职。/所以自动化非常棒,/有利于我们的职业。/有很多令人兴奋的事/正在发生。/这只是其中一些正在发展的技术。/但所有这些,/所有的这些技术/已经出现很长时间了。/这是互联网,/社交网络,/您的手机,/不好意思,/这个饼图不太

71

好，/看起来不太清楚。/

20:20—21:36

Then we have these things over here/which are the things that are coming right now. /Then you're starting to see these automation tools. /So we are starting to see things/like Predictive Analytics. /Predictive Analytics/will look at the candidate, /and say, "There is a 60% chance." /For example, /they will say, / "There is 60% likelihood/that this person will be a good employee. /But this person is 90% likely/to be a good employee, /and this person is only 20% likely/to be a good person for you to work within your company." /That's called Predictive Analytics. /And by using the data, /you can actually predict/which one of your candidates/will be the best person/to hire in the company. /It's already happening. /There is [are] tools/in the exhibit hall. /In the expo hall, /you can talk to [them] about that. /Then we have... /Where are we? /Sorry. /Where am I? /Here we are. /OK. /

然后这儿的这些工具/马上就要面世，/然后您看到这些自动化工具，/所以我们看到一些工具，/诸如预测分析。/预测分析/将观察求职者，/然后说："有60%的几率。"/例如，/预测分析会说：/"有60%的几率/这个人会是名好员工。/但另一个人有90%的几率/是好员工，/还有这个人只有20%的几率/能成为你们公司的好员工。/这就是预测分析，/通过使用数据，/您可以预测/您的哪一位求职者/将是最佳人选、/可以录用。/这个已经在应用了。/有这样的工具/在展厅展出。/在展厅里，/你们可以和他们聊聊这些工具。/我们还有……/说到哪了？/抱歉，/我说到哪了？/这儿。/好的。/

21:37—23:07

Then we have things like the Internet of Things. /If you have it in your phone, /it can tell you/how far you walk today. /And if you use that, /look at your phone/and see/how far did I walk today, alright, /how many kilometers have I walked. /That is the Internet of Things. /I can track/what you do. /I can track/how far did you walk today. /Maybe I want to hire people/who are very active. /I look at this data/and I say, / "You never do anything. /You didn't even walk anywhere/for a week, /alright? /So I don't want you to work in my company/because you are not active." / OK? /So when will we be able to do this? /We can do this right now. /It's a bit scary. /But we can begin to watch your heart rate, /because I only want to hire healthy people, /and this person is not that healthy. /We can begin to do this/because of the things that we are starting to wear. /Your phone knows more about you/than your mother, /OK? /So, /it's a very intelligent device/that you are carrying around, /but

第四单元 人力资源 Human Resources

we don't know it. /Most of us don't even know/how much this phone knows/about what we do. /That's the Internet of Things. /So/we are gonna begin/to use that information/to help us/to make decisions/about people/and whether we should hire them or not hire them. /And we can use the Internet of Things/to help us with that. /

然后我们有物联网。/如果您有一个手机应用,/这个应用可以告诉您/今天走了多远。/如果您使用这个应用,/查看您的手机,/看看今天您走了多远,/走了多少公里。/这就是物联网。/我可以追踪/您做了什么,/我可以追踪/您今天走了多远。/可能我想聘用的人/是非常有活力的,/我查看这些数据,/然后说:/"您什么都不做,/您哪儿都不去,/连续一周都是这样,/对吧?/所以我不想聘用您,/因为您没有活力。"/对吧?/我们什么时候能做到这样呢?/我们现在就可以。/听起来点吓人。/但我们可以开始关注您的心率,/因为我只想聘用身体健康的人,/而这个人不够健康。/我们能够获得这些信息,/是基于我们佩戴的电子产品。/您的手机更加了解您,/比您妈妈还要了解,/对吧?/因此,/这是一个非常智能的设备,/您可以随身携带,/但我们对它却不了解。/我们大多数人甚至都不知道/这台手机有多么了解/我们在做什么。/这就是物联网技术。/因此,/我们将开始/使用这些信息/来帮助我们/做决定/选人,/帮我们决定是否要聘用。/我们可以利用物联网技术/帮我们做出决定。/

23:08—23:16

Then we have robotics/and we've already talked about the robots/that can do many of the jobs we have, /can help us do many of the jobs. /

然后我们有机器人技术,/我们已经讲了机器人/可以做很多我们的工作,/可以帮我们做很多事。/

23:16—24:12

And we have Virtual Reality/and Augmented Reality. /So Augmented Reality means, /like if you are walking down the street, /you can have something on your glasses, /you can wear glasses. /And you look at a building, /it will tell you the name of the building, /and you just see it/right in front of your eyes. /If you go on a tour to a new country, /it might be able to translate for you immediately. /I can speak to you in English, /and you would hear me speak in Chinese, OK? /And you will speak me in Chinese/and I would hear you in English instantly. /Automatic. /Alright? /This is all coming/within the next two to three years. /You will see this. /It will also, /when you walk down the street/in a new city, /you will see a map/right here in front of your eyes, /you can follow the map/to where you want to go. OK? /

我们有虚拟现实/和增强现实。/所以增强现实是指,/比如您走在街上,/您可

73

以在眼镜上添加一些东西，/您佩戴这副眼镜。/看到一幢建筑物，/眼镜会告诉您建筑物的名字，/您会看到这个名字/直接呈现在您眼前。/如果您到一个陌生的国家旅游，/眼镜可能会即时为您翻译。/我可以跟您说英文，/而您听到的是中文。/您跟我说中文，/我会立马听到英文。/这是自动翻译的。/明白吗？/这将发生/在未来两三年的时间里，/你们会看到这些。/而且，/当您走在大街上，/在一个陌生的城市，/您会看到一幅地图/展现在您眼前，/您可以按照地图/去您想去的地方。/

24:13—25:23

And this can help to give your candidates an experience/of what it is like to work in this company. /The candidates/can actually see people working. /They could actually experience/what's going on in your company. /I saw one of these/in Australia in a mine/where they get coal, /a coal mine. /And in the coal mine, /they have the candidates. /First of all, /the turnover rate in a coal mine/is very very high/because working in a coal mine/is not a good job. OK? /It's a very difficult job. /And so people who start the job, /they work for one week/or one day, /and they leave. /And so now each candidate/goes through Virtual Reality, /where they put them into a coal mine/with this pair of glasses you wear. /I went through this myself. /It's very interesting. /You walk into the coal mine. /It's completely dark. /You have to do the work/that a coal miner would do. /And many people who apply for the job, /they say, / "I don't want this job anymore, alright? /This is a really bad job. /I want to do something else. /OK?" /

这个也能让求职者体验/在贵公司工作是什么样的。/求职者/能真正看到工作场景，/他们能真正体验/贵公司正发生的事情。/我就见过这样的应用，/在澳大利亚的一个矿场，/他们在那里挖煤，/那是个煤矿。/煤矿上/来了一些求职者。/首先，/煤矿上人员流动率/非常高，/因为在煤矿工作/不是一份好工作，对吧？/工作很艰苦。/所以刚入职的人，/他们工作一周/或一天，/就离职了。/因此现在每位求职者/都通过虚拟现实，/置身于煤矿里，/戴上这副眼镜就能实现。/我自己就体验过，/很有趣。/走进煤矿，/周围完全是黑的，/您要干活，/做矿工做的事情。/很多求职者/说：/"我不想再干这个活儿了，好吗？/真的太辛苦了。/我想做点别的，/可以吗？"/

25:25—25:39

So immediately/you can hire better people/to work for you/by using this kind of technology/to help you to find these people. /So basically, /automatically it helps you to get rid of people/that aren't going to be happy in your company. /

因此马上/您就能招到更合适的人/来工作，/利用虚拟现实技术/就可以帮您找到这些人。/所以基本上，/虚拟现实能自动帮您剔除一些人，/那些不会喜欢这份工作的人。/

25:40—26:17
And then we have Chatbots. /And Chatbots are tools/that talk to you online, /but you think it's a person. /You already have them. /I'm sure you have them. /If you go to a website, /and you don't know/how to use some software. /And you might see/ "chat with somebody", / "ask somebody", /and you type in, / "I'm not sure/how to open the window". /And comes back says, / "just click on such and such a thing". /OK? /That was not a person. /That was a Chatbot. /That was a computer. /OK? /

我们还有聊天机器人。/聊天机器人是一种工具，/能和您在线聊天，/但您会以为它是个人。/您已经跟聊天机器人聊过天了，/您一定聊过。/如果您访问某个网站，/但您不知道/如何使用某个软件。/您可能会看到/"发起聊天"/"向我咨询"的提示，/然后您输入/"我不确定/如何打开窗口"。/然后就有回复说，/"只要点击这个还有这个就可以"。/对吧？/回复您的不是真人，/而是聊天机器人，/是一台电脑。/是吧？/

26:17—27:03
And if you go for a customer support in a company/right now today, /probably at least 50% of the answers you get back/come from a Chatbot. /So imagining recruiting, /if I say, / "How much do you pay people in your company?" /Then this Chatbot/will answer that question for a candidate. /Anything a candidate asks, /the Chatbot/would be able to answer that candidate. /That's again, /frees up your time/for not having to do that/and makes a better experience/for the candidate. /They are much happier now, /because they don't have to do that anymore. /So/the Chatbot/is coming quickly to recruiting. /I think you'll see that very soon/in many many of the career sites, /the online part of the recruiting process, OK? /

如果您寻求某家公司的客户支持，/就现在，/可能至少50%的回复/都来自聊天机器人。/设想在招聘中，/如果我说：/"贵公司薪酬是多少？"/然后聊天机器人/就会回复求职者的问题。/求职者询问任何问题，/聊天机器人/都能回答。/这样/又可以节省您的时间/不用去做这些事情，/而且可以提供更好的体验/给求职者。/招聘人员也更开心了，/因为他们不用再做这些事情了。/因此，/聊天机器人/将很快进入招聘领域。/我相信您很快就能看到，/尤其是在许多求职网站上/及网上招聘流程中。/

III. 实战练习二

1. 演讲背景

下文是未来人才研究机构的创始人兼主席在"中国（珠海）国际人力资源科技博览会"的研讨会上发表的演讲。他在演讲的第二部分分享了未来五年到十年会出现的招聘自动化工具，例如：招聘系统、机器人人才经理、DNA 分析、被动评估、解析工具、生物统计分析、语义分析、情感分析、心理分析、自动评估、Crystal 邮件辅助工具、评估应届大学生的工具等。在与求职者互动方面，可以使用社交媒体、聊天机器人、化身、求职者关系管理工具等。

2. 预习词汇

candidate 求职者
pop out 弹出
algorithm 计算程序；（计算机）算法
formula 公式
saliva 唾液
passive assessment 被动评估
parse 解析
biometric analysis 生物统计分析
semantic analysis 语义分析
Chatbot 聊天机器人
avatar 化身
CRM/customer relationship management 客户关系管理

3. 演讲文本

00:00—00:36

Then we have what's emerging, /what's coming next. /What will you see five years from today? /What are you going to see? /You're going to see/completely automated conversation/between a candidate and you. /You won't even need to be there anymore. /It will be all automatic. /The candidate/will ask questions, /the computer/will be able to answer those questions, /just like on your phone, /you can talk to your phone. /It's gonna be the same thing/with getting the information about working in your company. /And that will all be done automatically. /

新事物正在兴起，/正在到来。/您会在五年后看到什么？/您会看到什么呢？/

您会看到/完全自动的对话/出现在求职者和您之间。/您甚至不需要在场,/完全是自动的。/求职者/提出问题,/电脑/能回答这些问题,/就像您的手机一样,/您可以和手机对话。/同样,/在了解贵公司工作情况方面也是如此。/全都是自动完成的。/

00:37—01:37

You are going to see systems/that when they see somebody/come to the website. /Let's say/that I am coming to shop, /I want to buy something. /And this computer/instantly goes out/and says, / "Who is this person?"/And they do a quick look at/who I am. /And they say, / "Oh, this person/might be a good person/to work in our company. /This person/is not looking for a job. /This person wants to buy something." /But suddenly, /in the screen/pops out a little window, /it says, / "Would you like to work at our company?" /and starts to give them some information/about your company. /Think of how many more people you could hire/if that happened. /These people/are obviously interested in your company, /because they are buying something from you. /They know who you are/because they are already on your website. /But you don't even know today, /you don't know/that they are there, /because shopping/is totally separate from recruiting. /

您会看到这样的系统,/就是在他们发现有人/访问网站的时候。/假设/我想购物,/打算买点东西。/这台电脑/立即登场,/说:/"这人是谁?"/电脑快速地查看/我的信息,/说:/"哦,这个人/可能是合适人选,/适合在我们公司工作。/但这个人/不是在找工作,/而是想买东西。"/但突然,/电脑屏幕上/弹出一个小窗口,/上面写着:/"您愿意到我们公司工作吗?"/然后提供一些信息,/介绍贵公司。/想想您能招多少人啊,/如果真能这样操作的话。/这些人/显然对您的公司感兴趣,/因为他正从您那儿买东西。/他们了解你们公司,/因为他们已经登陆你们的网站。/但您今天甚至不知道,/不知道/他们已经在那里了,/因为购物/与招聘完全分离。/

01:37—02:09

But what if/I can put the two together? /So every time/somebody comes, /I can talk to them and say, / "Maybe/you might want to work here. /I know/you are an engineer. /This is what we have for engineering jobs." /Personal, tailored to them/and specific for them/and they will be very surprised, /because they just want to buy something/and suddenly/you say/you are interested in hiring them. /So this is really useful stuff, /really useful. /That's coming soon, coming soon. /

但是如果/我能把这两者结合在一起呢?/那么每次/有人来,/我都可以跟他们说：/ "也许/您想来这儿工作。/我知道/您是工程师。/这就是我们为工程师提供的职位。"/信息个性化，量身打造，/也很具体，/他们会非常惊讶，/因为他们只是想买东西，/突然/您说/您有兴趣聘用他们。/因此这是非常有用的系统，/非常有用。/很快就会出现。/

02:10—02:57

This algorithm/that automates everything. /And algorithm/is a fancy word for a formula. /Like a math formula:/A + B + C = D. /Algorithm/is the same thing. /It says, / "If somebody does this, /has this background, /is like this, /then this, /we will offer them a job or whatever." /So/all of the new software tools/are based on algorithms, /information about the people who are coming, /and then being able to talk to you from that/and recommend/this person/will be a good person for this job. /So this is powerful technology/that's coming. /

这个算法/能使一切自动化。/"算法"/是公式的高级说法。/就像一个数学公式，/A + B + C = D。/算法/也是如此。/算法说：/ "如果一个人做了这个，/有这样的背景，/是这样的，/还有这样，/我们就会聘用他或者怎么样。"/因此，/所有新的软件工具/都是基于算法，/基于访客信息，/然后软件能够与您交谈，/并推荐说/这个人/会适合这份工作。/这是一项强大的技术，/即将面世。/

02:58—03:38

Then there is gonna be robotic talent managers. /These already exist to some degree. /These are little robots/that roll around on the floor, /and they might be here in this conference/and they might roll up to you/and say, / "Hi. /I am robot A, /and I am from this company. /I'd like to talk to you." /And it would analyze you, /talk to you/and then send all the information back to the company. /So you don't have to come, /you can just bring a robot. /I saw one of these. /I've seen two of these now. /They are very cute. /They are round. /They stop you, /ask you questions/and talk to you. /But this is the future. /This is what's going be there in the future. /

然后会有机器人人才经理。/这在某种程度上已经存在了。/这些小机器人/在地上转来转去，/他们可能就在这儿参加这个会议，/他们可能会转到您身边/说：/ "嗨！我是机器人A，/我来自这家公司，/我想和您聊聊天。"/它会分析您，/和您交谈，/然后把所有的信息发送回公司。/所以您不必来参会，/可以只带一个机器人过来。/我看到了一个，/现在看到两个，/它们非常可爱，/都是圆的。/他们会拦住您，/问您问题，/和您说话。/但这是未来的事情。/这是将来会发生的事。/

第四单元　人力资源 Human Resources

03:39—04:29

And then maybe 10 years from now, /we will have DNA analysis, /where they will actually perhaps take and ask you, / "Would you submit/some of your saliva/or some of your skin? /And we're gonna analyze/your DNA." /Because we know/people whose DNA is like this/are better employees/than people whose DNA is like that. OK? /This is very very scary, /but this is where we are heading, /this is the future that we're going into. /So the future for HR/is very exciting. /It's also somewhat frightening/because it's we have never been there before. /We don't know what to do. /This is so new. /We have no way to think about this, /because we haven't done it before. /So/it's gonna be exciting, OK? /

　　也许十年后，/我们将进行 DNA 分析。/他们可能会问您：/ "您能提交/一些您的唾液/或皮肤吗？/我们会分析/您的 DNA。" /因为我们知道/人们的 DNA 像这样的/会是更优秀的员工，/比那些 DNA 像那样的人更优秀。/这一技术非常吓人，/但这正是我们前进的方向，/是我们要面临的未来。/所以人力资源的未来/非常令人兴奋。/这有点让人恐慌，/因为我们从未经历过，/不知道该怎么办。/这太新鲜了。/我们没有办法考虑这个问题，/因为我们没这么做过。/所以，/这会很刺激。/

04:31—05:24

So basically, /in the future/this is my belief. /The web, /the Internet/will be your CV. /You won't need a CV, /because I will know everything about you/from what you do on the Internet. /I know what you buy. /I know which websites you like the most. /I go to Renren/or Weibo/or Alibaba/and I find everything about you. /And then I've already known all of these. /So I don't need to talk to you, /because I've already known everything. /I know how much money you spend; /I know what you buy; /I know what color you like the best. /I know everything about you, /all because of what you do on the Internet. /So having a CV, /having an interview/is just really useless. /I've already had it all. /It wastes my time. /

　　所以基本上，/未来/我相信会是这样。/网络，/互联网/将成为您的简历。/您不需要简历，/因为我会知道您的一切，/只要了解您在互联网上做了什么。/我知道您买了什么，/最喜欢哪个网站。/我上人人网、微博、或者阿里巴巴，/了解有关您的一切，/然后我就了解了所有这些信息。/所以我不需与您沟通，/因为我已经知道了一切。/我知道您花了多少钱，/买了什么东西，/最喜欢什么颜色。/我知道您的一切，/这都是从您的上网历史记录了解到的。/因此简历、面试/都没有用。/我已经掌握一切信息了。/看简历或面试只会浪费我的时间。/

05:25—05:58

So/in the future/this is where we are gonna be. /So we automate assessment. /If we look at the assessment side of it, /how do you select good people? /And there is so much excitement going on here. /In the old days, /we did this stuff. /We interviewed, /we observed people, /we tested them, /we put them on the job/and we see how did they work on the job. /Very inefficient, /very slow, /and not very accurate, OK? /

因此，/未来/这就是我们前进的方向。/我们自动化评估。/来看看评估方面，/您是如何挑选优秀的员工的呢？/其实有很多激动人心的部分。/过去，/我们自己评估。/我们面试，/观察求职者，/测试他们，/让他们进入工作岗位，/观察他们工作表现。/这样效率很低，/进展很慢，/结果不是很准确，对吧？/

05:58—06:41

Today/we're having a new whole world. /We all hear Passive Assessment. /And what I was just talking about, /where the web is your CV, /this is Passive Assessment. /I don't need to see you. /I don't need to talk to you. /I can learn everything about you, /OK? /So/I can do this/by matching you. /And by matching, /I mean, /I look at all the things/that I learn about you from the Internet. /I see your skills. /I see your interests. /And I look at the jobs I have in my company, /and I match them together, OK? /If you go to the expo hall, /there are many many products/already do this, OK? /Already do this now, OK? /

今天，/我们有了一个全新的世界。/我们都听说过"被动评估"。/我刚才说的/网络是您的简历，/这就是被动评估。/我不需要见您，/不用和您交谈，/就可以了解您的一切，/对吧？/因此，/我能做到这些，/只需要对您进行匹配。/匹配，/我的意思是，/我查看信息，/这些信息都是从互联网上了解到的，/我能看到您的技能，/您的兴趣。/我再查看我们公司的职位，/再将您与职位进行匹配。/如果您去展厅，/那里有很多产品/已经能够做到这样。/现在已经可以这样做了。/

06:41—07:38

And then we have Parsing. /And "parsing" /simply means/that we take the information/and the computer can analyze it/word by word/for competency, /for skills and so forth. /They can even determine your personality/from this, OK? /There are new tools now/that I am using as I'm writing an email. /If I write an email to you, /it gives me advice/about what to say in the email/to match your personality. /So it will say, / "This person like you to be very friendly/and ask a lot of questions/about their family, /and everything about them." /And I do another email/and say, / "This person doesn't like that. /They want you only to use bold points. /And just quickly tell them/what you want." /So everybody has a different way/of using email. /This will give you advice/on how to do that. /This is all done/through some of these tools, OK? /

然后我们有解析。/"解析"/就是指/我们获取信息,/然后计算机可以进行分析,/逐字逐句/分析能力、技能等等。/他们甚至可以确定您的性格,/就是通过解析来确定。/有些新的解析工具,/我在写电子邮件的时候会用。/如果我给您写电子邮件,/解析工具会建议我/在邮件中说什么,/来匹配您的性格。/解析工具会提示说:/"这个人希望您表现得非常友好,/问很多问题,/询问关于家庭/以及关于他们的一切。"/我又写一封电子邮件,/解析工具提示说:/"这个人不喜欢问很多问题,/他们只想您要点明确,/简洁地说明/您想要什么。"/所以每个人都有自己的方式/来使用邮件,/解析工具会建议/您如何做。/完成这些/都需要解析工具。/

07:38—08:29

Then we have Biometric Analysis. /Biometric Analysis/is analyzing your face/when you are interviewing/to learn your emotions/and whether or not you're lying or telling the truth. /And this already exists. /This is the product/that you can purchase today/for recruiting. /When you do a video interview, /it reads your face, /the candidate's face/and then it says, /"When you asked them these questions, /they were lying to you. /And when you asked them this question, /they didn't like what you ask. /They were angry/or they were upset." /And they can tell this/by the small, /very invisible movements that we do on our face/and we don't know we are doing it. /And the computer can see it, alright? /So this is Biometric Analysis. /This is coming. /

然后我们有生物统计分析。/生物统计分析/是分析您的面容,/在面试时进行分析,/以了解您的情绪/以及您是否撒谎。/这种技术产品已经有了。/这款产品/您现在已经可以购买,/用于招聘。/视频面试时,/它会读取人的面容,/求职者的面容,/然后会说:/"当您问求职者这些问题时,/他们在撒谎。/当您问他们这个问题时,/他们不太喜欢这个问题,/他们感到生气/或者沮丧。"/技术产品可以分辨出这些,/只需通过分析这些细小、/几乎看不见的面部动作,/求职者都不知道他们会有这些动作。/电脑却能看到。/这就是生物统计分析,/这项技术即将问世。/

08:30—08:53

Then there are Semantic Analysis, /where I can actually understand/what you are saying, /where the computer is now able to understand. /When you say, /"I don't like this/or something like this."/And it knows what you mean. /And then it can give a response back/based on whether or not it knows/if you like something/or don't like something, alright?/

然后有语义分析,/也就是我可以真正理解/您在说什么,/计算机现在能明白。/当您说:/"我不喜欢这个/或像这样的东西。"/它能明白您的意思。/然后计算机可以做出回应,/这是根据它所了解的/您喜欢什么/或者不喜欢什么。/

08:53—09:32

And Sentiment Analysis/is when it goes out to,/like Renren,/and it looks everything you ever wrote on Renren. /And it says,/"This person is very unhappy."/or "This person is depressed."/or "This person is very analytical."/But it can analyze that/from what you put on something/like a social network,/what you put on the social network, OK?/So this is all available today. /All of this is right now today. /And these tools right here/that you can use already do some of this, OK?/So/this is just the beginning of the future, OK?/This is the beginning. /

情感分析/是用于,/比如说人人网,/情感分析工具查看您在人人网上的所有文字,/判断说:/"这个人非常不开心。"/或"这个人很消沉。"/或"这个人很善于分析。"/这个分析/是基于您发布的信息,/比如发布在社交网络上,/基于您在社交网络发布的信息。/这些信息现在都能获取。/如今这些都有。/这些工具/已经可以用于其中一部分分析了。/因此,/这仅仅是未来的开始。/只是开始。/

09:32—10:04

This is Laszlo Bock,/the Vice President/or the President/of Human Resources for Google,/and this is his statement that/"Interviews are a waste of time."/Alright?/Total waste of time. /You want nothing from the interview/and you need to use some sort of assessment test/or technology,/if you are going to really be successful/and selecting good people/to work in your company, OK?/

这是Laszlo Bock,/一位副总裁/或总裁,/管理谷歌的人力资源部,/这是他说的:/"面试浪费时间。"/对吧?/完全是浪费时间。/您完全不需要面试,/您需要的是使用某种评估测试/或技术,/才能真正取得成效,/挑选优秀的人才/到您公司工作。/

10:04—11:56

So this is the Psychological Analysis/of different forms of selection. /So/if you use age/as a way to hire somebody,/a perfect success would be 1.0. /That would be perfectly successful. /So the best we can get here/is this general test of you IQ,/which

第四单元　人力资源 Human Resources

is about 0.5 predictive. /Now if you flip a coin, /you get 0.5, OK? /Flipping a coin is 0.5, /OK? /So all of the things that we do, /everything we do here, /none of them by itself is very useful. /We have to do many of these things/to get over 0.5, /and if you are not over 0.5, /you are wasting your time. /And so/when you use assessment/like what we are talking about here, automated assessment, /when you are doing online analysis/of people's capabilities, /you can bring that up/to 0.7 or 0.8, /so this is one of the reasons/why I think we have to use automated assessment/and stop doing what we are doing today. /What we're doing today/is wasting a lot of time/that we could be using to do other things/that are more useful/and will make us more successful in our company, OK? /So Passive Assessment. /This is what I just talked about, /I'm not going to go through this again, /because we've just talked about it. /And this is the explanation/of what I was putting on that slide before, OK? /

　　这就是心理分析，/有不同的选择形式。/所以，/如果您用年龄/作为招聘的方式，/最完美的结果是1.0，/这就非常成功了。/最好的实现方式/就是整体测试您的智商，/预测值大约为0.5。/现在如果您掷硬币，/您得到0.5，/掷硬币是0.5，/对吧？/所以我们所做的一切，/我们在这里做的所有的事，/每一件都没什么用。/我们要做很多，/才能超过0.5。/如果您还不到0.5，/您就是在浪费时间。/因此，/当您使用评估，/就像我们正在讨论的自动评估，/当您在网上分析/人们的能力时，/您可以将其提高到/0.7或0.8，/所以这就是为什么/我认为我们要使用自动评估，/停止我们在做的事情。/我们今天所做的事/浪费大量时间，/我们可以用这些时间来做其他事，/做更有用、/让我们公司更有成就的事。/所以被动评估，/这就是我刚才所说的，/我不打算再讲一遍，/因为我们刚刚讲过。/这解释了/我之前放在幻灯片上的内容，好吧？/

12:00—13:24
　　So/by using automated assessment, /you remove all the biases, /all the things we think are true/but cannot prove. /We get rid of this, /we remove this, /OK? /It provides an equal assessment of each person. /Now think about it right now, /when you interview six or seven people. /Today you are in a good mood/and you are happy when you interview the people. /I interview two people today, /and I am in a good mood. /Then I interview somebody tomorrow, /and tomorrow I am tired, /I am sleepy, /and I am not happy. /Do those people/get the same interview? /Do they have the same sort of chance/of getting a job? /And the answer is, / "No, they don't." /Because so much of it/changes day by day/depending on how the recruiter feels, /what kind of mood you are in/and so forth. /With assessment, /it's always the same. /Everybody gets exactly the same chance/to be assessed, /fairly and equally, /OK? /

And then so it's much more objective. /Right now, /the way we choose people/is not objective at all. /It's based on nothing, /on no data, /just on assumptions, /OK? / So the first thing/I think/is that you really have to think about/using more of the assessment tools/that exist today, /and replace what you're now doing in person, /OK? /

因此, /通过使用自动评估, /您消除了所有的偏见, /所有我们认为是真实的/但无法证实的东西。/我们将其摒除, /去除掉, /好吗？/自动评估平等地评价每个人。/现在想想, /当您面试六七个人时, /今天您的心情很好, /很开心地面试。/我今天面试两个人, /我心情也很好。/然后我明天面试, /明天我累了, /我困了, /而且我心情不好。/明天那些人/会有同样的面试吗？/他们有同样的机会/得到工作吗？/答案是/"不, 不一样。"/因为很多事情/每天都在改变, /取决于招聘人员的感受、/心情/等等。/采用自动评估的话/就不会变。/每个人都得到同样的机会/进行评估, /公平和平等地评估, /好吗？/这样更客观。/现在, /我们选人的方式/根本就不客观, /没有依据, /没有数据, /只是依据假设, /对吗？/所以首先, /我认为/您真的应当考虑/使用更多的评估工具, /使用现有的评估工具, /取代您现在亲自做的事情, /好吗？/

13:24—13:51

These are some of tools/that are doing this. /I know it's very hard to see these. /This one will give an analysis/of your personality. /These are tools/to analyze your personality. /This is the tool/that does the Biometric Analysis of your face. /This is a video interviewing tool. /So these are all tools that automate/a lot of what we are doing here. OK? /

这些工具/都可以用来面试。/我知道很难看清楚。/这一个会分析/您的性格。/这些工具/会分析您的性格。/这个工具/是做面部生物统计分析的。/这是视频面试工具。/这些工具都自动化了/很多我们现在在做的事情。/

13:51—14:11

Then there are many other tools here. /We have Crystal. /Crystal is the tool/that as you are typing an email, /it gives you the personality/of the person that you are writing the e-mail to. /That's called Crystal. /And I don't know/if any of these are available in Chinese, /but they certainly are in English. /

这儿还有很多其他工具。/我们有Crystal。/Crystal这个工具/在您写电子邮件时, /它会告知您性格特征, /收件人的性格如何。/这就是Crystal。/我不知道/这些工具是否有中文版的, /但肯定有英文版的。/

84

第四单元　人力资源 Human Resources

14:11—15:14

So there is a lot of tools out there/that are doing this. /IBM has a very powerful tool/called "Watson". /And "Watson" /is being used/to analyze people/for jobs/and can actually predict/your personality/and your success in the job/based on looking at many different factors/about your life/and your personality. /So all of these things are already here. /And they are gonna just be part of the recruiting/within the next year or two. /So/if you are not doing it already, /you should start to think about these things. /This is "Watson". /This is a personality profile/based on what people have said in a social network. /It goes out to any social network, /analyzes everything that you've said in the social network/and then presents the personality portrait of you from that. /And this is available right now today/from IBM. /So these things are there right now. /It's not the future. /It's today. /

所以有很多工具/在做这件事。/IBM 有一个非常强大的工具/叫做 Watson。/Watson/被用来/分析人/在工作中的表现,/可以预测/您的性格/和您在工作中的成就,/这都是依据多种不同因素/比如您的生活/和性格来预测的。/所有这些工具都已经面世了。/他们将参与招聘工作,/在未来一两年内应用。/所以,/如果您还没有着手用这些工具,/您应该开始考虑一下了。/这就是 Watson,/一个性格档案,/它是基于人们在社交网络中的言论而建立的。/它会进入所有社交网络,/分析您在社交网络中所有的言论,/然后呈现您的人格肖像。/这个已经可以使用了,/由 IBM 公司提供。/所以这些东西现在已经有了。/这不是未来,/就在当下。/

15:19—15:47

This is one/for assessing new college graduates, /fresh graduates from university. /This will assess them/and give you recommendation/about whether or not you should hire them. /So these are all kinds of tools, /all things coming for everything/from engineering/to software programmer/to a new college graduate. /We have software tools/for assessing all of these people/over and over/in many different ways, OK? /

这个工具/是用来评估应届大学毕业生/和刚毕业的大学生。/这会对他们进行评估,/建议您/是否应聘用他们。/这些是各种各样的工具,/用来进行各种评估,/包括工程师、/软件程序员/以及刚毕业的大学生。/我们有软件工具/评估这些人,/反复评估,/方式各式各样。/

15:50—16:33

So what's the danger? /Everything has a bad side, too. /And the danger is/that some of these tools/may have their own bias, /because somebody had to write the

85

formula, /that algorithm. /We don't know. /Maybe that formula is wrong. /So we have to constantly test/what we're doing, /we have to constantly make sure/what we are doing. /Sometimes it uses a language/that people don't understand/or it's not their native language. /So for example, /if you take a personality test/in English, /it might be a different result/than if you took a personality test in Chinese/because English is not your native language. /

那么有什么风险呢?/任何事物都有坏的一面。/风险在于/有些工具/可能有自己的偏见,/因为有人要去写公式、/写算法。/我们不知道,/可能这个公式是错误的。/所以我们要不断地测试/我们做的事情,/要不断地确定/我们做的是对的。/有时它使用的语言/是人们不理解的,/或者不是他们的母语。/举个例子,/如果您进行性格测试,/用的是英语的话,/可能会有不同的结果,/不同于您用汉语进行性格测试的结果,/因为英语不是您的母语。/

16:34—17:05

So/that also gets cultural bias. /So I might have a different culture in my life/than you have in your life. /And when I ask certain questions, /you would always answer the questions/based on our own culture. /So the tests have to be accurate/for your culture, OK? /So these are the dangers of a passive assessment. /But the benefits are great, /much greater benefits than danger. /But you have to always think about both sides/of everything that you do. /There is good and there is bad/to everything that we do, /OK? /

因此,/这也会导致文化偏见。/所以我可能有不同的文化,/与您生活中的文化不同。/当我问某些问题时,/您回答这些问题/总会基于您自己的文化。/所以测试必须是准确的、/符合您的文化的。/所以这些都是被动评估的风险。/但好处很多,/利远大于弊。/但是您要时刻考虑两面性,/做任何事情都要考虑。/有好也有坏,/任何事情都这样,/对吧?/

17:06—17:33

So let's look at engagement. /Now today/when we talk about engagement, /basically/we mean face-to-face talking to people. /I can do my talk to you. /We are engaging with each other, /OK? /If you meet somebody, /you go to a party, /you go to a restaurant, /you sit down with your family, /you're talking, /that's engagement. /Alright? /

我们来看看互动。/现在,/当我们说到互动时,/基本上/我们是指面对面交谈。/我可以跟您说话。/我们在互动,/对吗?/如果您和某个人见面,/去参加聚会,/去餐馆吃饭,/和您的家人相聚,/您们在聊天,/那就是互动。/对吧?/

第四单元　人力资源 Human Resources

17:33—18:01
　　So/when we say we want to engage with candidates,/we mean/I want to talk to the candidates,/I want to see the candidates./And many recruiters say,/"I cannot automate that./That's what I do./That's what recruiting is all about./It's me talking to candidates./If I can't talk to candidates,/then I should find some other work to do."/Maybe that's true for some people./But I think/there are ways/that we can automate a lot of what we do with that./

　　因此,/当我们说想和求职者互动时,/意思是/我想和求职者谈谈,/我想见见求职者。/许多招聘人员说:/"我不能将其自动化。/这是我的工作,/这样才是招聘,/是我在跟求职者谈话。/如果我不能和求职者交谈,/我就应该换一份工作。"/也许对某些人来是这样。/但我认为/有很多方式/我们可以用来自动化我们的工作。/

18:02—19:20
　　So this is what we kind of do now./What's coming here/are social media./So you can communicate with candidates easily/on social media./And it's becoming the most common way/right now/in most countries in the world./The most common way/to communicate with a potential employee/is through social media./And there is many difference./Every country/has its own version./China has its own./Europe has its own./America has its own./So it doesn't matter what it is./It's the point/that people are using social media./So that's a way to engage with people./but you never see/many of these candidates./You will never see them,/but you can really have a conversation with them./I don't know in China,/but in the US,/many people,/or many boys and girls are dating each other/in social media,/and they've never seen each other, alright?/So eventually,/I guess/they will see each other someday./But for a long time/when they begin,/they just talk to each other on social media,/and they don't actually meet each other./So it's the same thing./If you can date someone/with social media,/then you should be able to hire somebody/using social media,/OK?/

　　这是我们现在在做的事。/接下来/是社交媒体。/所以您可以与求职者轻松地交流,/通过社交媒体就能交流。/这正成为最常见的交流方式,/目前来说,/世界上大多数国家都在用社交媒体。/最常见的方式、/用来与潜在员工沟通的/就是社交媒体。/有多种不同的社交媒体。/各个国家/都有自己的社交媒体。/中国有自己的,/欧洲有自己的,/美国有自己的,/是什么并不重要,/重要的是/人们都在用社交媒体。/所以这是一种与人互动的方式。/但您永远都不会见到/其中很多的求职者。/您永远不会见到他们,/但您确实可以与他们交谈。/我不知道在中国如何,/但在美国,/很多人,/许多男孩女孩约会/都是在社交媒体上,/他们从来没

87

有见过面。/最后,/我想/他们总有一天会见面的。/但很长一段时间,/就是在刚开始的时候,/他们只是在社交媒体上聊天,/实际上并没有见面。/同样的道理,/如果您约会/可以用社交媒体,/那您招聘/也可以用社交媒体,/对吧?/

19:20—19:40

Automated messages. /We have already talked about/the Chatbots, /alright? /This is what a Chatbot can do. /It can send automatic messages/to a candidate/based on what the candidate wants, /not what you want. /So/it can really communicate personally/to the candidate, alright? /

自动发送消息。/我们已经讲过/聊天机器人,/对吧?/这就是聊天机器人能做的事。/它可以自动发送消息/给求职者,/是基于求职者的需求,/而不是您的需求。/因此,/聊天机器人真的能进行个性化交流,/与任何求职者都可以。/

19:41—20:49

And Avatars. /Avatars are really automatic devices/on the computer/that pretend to be you, alright? /The candidate would think/it's you, /but it's really your virtual self. /It's your online self, /not really you. /And this is again, /this is coming in the future. /I've already seen/some of this. /It would say, / "Hi, /I'm Kevin. /How are you?" /But it's not me. /It's my online Kevin, /not my real Kevin, /alright? /But to the candidate, /they think it's me. /They think they are talking to me, /but actually/they are talking to a computer. /So/these are the things/that are coming to engage/in automatic engagement with candidates. /So if we really want to create/the optimal candidate experience, /the very best possible experience for a candidate, /then these are the things/we have to do with technology that supports us, OK? /

还有化身。/化身是一种自动装置,/安装在电脑上,/可以假装是您。/求职者会认为/是您本人,/但实际上是虚拟的您。/是线上的您,/不是真实的您。/同样,/化身未来将面世,/我已经见过/其中一些。/它会说:/"嗨,我是凯文,/您好吗?"/但这不是我,/是线上的凯文,/不是真正的凯文,/好吗?/但对求职者来说,/他们认为是我,/他们认为他们是在跟我说话,/但实际上/他们在和电脑交谈。/因此,/就是这些工具,/它们将参与/和求职者的自动交流。/所以如果我们真的想创造/最优求职体验,/创造最佳求职体验,/那么可以使用这些工具,/我们需要有技术支持。/

20:49—21:17

So/first of all, /emotion. /How do I feel as a candidate? /Do I feel happy? /Do I feel like/I want to work in this company? /If I feel good, /I can just... /Some of the slide/is not showing. /That should be there. /Maybe I have to get one more time done. /Here we go. /These are the technologies/that help you to do this. /

因此，/首先/是情感。/作为求职者我感觉怎样？/我感到高兴吗？/我觉得/我想在这家公司工作吗？/如果我感觉很好，/我可以……/有些幻灯片/显示不出来，/本来应该有的。/可能我要再播放一次。/可以了。/这些技术/能帮您做到这一点。/

21:17—21:43
So we are emotional. /We have candidate relationship management tools. /There are many CRM tools/in the expo hall today. /These help you/to talk to candidates virtually, OK? /They are automatic email, /periodic reminders, /Chatbots, /all kinds of things/that will help make a candidate/feel good about your company, alright? /

所以我们是有情感的，/我们有求职者关系管理工具。/很多客户关系管理工具/都陈列在今天的展厅里，/可以帮您/和求职者进行虚拟交谈。/有自动电子邮件、/定期提醒、聊天机器人，/各种各样的工具，/能够使求职者/对您的公司感觉良好。/

21:43—21:57
Then they have to be, /there is virtual stuff you can do/with social media, /instant messaging, /video-conferencing. /So you can continuously communicate with them virtually/and create a virtual world for them. /

然后是，/您可以做些虚拟的事情，/可以用社交媒体、/即时通讯、/和视频会议。/所以您可以不断地与他们进行虚拟交流，/为他们创造一个虚拟世界。/

21:57—22:29
Then there's many candidates wondering, /"What's my future in your company? /If I come to work here, /what will happen to me/in three years or five years?" /So/now you can begin to tell them/about career path. /You can help them/to learn about themselves, /and say, /"You know, /you would be good for this job/in two years." /or "If you would get this skill, /then you could do this job in our company." /So it can help a candidate/understand more about themselves. /So they understand their career opportunities. /

那么很多求职者可能会想知道：/"我在贵公司的前景如何？/如果我来这里工作/会怎么样？/三五年后会怎样？"/因此，/现在您可以告诉他们/职业规划，/您可以帮助他们/了解自己，/告诉他们：/"您知道，/您会胜任这份工作的，/只需两年。"/或者"如果您能掌握这个技能，/您就可以在我们公司做这项工作。"/所

以这能帮助求职者/更了解自己,/让他们了解他们的职业机会。/

22:30—23:01

Intellectually, /I can help them/to find more information about the company. /I can help them/to learn more about the work that we do. /I can help them/get smarter about/what they can contribute. /And then physically, /I can monitor/stuff on their phone. /I can help them/to become healthier. /I can get them to be more active, /to lose some weight, /to become a better, healthier employee. /So/with automated tools, /I can create/a really good candidate experience/if I use the automated tools. /

认知方面,/我可以帮他们/进一步了解公司。/我能帮他们/进一步了解我们的工作。/我能让他们/更了解/他们能为公司做什么。/身体方面,/我可以监控/他们手机上的东西,/我可以帮助他们/变得更健康,/让他们更活跃,/让他们减肥,/成为更好、更健康的员工。/因此,/使用自动化工具,/我能创造/非常好的求职体验,/前提是我要使用自动化工具。/

23:02—23:40

So/the future of automation/is amazing. /I think/we are gonna find an amazing future. /I think/you're gonna be very excited/about what's coming in terms of the technology and the tools. /But none of it is useful/if you don't use it. /So/you have to decide/that I want to use this/and I will start to do it, /even if it's a little bit. /But the technologies are already there, /it's your choice to use it. /So thank you very much! /

因此,/自动化的未来/很让人惊叹的,/我想/我们会看到一个了不起的未来。/我想/你们会非常兴奋,/对未来的技术和工具感到兴奋。/但一切都没有意义,/除非您加以利用。/因此,/您要下决心,/您要想去使用,/您要开始去用,/即使用一点点也可以。/但技术就在那里,/用不用取决于您。/谢谢大家!/

第五单元　行业介绍
Introduction to Industries

I. 从句视译

英语句子的一大特点就是从句，而我们一般认为汉语是没有从句这一概念的。在笔译中，处理从句的常用方法就是语序调整，而在视译中，要遵循顺译原则，因此需要注意从句的翻译，尤其是定语从句、同位语从句和状语从句的翻译。

1. 定语从句

英语中定语从句的位置是在中心词之后，而汉语中并没有定语从句，定语的位置往往是在中心词前面。在笔译中常对有定语从句的英语句子进行语序调整，在视译中，需要遵循顺译原则，一般在定语从句处断句，从句拆分出来另行翻译，遇到较长的从句更是如此。

【例1】Climate change would have an impact/on the global economy/that was equivalent to/the two World Wars of the 20th century. /

译文1：气候变化会对全球经济产生相当于20世纪两场世界大战的影响。

译文2：气候变化会影响/全球经济，/其影响相当于/20世纪两场世界大战。/

在视译中为了节省时间，往往不会大幅度调整语序，因此译文2选择将定语从句和中心词断开，从句单独成句，并增加了"其"指代前文提到的气候变化。

2. 同位语从句

同位语从句一般都是位于所说明的名词后面，和定语从句位置一样。在视译中也是在从句处断开，可加入必要的成分进行衔接。

【例2】We have to agree with his conclusion/that the price of oil products will continue to rise/at least for another decade. /

译文1：我们不得不同意他关于石油产品价格至少在未来十年里会继续攀升的结论。

译文2：我们不得不同意他的结论，/即石油产品价格会持续攀升，/至少在未来十年是这样。/

译文1是笔译的版本，需要进行大幅度的语序调整。译文2则在conclusion处将同位语从句与中心词断开，同时加上了"即"，将从句内容与中心词衔接起来，这样译文听起来就比较流畅。

3. 状语从句

状语从句在英语中的位置可以在句首，也可以在句末，在视译中，无论状语在什么位置，都要顺着句子顺序翻译。

【例3】Your conference will be a great success/if it contributes in important ways/to assisting countries in our region/to develop the sophisticated knowledge assets/needed to combat poverty/and to reduce inequality/for our people. /

译文1：如果本次大会能做出重大贡献，帮助本地区国家发展其在消除贫困、打破不平等所需的先进知识，这就会成为一次非常成功的大会。

译文2：本次大会将取得巨大成功，/只要大会能做出重大贡献，/帮助本地区国家/发展先进的知识资产，/战胜贫困，/消除不平等，/造福人民。/

例3中的条件状语位于句末，按照中文的习惯，往往会先说清楚条件，再说结果。译文2遵循视译原则，使用合适的衔接词，按照原文语序进行翻译。

由以上三种从句的分析可见，无论英语句子使用了什么从句，视译都会在从句处断开，使从句在译文中单独成句。

II. 实战练习一

1. 演讲背景

全球前四大市场研究公司之一的捷孚凯公司代表应邀参加"广交会英国国际市场论坛"，并发表主旨演讲。他的演讲涵盖三大主题：英国脱欧的影响；目前英国家电市场的关键趋势；互联网改变了英国消费者的行为。他认为英国脱欧并没有给英国市场带来负面影响，受访消费者表示，即使他们认为通胀率和生活成本都会上升，但依然愿意花钱购买家电和消费品。各种品类的大小家电都呈现出强劲的增长势头，电器的容量、技术含量和效率都刺激了消费者需求。最后，他还提到了消费者购买家电的渠道逐渐从实体店转移到网购。

2. 预习词汇

GfK 捷孚凯公司
Brexit 英国脱欧
built-in appliance 嵌入式电器

integrated appliance 集成电器
Lisbon Treaty《里斯本条约》
fridge freezer 立式冰箱
hub 中心
Hinckley Point 欣克利角核电站
inward investment 外来投资
sterling 英镑
pick-up 改善；提高
disposable income 可支配收入
tally 记录
garden shed 花园工具棚
year-on-year 较去年同期
hob 炉架
cooker hood 抽油烟机
freestanding（家具或设备）独立式的
consumer durables 耐用消费品
underpin 加强
quarter-on-quarter 季度环比
month-on-month 月度环比
tumble dryer 滚筒式干衣机
electric induction hob 电磁炉
smart appliance 智能家电
connected appliance 联网家电
part and parcel 重要部分
heat pump tumble dryer 热泵滚筒干衣机
Omni-Channel 全渠道销售
outstrip 超过
esoteric 只有内行人才懂的，小众的
wearable 可穿戴设备
tracker 追踪器
hype 天花乱坠的广告宣传；炒作
mousetrap 捕鼠夹

3. 演讲文本

00:00—00:17
Good morning, /ladies and gentlemen. /And firstly, /let me thank/the organizers

of the Canton Fair/for inviting us/to participate once again. /This is the 5th year/in which GfK has participated with the Canton Fair. /We are very proud/of that partnership. /

早上好,/女士们、先生们。/首先,/感谢/广交会的主办单位,/邀请我们/再次参加广交会。/这是第五年/捷孚凯公司参加广交会了。/我们非常自豪/能与你们合作。/

00:17—00:57

My job today is/to talk to you/a little bit about the potential opportunities/within the home appliances market within the UK. /Just a little introduction/to who GfK are. /We are a global organization, /market research business, /working across 80 countries worldwide. /And our job is/to provide insights/to businesses/into what consumers think/and what consumers do. /And it's probably never been more important to do that. /For businesses across the world, /we have huge amounts of change/both economic and technological. /

我今天的任务就是/告诉大家/一些潜在的机会,/存在于英国家电市场的机会。/先简单介绍一下/捷孚凯公司。/我们是一家全球性机构,/专注市场研究,/业务遍布世界80个国家。/我们的工作就是/提供有价值的信息,/告诉企业/消费者在想什么、/做什么。/这或许是最重要的事情了。/对全世界的企业来说,/我们为其带来大量变革,/促进盈利、提升技术。/

01:01—01:56

So to give you an understanding/of what we are going to be discussing today, /first of all, /we will take a look/at what impact the Brexit decision has had. /This is the referendum/that the UK has decided now/to leave the EU/within the next two to three years. /We will also discuss/what are the key trends/within UK home appliances right now. /We will talk about the Internet. /Online has been a real game changer/for UK consumers and indeed UK retailer manufacturers/over the last ten years. /I will talk a little bit more/about the current dynamics within that area. /And finally, /we will have a little look at/what the future holds, /and in particular, /the importance of smart home appliances/within the UK market in the coming years. /So there are three key themes/that I want you to take away with you today. /

先让大家了解一下/我们今天要讨论的内容。/首先,/我们将看看/英国脱欧这一决定带来的影响。/这是公投的结果,/英国已经决定/脱离欧盟,/并在未来两到三年完成。/我们还将讨论/有哪些关键趋势,/目前英国家电市场的走向。/我们还会讨论互联网。/互联网已经真正改变了游戏规则,/改变了英国的消费者和零售型

第五单元 行业介绍 Introduction to Industries

制造商，/尤其是在过去十年里。/我还会讲到一些/有关这个领域最新发展。/最后，/我们还会展望/未来的局势，/尤其是/智能家电的重要性，/在英国市场未来几年有多重要。/所以一共有三个关键主题，/这是我希望大家今天能够收获的。/

01:56—02:47

First of all, /is the Brexit actually may bring/opportunity as well as the challenges/that we face in the negotiations? /There are lots of opportunities/for foreign investors/and indeed foreign trade/in the UK/in the coming years. /Secondly, /built-in appliances. /There are a number of different appliances/within the UK. /But built-in appliances, integrated appliances/have a very bright future in the UK. /Even in tough times, /they have been very resilient/and then they now make up/an enormous amount of value/within the UK home appliances market right now. /And finally, /most importantly, /for the future, /British consumers/are among the most connected, /not just in Europe, /but also worldwide. /And this is particularly important/when it comes to considering/manufacturers' behavior, /but also shoppers' behavior in the UK. /

首先，/英国脱欧真的会带来/机遇和挑战，/影响我们的谈判吗？/有很多机会/外商投资者是可以利用的，/当然外贸/在英国/未来几年也是大有可为。/其次，/是嵌入式家电。/有很多不同种类的电器/在英国市场销售。/但是嵌入式电器和集成电器/在英国前景非常光明。/就算是在经济不景气的时期，/它们也很有弹性，/如今也占据着/巨大的价值份额，/是英国家电市场的大户。/最后，/最重要的是，/未来，/英国消费者/是互联程度最高的群体之一，/不仅是在欧洲，/在全球范围内都是如此。/这一点尤其重要，/特别是当我们谈到/制造商行为/以及英国消费者行为的时候。/

02:47—03:56

So, talking a little bit/about what impact Brexit has had, /I will just give you a little bit of background/to those who are unfamiliar with the term "Brexit". /This is Britain's exit from the European Union. /And over last summer, /we held the referendum in the UK/and the result confirmed/that just over half of Britains/voted to leave the European Union. /Our government then enacted this/and in 29th of March, 2017, /Article 50 of the *Lisbon Treaty*, /a core part of the European Union Constitution, /was triggered by Theresa May/and confirmed that the UK will leave the European Union. /And we now have two years/of negotiation with the European Union/and talk about citizens' rights/and talk about our transition/from the European Union into our own self-contained unit, /and how we will trade/indeed with Europe and the rest of the world. /Currently, /trade negotiations are a little static. /However, /

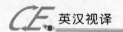

within two years, /we believe that we will have an agreement. /

谈到/脱欧带来的影响，/我会先简单介绍一下背景，/照顾在场不了解英国脱欧的听众。/脱欧就是英国脱离欧盟。/去年夏天，/我们在英国举行了公投，/结果是/仅有超过半数的英国民众/投票赞成脱欧。/政府随后通过了这一结果，/并在2017年3月29日，/《里斯本条约》第50条，/也就是欧盟宪法的核心部分，/由首相特雷莎·梅启动生效，/确认英国将脱离欧盟。/现在我们有两年时间/来和欧盟谈判，/谈判公民权利，/谈判我们的转变，/从欧盟成员国过渡到独立的身份，/谈判我们将如何贸易，/如何与欧洲以及世界其他地区进行贸易。/目前，/贸易谈判进展缓慢。/但是，/在未来两年内，/我们相信一定能达成协议。/

03:56—04:41

But the question/that a lot of people, /of course, /are naturally asking is:/will this negatively impact/foreign imports to the UK? /So my argument, /very clearly, /is/the UK is a very good bet for investment/despite this challenging times. /The home appliances, /during the worst times of the recession, /back in 2007 to 2011, /home appliances was incredibly resilient. /Both major appliances, /like washing machines and fridge freezers, /small domestic appliances, /like kettles, /coffee machines, /toasters/and irons, /were all extremely robust/and performed very well, /particularly in value/over those difficult years. /Consumers/effectively/still wanted to go out and buy. /

然而有一个问题/是很多人/理所当然/自然会问到的，/即脱欧是否会冲击/英国的外贸进口。/我的观点/非常明确，/那就是/英国是个明智的投资选择，/哪怕现阶段困难重重。/家用电器，/在经济最萧条的时候，/也就是2007到2011年那段时间，/家电表现非常坚挺。/大家电，/像洗衣机和立式冰箱，/小家电，/像热水壶、/咖啡机、/烤箱/和熨斗，/势头都非常强劲，/销量也很好，/尤其是市场价值，/并挺过了那段艰难的时期。/消费者/实际上/仍想要出门购物。/

04:41—05:36

From a wider macro economic perspective, /at the moment, /London has stated/it wants to be the second biggest global hub/for raising funds in Chinese currency worldwide. /Hinckley Point, nuclear power plant, /which Director Huang mentioned in his speech earlier, /is the largest infrastructure investment/by China in Europe. /That's very significant. /But it also shows/the partnership and commitment/that the UK has to inward investment. /And while sterling weakened/initially after Brexit, /it has rebounded. /And the next two years/could also yield greater exchange opportunities/for RMB in the future. /The UK has also stated/a fundamental need and desire/to

第五单元 行业介绍 Introduction to Industries

encourage foreign direct investment/from China. /And Mr. Mellon and his colleague/ earlier specifically alluded to that fact. /

  从更宏观的经济角度看,/当前,/伦敦声明/计划成为全球第二大中心,/在全世界范围内募集人民币资本。/欣克利角核电站,/黄处长在前面的讲话中也提到了,/它是最大的基础设施投资项目,/由中国在欧洲投资兴建。/该项目意义重大。/它也体现了/合作关系和承诺,/是英国对外来投资的承诺。/尽管英镑贬值了,/在脱欧初期就贬值,/但现在已经回弹了。/接下来两年/会有更多的兑换机会,/供人民币和英镑兑换。/英国也声明/其最基本的需求和期望/是鼓励外商直接投资,/吸引中国投资者。/梅隆先生及其同事/刚刚也明确提到了这一点。/

05:36—06:29

  From the home appliances market,/it is actually worth/over 3.7 billion pounds/in the UK right now,/across major domestic appliances and small domestic appliances,/very much driven/by this change in shopping behavior/to Internet retail. /And UK appliances/have been becoming very price-polarized. /And this actually gives an opportunity/for manufacturers/to tap into aspirational consumers/at a more affordable price. /Consumers don't change/what they want. /They don't want a white box/for a washing machine or a fridge freezer any more. /They want style,/they want good looks/and they are prepared/in many cases/to pay for it. /But even so,/there are lots of opportunities/for providing that type of quality,/that type of design/at a more affordable price. /

  从家电市场来看,/实际上价值/超过了37亿英镑,/贡献给了当前的英国市场,/包括大家电和小家电,/很大程度上是由于/购物行为改变,/转变为互联网零售。/英国家电/价格分化越来越明显。/事实上这提供了一个机会/给制造商/去发掘高要求的消费者,/为他们提供更优惠的价格。/消费者不会改变/他们的追求。/他们不再想要一个白色外壳/罩着洗衣机或冰箱。/他们想要造型,/想要好看的外观。/他们已经准备好,/在很多情况下,/愿意为之付费。/尽管如此,/还是有很多机会/可以提供高质量、/有设计感的产品的,/同时价格更优惠。/

06:29—07:20

  And having a look at prices over time/for the UK in major appliances trajectory/since the start of this year. /Actually,/the mid-range products,/which have dominated the market,/between 300 and 450 pounds,/have actually dropped. /And the price polarization/has come in/that actually/products above 450 pounds/or below 300 pounds at the entry level,/have performed exceptionally well/over the last seven to eight months. /As a result,/this has a direct opportunity/for investors/who are

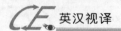

manufacturers/within home appliances, /who are looking to, /effectively work better/ with manufacturers in the UK/and consumers/and attract consumers/to some of those lower price point products/and also products at the premium end. /

我们看看价格在时间上的变化, /看看英国大家电的价格轨迹, /从今年年初以来的变化。/实际上, /中档产品/是市场的主角, /价位在 300 到 450 英镑之间, /价格已有所下降。/而且价格分化/也出现了, /实际上/高于 450 英镑的产品/或者低于 300 英镑的入门级产品, /销量非常好, /特别是在过去的七到八个月内。/因此, /这直接提供了机会/给投资者, /他们也是制造商, /在家电领域/他们期望/高效、更好地/与英国制造商合作, /服务消费者, /吸引消费者/关注价位较低的产品/和高档产品。/

07:20—08:26

Having a few look at the key economic indicators/for the UK. /So interest rates/ remain relatively low. /It's been flat/for many years. /The Bank of England/has kept that rate/and only changed last year. /There are expectations as well/that there may be a small rise/within the next 12 to 18 months. /Well, inflation. /Inflation has dropped considerably/from where we were in the late 80s/and even during the mid 2000 to 2010 period. /But the reality is/the inflation may increase further/due to some of the situation in the UK. /But historically, /for home appliances/and for many of the other consumer products/we look at at GfK, /it's only made a very small impact/on the pick-up of sales by consumers. /The UK, /ultimately, /has grown its disposable income/of nearly 320 billion pounds. /That's a huge amount of potential/to tap into within the UK. /

我们再来看一下关键的经济指标/在英国有哪些。/利率/一直相对较低, /保持不变/已经好多年了。/英格兰银行/一直控制着利率不变, /直到去年才有所变化。/人们也预期/利率可能会小幅度上升, /未来的 12 到 18 个月内会上升。/至于通货膨胀, /通胀率已经大幅下降, /低于上世纪 80 年代末, /甚至低于 2000 年年中到 2010 年这段时间。/但事实是/通胀可能会进一步加剧, /这是英国的一些形势所导致的。/但从历史上看, /对于家电产品/和很多其他消费品来说, /捷孚凯公司调查发现/通胀的影响微乎其微, /对消费者销售量提升影响甚小。/英国/最终/增加了可支配收入, /达到将近 3,200 亿英镑。/这是的巨大潜能, /可以在英国市场开发。/

08:26—09:31

One of the pieces of research/that we do within the UK/and indeed for the European Union/and the Organization for Economic Cooperation and Development/is we measure consumer confidence, consumer sentiment/within the UK and many other

第五单元 行业介绍 Introduction to Industries

countries. /And one of the questions/that we ask/as part of our Consumer Confidence Index/is "Will prices change/in the next 12 months?" /Before the referendum, /in June, 2016, /a number of people suggested/that actually there was only going to be/a very small or slow increase/in average prices/over the coming 12 months. /Only 12% of the UK consumers/that were surveyed/suggested that there was going to be a fast increase/in average prices. /After the referendum, /and come last month, /August, 2017, /we actually see/that now, nearly 30% of UK consumers/that were surveyed/believe that there is going to be a fast increase in average prices. /So this tally/is very closely with our expectation/that yes, inflation will increase. /

有一项研究/是我们在英国做的，/也是为欧盟/和经济合作与发展组织做的研究，/我们测量了消费者信心、消费者态度，/研究范围是在英国和很多其他国家。/其中有一个问题/我们提问/是为了衡量消费者信心指数，/这个问题是："价格变化/在未来12个月里会发生吗？"/在公投之前，/即2016年6月，/很多人认为/事实上只会有/很小或者缓慢的增长，/平均价格/在未来12个月内上涨不明显。/只有12%的英国消费者/受访时/认为会有很快的上涨，/平均价格会快速上涨。/公投之后，/上个月结果出来，/也就是2017年8月，/我们事实上看到，/现在将近30%的英国消费者/受访时/相信平均价格会快速上涨。/所以这个记录/非常接近我们的预测，/即通胀率会上升。/

09:31—10:12

And looking at the cost of living/compared to 12 months ago, /26% of consumers/that were surveyed/in June, 2016, /before the referendum to leave Europe, /suggested that the cost of living/is going to be a lot higher. /Now, in August, 2017, /45% of consumers believe that, /actually, the cost of living/is going to be a lot higher. /So a lot of people/have expectations/that prices will move higher. /They have an expectation/that disposable incomes will be stretched. /And Nonetheless, /consumers continue, /as we've seen time and time again, /to spend within home appliances/and the consumer products market. /

再看看生活成本，/相比12个月前，/26%的消费者/在我们调查中，/在2016年6月/公投脱欧之前，/认为生活成本/会大幅度增加。/现在，2017年8月，/45%的消费者认为/事实上生活成本/还会变得更高。/所以很多人/预测/价格还会走高。/他们预计/可支配收入得省着点花。/不管怎样，/消费者会继续，/正如我们一次次看到的那样，/花钱购买家电/和消费品。/

10:12—10:57

So another key question/that we ask/is whether it is the right time/to make a major purchase. /And compared to 2010, /right through to 2014, /where consumers were very very fundamentally opposed to/spending on major purchases, /actually, /we are now in a situation/where consumers are far more positive/about making a major purchase of appliance. /There is anything/from washing machine/through to a car, /through to buying a garden shed. /But in any of these major purchase situations, /despite the fact/ that we had some bumps/along the road/in recent months, /consumers still remain positive in their sentiment/about spending on major purchases/in the near future. /

另一个重要的问题，/我们提问/的是现在是否是正确的时机/去购买大宗产品。/相比2010年，/一直到2014年，/这段时期消费者坚决反对/大宗消费，/而事实上，/我们现在的情况是/消费者的态度已经积极了很多，/可以接受购买大家电，/无论是/购买洗衣机/还是汽车，/或是一间花园工具棚。/但是在任何这种大宗消费情景中，/尽管/我们面临一些困难，/一路上不是很顺利，/尤其是最近几个月以来，/但是消费者仍然保持积极的态度，/愿意购买大宗产品，/近期都会购买。/

10:57—12:06

Just to explain a little bit/about this chart. /This is looking/at the first half of the year/within the UK/and this is focusing specifically/on the major domestic appliances market/within the UK. /Overall, /we've seen a value growth, /a value increase of 1%/in the first six months of this year. /This is not as high as it has been. /But the fact that/we are still seeing robust growth/12 months after that referendum/continues to show/the positive flow of mind/in which consumers are/in the UK right now. /Of the mix of products/within home appliances, /we have nearly 500 million pounds/which is spent/in the UK alone/on washing machines. /We have the second biggest category/ with refrigeration or cooling, /where 460 million pounds/is net spent year-on-year. / And increasingly, /we can see other areas, /some of the more premium ends, /some of the areas which are more European in nature, /such as built-in cooking/has actually helped to drive a lot of this value growth/over time. /

简单解释一下/这个图表。/描述的是/今年上半年/在英国的情况，/特别关注的是/大家电市场/在英国的情况。/总的来说，/我们看到价值是在增长的，/增长了1%，/这是今年前6个月的情况。/这个增幅不如之前大。/但事实上，/我们还是能看到强劲的增长，/即便是公投后的12个月里，/这再次体现了/积极的心态，/消费者一直很积极，/目前对英国市场仍有信心。/不同品类的商品中，/在家电领域，/我们已经有将近5亿英镑/是花费在/英国国内/洗衣机的购买上。/我们第二大品类/是冰箱或制冷柜，/有4.6亿英镑的/年度净消费量。/同样在增长的，/我们可以看到其他品类，/有些是偏高档的，/有些是更具欧洲特色的，/例如

第五单元 行业介绍 Introduction to Industries

嵌入式厨具/实际上就大大带动了价值增长,/贡献越来越大。/

12:06—13:07

If we take a look at volume/and value growth/year-on-year,/you can see/that volume still remains/relatively low,/not as low as many other European countries,/but it still remains/a little softer/than it has been in previous years. /But value from many areas, /including washing machines, /dish washers, /and also the crucially, /the premium built-in categories/in ovens, /in built-in hobs/and cooker hoods, /still remain relatively robust. /And what you also noticed/from the very far right of the chart, /is the average price continues to grow/very strongly year-on-year. /And in fact, /across both freestanding/and built-in appliances, /average price/has been increasing very strongly. /We now have freestanding appliances growing/to nearly 4.5 to 5% on average/across major appliances, /but built-in appliances, /that figure rises to 7 to 7.5%, /so again, /fueling a lot of the value growth and development/within the UK right now. /

如果我们看数量/和价值的增长,/相较去年同期,/您会发现/数量还是维持/在相对较低的水平,/尽管不像其他欧洲国家那般低,/但还是/不够强劲,/相比前几年弱一些。/但是很多品类的价值,/包括洗衣机/和洗碗机,/以及很关键的,/高档嵌入式家电,/包括烤箱、嵌入式炉架/和抽油烟机,/还保持相对强劲的势头。/大家也注意到,/在图表的最右侧,/平均价格继续攀升,/相比去年同期增长势头很猛。/事实上,/无论是独立式/还是嵌入式家电,/平均价格/都上涨得很快。/现在独立式电器价格增长/平均接近4.5%到5%,/主要是大家电,/但嵌入式家电/价格增长高达7%到7.5%。/所以这再次表明,/家电大大促进了价值增长和经济发展,/是英国当前发展的动力。/

13:07—14:41

So what are the key trends/within UK home appliances/and what does all this mean/for the success/for Chinese manufacturers/working in the UK/in the next few years? /Well, if we take a look/at all of the areas/that we track at point of sale/within the UK, /we can see/that actually home appliances, /are generally, /during tough times, /fairly resilient, /compared to a lot of other markets. /In the bottom right-hand corner, /you have the total overall consumer durable spend/for both the last 12 months, /the year to date up to August, 2017. /And also in green, /you have the quarter-on-quarter. /So, Q3 versus Q3 last year. /And overall, /hopefully, /UK market consumer durables/have grown in the last quarter/by 3% in value terms. /On the year, /it's grown by around about even 2%. /And if you take a look at major

101

appliances, /major domestic appliances, /denoted as MDA, /and small domestic appliances, /denoted as SDA, /to the left of the screen, /you can see that actually on that quarter, /we've all remained relatively robust:/5% growth/for small domestic appliances quarter-on-quarter/and 2% growth quarter-on-quarter/for major domestic appliances. /Even the long term/also still remains relatively strong. /Despite the fact/that you have other areas, /such as CE, /which is consumer electronics, /such as TV, /actually seeing some degree of decline. /

那么有哪些关键趋势/存在于英国家电市场之中?/这些趋势意味着什么?/是否有助于成功?/能否帮助中国制造商/在英国/未来几年获得成功?/如果我们看一下/所有这些家电品类,/从销售来看,/在英国,/我们会发现/事实上家电/总的来说/在艰难时期/依然相当有韧性,/比其他很多行业都要好。/在右下角,/大家可以看到总的耐用消费品消费额,/时间是过去的12个月,/一直到2017年8月。/还有绿色部分,/表示季度环比数据。/这是今年第三季度和去年第三季度的比值。/总体而言,/还是充满希望的,/英国耐用消费品市场/上一季度增长了/3%的价值量。/与去年同期相比,/增长了大约2%。/如果大家再看看大家电,/大型家用电器,/标为MDA,/还有小家电,/标为SDA,/在屏幕的左边,/大家可以看到事实上在那个季度,/都表现得相对强劲:/5%的增长/是小家电的季度环比增长率,/2%的季度环比增长率/是大家电的。/甚至长期来看/还会保持相对强劲的势头。/尽管事实上,/大家还可以看到其他领域,/比如CE,/即消费电子产品,/比如电视机,/实际上有一定程度的下滑。/

14:41—15:25

Effectively, /and this is the reason/why major appliances and small appliances/are so resilient/during tough times. /It's a consumer's look to a replacement market. /If that kettle breaks, /UK consumers/will buy another one, /as the same for washing machines. /For small appliances, /generally, /a lot of the time, /outside the replacement, /consumers are also looking/to refresh their kitchen/in new ways/and more affordable ways. /Small domestic appliances/allow the opportunity to do that. /Equally, /for major domestic appliances, /the strong replacement market, /which I mentioned earlier, /generally, /tends to underpin/and continue to have very very strong growth/even though there may be challenging times ahead. /

事实上,/这就是为什么/大家电和小家电市场/如此坚韧/并挺过了艰难时期。/因为消费者在寻求替换市场。/如果热水壶坏了,/英国消费者/会买一个新的,/洗衣机也一样。/小家电,/总的来说,/在很多情况下,/除了替换,/消费者也在考虑/更新他们厨房/以新方法/和更低价的方式。/小家电/就有机会做到这一点。/同样地,/对于大家电来说,/强大的替换市场,/我前面也有提到,/总体而

第五单元 行业介绍 Introduction to Industries

言,/倾向于加强/且将继续强有力地增长,/尽管可能未来仍充满挑战。/

15:25—16:03

And looking at the more recent picture. /This is looking at value growth, /on a month-on-month basis. /And for small domestic appliances, /like coffee machines and vacuum cleaners, /we've seen a short return to growth/over the last three months in value. /For major domestic appliances, /such as tumble dryers, /refrigeration/and built-in cooking, /which have particularly rebounded/in the last few months. /We are also, /after a brief tumble in the market/at the end of last year, /we are also beginning to see this recover, /recording 5% growth nearly/for June 2017. /

我们来看看更近期的情况。/这个是价值增长,/月环比的数据。/关于小家电,/像咖啡机和真空吸尘器,/我们看到了短期的增长反弹,/这是过去三个月的价值变化。/至于大家电,/像滚筒式干衣机、/冰箱、/嵌入式厨电,/都有明显反弹/出现在过去几个月里。/我们也/在经历了短期的市场回落之后,/在去年年底,/我们也开始看到回升,/有接近5%的增长/是在2017年6月份。/

16:03—16:49

And there are three areas/which really drive a lot of the replacement market/and the demand for home appliances in the UK. /This is capacity, /in the first instance, /so you have areas/such as the American-style fridge freezers, /now worth 221 million pounds in the UK/and growing at 1% annually. /You have very large capacity washing machines, /8-kilogram and 9-kilogram washing machines/and above, /very popular in the UK/and continue to grow/and become the biggest part of the market, /continuing to grow 18%/in value year-on-year. /You also have more premium-range cookers, /very popular among UK consumers/outside of the built-in cooking market, /which also continue to grow/at a very healthy 5%. /

有三种因素/真正带动了替换市场/和英国的家电需求。/这是容量,/这是第一个因素,/大家可以看到各种品类,/比如美式立体冰箱,/现值2.21亿英镑的英国市场价值,/年增长率1%。/还有大容量洗衣机,/容量8公斤和9公斤的洗衣机/以及更大容量的,/在英国非常受欢迎/并且继续在增长/占据了最大的市场份额,/继续增长18%/的年同比价值增长率。/还有更高端的厨电,/也非常受英国消费者欢迎,/也就是非嵌入式厨电,/也持续增长,/稳健增长5%。/

16:49—17:38

The second trend/which we noticed/within the UK market/is around technology, /not just in smart home/but also for areas/such as electric induction hobs, /which now make up nearly 80 million pounds/in the UK market. /Pyrolitic that is self-cleaning ovens/within the UK market/now also account for around 79 million pounds/and growing at a very strong 36% year-on-year. /And then coming back to smart appliances, /connected appliances, /we also see/extremely strong growth for that. /In fact, /over the last four or five years, /we've seen/the market growth/from smart appliances in the UK/from only 10 to 12 million pounds/to nearly 100 million pounds annually. /And that growth is continuing/at 100% year-on-year. /

　　第二个影响趋势/我们注意到/在英国市场/是有关技术的, /不仅是在智能家居方面, /还有其他领域, /例如电磁炉, /现在占有将近8000万英镑/的英国市场价值。/高温分解自洁炉/在英国市场/目前占有约7,900万英镑的价值, /增长迅猛, 达到36%的年度增长率。/再看回智能家电, /联网家电, /我们也可以看到/特别强劲的增长。/事实上, /在过去四五年里, /我们看到/市场增长/来自于英国的智能家电, /从原先只有1,000万至1,200万英镑/增长到现在每年近1亿英镑, /增长继续/保持100%的年增长率。/

17:38—18:28

　　And finally, /efficiency/is also very important. /So we now have/technology/such as heat pump tumble dryers, /growing very strongly/at 32%, /also worth a significant amount of consumer wallet. /Equally, /you have low-capacity dish washers, /which are also extremely popular/within the UK right now, /and that's making up nearly three times/the level of heat pump tumble dryers, /with 154 million pounds year-on-year. /And also high-energy-efficiency rated products. /This is to some extent/part and parcel of the fact. /Consumers are buying these types of products/because they want good-looking, /energy-efficient/and high-technology appliances. /And with those high-technology appliances, /energy efficiency generally comes part and parcel of that. /

　　最后, /效率/也非常重要。/我们现在有/高科技产品, /像热泵滚筒干衣机, /增长迅猛, /达到32%, /也备受消费者青睐。/同样地, /还有小容量洗碗机, /也很受欢迎, /是英国目前的热门产品, /占了将近三倍/于热泵滚筒干衣机的市场价值, /高达每年1.54亿英镑。/还有高能源效率的产品。/这在某种程度上是/相当重要的。/消费者购买这些类型的产品/因为他们想要好看的、/高能效的/和高科技的电器。/而且在高科技电器中, /能源效率通常是重要的考量因素。/

18:28—19:30

　　So if we take a look/at the long term/for major domestic appliances over time, /first of all, /for washing machines, /you can see/that we're continuing/to see growth year-on-year. /So from January to December 2016, /through to the last 12-month period/between July 2016 and June 2017, /we've now reached/one billion pounds/for the washing machines market in the UK. /For refrigeration, /we are remaining relatively stable/but still very strong/at 900 million pounds. /And you will also notice/in the dark red, /the yellow, /the pink/and the orange colors/at the bottom of this chart, /the freestanding cooking, /built-in cooking/and built-in hobs/and cooker hoods/also very strong growth/over the last four or five years. /In fact, /the last 12 to 10 years/have seen enormous growth/within the major appliances market. /And again, /a lot of this is testament/to the strong replacement market/that underpins the UK climate. /

所以如果我们看一下/长期的情况，/看看大家电的趋势，/首先，/是洗衣机。/大家会发现/我们继续/看到每年都在增长。/所以从2016年1月到12月开始，/在过去12个月内，/即2016年7月到2017年6月，/我们现在已经达到/10亿英镑，/这是洗衣机在英国市场的价值。/至于冰箱，/我们保持相对平稳的状态，/但还是很强大，/达到9亿英镑。/大家也注意到，/在深红色、黄色、粉红色/和橙色部分，/在图表的底部，/立式厨电、嵌入式厨电、嵌入式炉架/和抽油烟机/增长都很强劲，/特别是过去四五年里。/事实上，/过去10到12年间/已经有巨大的增长/来自大家电市场。/再一次，/这些都证明了/强大的替换市场/支撑着英国的市场表现。/

19:30—21:38

We touch a little bit/about built-in appliances. /And the built-in appliances, /indeed the major domestic appliances overall, /are very strongly correlated/to housing transactions, /house moves within the UK market. /It's very much part of the UK culture/to purchase a home/rather than rent, /very different/to the culture in other parts of Europe/and that is something/which probably will not go away/even though property prices in the UK/are of record heights. /And there is a close relationship/as you can see/between the red line, /which is built-in sales for major domestic appliances, /and in the blue line, /housing transactions/over that period of time. /As housing transactions go up, /so the built-in appliances. /And particularly/around cooking, /refrigeration/and dish washers, /we see very very strong correlations/between those types of markets/increasing year after year. /In fact, /in total, /and this is a huge increase/over the last five or six years. /The built-in sales markets/for major domestic appliances, /or MDA/as we sometimes refer to it, /in the last 12 months, /is 1.3 billion pounds. /It makes up/a significant portion, /nearly a quarter/of the overall home appliances market/in the UK. /We also see/growth of 30%, /more than 30%

annually, /coming from built-in appliances/in the last 12 months. /Still a very robust environment/in which to do business within these markets. /And by category, /we also see/very strong growth that areas, /such as refrigeration, /growing at 17%, /for washing machines/that has a slice, /because built-in washing machines/are not as important/then not as big in the UK market/as they are in some other areas. /But for dish washers, /hobs, /and indeed for cooking and cooling, /which we've all seen, /is well over/and makes big contributions/to that one billion pound figure/that we saw earlier/for major appliances. /It's a huge, huge investment/by consumers in the integrated market. /

　　我们来讲一点/关于嵌入式家电的内容。/嵌入式家电,/应该说大家电总体上/紧密关联着/房屋交易,/与英国房屋搬迁息息相关。/这属于英国文化一部分,/人们会倾向于买房/而不是租房,/这不同于/欧洲其他地方的文化,/这个现象/不大可能会改变,/尽管英国房价/正处于历史新高。/还有一种紧密的联系,/就像你们看到的,/红线,/代表嵌入式大家电的销售量,/蓝线,/表示房屋交易/在对应时期内的变化。/随着房屋交易量上升,/嵌入式家电销售量也上升。/尤其是/厨电、冰箱、和洗碗机,/我们看到非常紧密的相关性/存在于这两类市场之间的,/且一年比一年紧密。/事实上,/总的来说,/这是很大的增长,/从过去五六年就可以看出来。/嵌入式家电的销售市场,/对于大家电来说,/或者MDA,/我们有时候也这么叫,/在过去12个月里,/销售额达到了13亿英镑。/这占据了/巨大的份额,/接近四分之一/的整个家电市场/在英国的价值。/我们还看到了/30%的增长率,/超过30%的年增长率/是来自嵌入式家电,/这是过去12个月的情况。/所以这仍是个强健的市场环境,/适合来此营商投资。/按品类来看,/我们可以看到/不同品类强势的增长,/例如冰箱,/增长率17%,/至于洗衣机,/也占有一些份额,/但因为嵌入式洗衣机/不像过去那般重要了,/所以也没有占那么大的英国市场份额,/比不上其他一些地方。/但洗碗机、炉架,/当然烹饪电器和制冷柜,/我们已经看到,/占的份额也很大,/贡献很多,/对10亿英镑这个数字贡献很大,/也就是我们前面看到的/大家电的市值。/这是一项巨大的投资,/是消费者对整个集成电器市场的投资。/

21:38—23:03

So how have regional brands/performed over time? /So in general times, /we're estimating brands/which are owned by Chinese companies, /other Asia-Pacific brands, /European brands/and US brands. /This is looking not in value, /but in volume share/of the UK market. /Five years ago, /the UK market/was dominated/by European brands. /62% of products/purchased in the UK/came from European brands, /9% from US brands, /only 5%, /currently, five years ago, /from Chinese brands. /If we fast forward to do 2017, /we see this has changed. /Chinese brands/ have increased by 3% to this point, /now making up 8%, /and very close to making up 9% of all sales in the UK. /European brands/have continued to increase/and there are a lot of them. /However, /Chinese brands increase particularly/against other Asia-Pacific brands as well. /And this provides a great springboard/for a lot of manufacturers from China/to use this opportunity/with price polarization, /with premium opportunities at the premium end/and opportunities at the entry level/to really come/and make a difference/and make them up in the UK. /

那么地区性品牌/在各个时期的表现如何呢？/在大多数时候,/我们评估这些品牌,/中国公司拥有的品牌、/其他亚太品牌、/欧洲品牌/还有美国品牌。/我们研究的不是市场价值,/而是销售量份额/占英国市场有多少。/五年前,/英国市场/的主角,/是欧洲品牌。/62%的产品/在英国卖出去的/都是欧洲品牌,/9%是美国品牌,/只有5%/在5年前/是中国品牌。/如果我们快进到2017年,/我们会看到这个数字发生了变化。/中国品牌/增长了3%,/现在的份额是8%,/并且很快就要占9%的英国市场总销量了。/欧洲品牌/份额也在持续上升,/品牌数量也非常多。/然而,/中国品牌增长最明显,/超越了其他亚太品牌。/这就提供了一个极佳的跳板,/帮助很多中国的制造商/利用这个机会/和价格分化的特点,/抓住高档市场的机会/和入门级产品市场的机会,/真正打入本地市场,/并做出一番成绩来,/占据英国市场。/

23:03—23:52

And then also talking a little bit/about online sales. /So it has been a real game changer in the UK. /If you take a look across Europe, /UK ranks currently second highest/in terms of internet penetration around population/in Western Europe. /And 92% in 2015 of the UK population/were connected online. /Netherlands was slightly ahead. /But if you take a look at/the number of households and the potential audience/ that you have in the UK, /there are only 7 million households/in the Netherlands, / while there are 26.5 million households/in the UK. /So relative to the size of population, /relative to the size of the number of households, /the UK, / effectively, /the biggest most important market/for online connectiveness in Europe. /

接下来讲一点/关于线上销售的。/这已经真正改变了英国的游戏规则。/如果大家放眼欧洲,/英国目前排名第二高,/互联网的人口普及率/在西欧是第二高。/2015年92%的英国人口/可以上网。/荷兰稍稍领先。/但是如果大家看看/家庭数量和潜在的消费者数量/在英国有多少,/只有700万户家庭/是在荷兰,/而2,650万户/是在英国。/所以在人口规模上,/在家庭数量上,/英国/实际上是最大最重要的市场,/是欧洲最大的线上销售市场。/

23:52—24:54

And if we take a look/at sales of major appliances/over that time, /online sales have boosted/the growth in UK major appliances, /where some areas/within, in store, /have declined. /We've actually seen/online growth remain robust, /throughout pretty much the whole assortment of major domestic appliances, /from tumble dryers, /where value approaches nearly half the market/being bought online, /through to built-in cooking/and built-in hobs, /historically, /products which consumers have wanted/to go in store/and touch and feel. /Now consumers/feel far more empowered/to purchase these things online, /because they understand more/because of the Internet. /They are able to research. /They are able to consider. /And as a result, /we've seen/a huge shift, /in the way that consumers are buying, /not just built-in products, /but home appliances in general. /22% of European online sales, /at the moment, /are made in the UK. /That is a big number, /ladies and gentlemen. /

如果我们看一下/大家电销售/在那段时间的情况,/在线销售促进了/英国大家电的销售,/但是有些品类,/在商店的销量/却下降了。/我们实际上看到/在线销售保持强劲势头,/涵盖几乎所有种类的大家电,/其中滚筒式干衣机/接近一半的市场购买额/来自线上购买。/嵌入式厨电/和嵌入式炉架,/以前,/这些产品,/是消费者想/去商店里/亲自触摸和感受的。/而现在消费者/更愿意/网上购买,/因为他们了解得更多信息,/这得益于互联网。/他们可以在网上搜索。/他们有考虑的空间。/因此,/我们看到了/巨大转变,/消费者购物方式发生了巨变,/不仅仅是嵌入式家电,/甚至所有家电都在网上购买。/22%的欧洲线上销售/目前/都来自英国。/这可是个庞大的数字啊,/女士们先生们。/

24:54—25:22

But Omni-Channel, /that is between true stores and also online, /also is vital/to achieve success in the UK. /Consumers are attracted/to experiences in store. /And indeed, /more and more consumers/are using both the Internet and physical store/in a more interactive way than ever. /And those kinds of products/that make an impact on/consumers in store/are just as likely to do well online as well. /

但是全渠道销售,/包括实体店和在线销售,/同样很重要,/有助于成功占领英国市场。/消费者会被吸引/去商店里体验。/确实,/越来越多消费者/既网购也在实体店购物,/越来越注重两者相结合。/那些产品/很吸引/实体店消费者的,/在网上也有可能会卖得很好。/

25:22—27:08

Black Friday, /to those of you/who are familiar, /is a peak sales period/in the

108

UK. /It was imported/from the US. /Amazon/was very well-known for it, /as was Walmart. /These were important to the UK. /Around about three years ago/and the UK consumers/have adopted Black Fridays/now as their own, /the single biggest trading day/in the UK/even outstripping Christmas/last year and the year before. /For 2015 and the first year/or 2014, /the first year that we had it, /most of those sales/were physical store sales. /Moving to 2016, /75—80% of all sales/across any product, /whether technical consumer products, /or clothing, /or any other types of luxury products, /was made online. /We had 6% market growth/because smart products/really took hold within the UK. /Overall growth/of 21% year-on-year. /And if you take a look/at some of the products/that did extremely well, /you have areas/like smart audio equipment, /wearables, /health and fitness trackers, /growing at 60%. /High and big screen TVs, /over 60 inches, /growing 135%/over that Black Friday period. /Cord-free vacuum cleaners, /incredibly popular in the UK, /and has really been very very strong in the UK/for a number of years/now grew 43%/over that period. /Smart and home computing/also grew in triple-digit. /And dental care, /even some of the more esoteric, /small domestic appliance areas, /also showed very strong growth/over this key Black Friday period. /

黑色星期五，/在座有些人/非常熟悉，/是巅峰销售期/的英国购物节，/引进/于美国。/亚马逊/曾因此闻名，/沃尔玛也是。/这些对英国都十分重要。/大约三年前，/英国消费者/引进了黑色星期五，/现在已成为我们自己的购物节。/其最大的交易日/在英国/甚至超过了圣诞节，/去年和前年都是如此。/在2015年以及第一年，/或者说2014年，/我们引入黑色星期五的第一年，/大多数销售/都在实体店进行。/到了2016年，/75%～80%的销售，/包括各类商品，/不管是技术类消费品，/还是服装，/或是任何其他奢侈品，/都是在线上完成的。/我们有6%的市场增长率，/因为智能产品/在英国确实占有一席之地。/总体增长/达到每年21%。/如果大家再看看/一些产品，/销量相当好，/您会发现有些品类/像智能音响设备、/可穿戴设备、/健康及健身追踪器，/销量增长60%。/高清大屏幕电视，/60英寸以上的，/销量增长了135%，/这得益于黑色星期五的促销。/无线真空吸尘器，/在英国备受青睐，/销售异常火爆，/热销了好几年，/销量增长43%，/也是因为黑色星期五的促销。/智能和家用电脑/增长率达到了三位数。/还有口腔护理产品，/甚至一些更小众的、/小家电产品门类，/也展现了强劲的销量增长势头，/也是得益于黑色星期五。/

27:08—27:55

And as I mentioned, /the shopping behaviors of consumers/have changed enormously. /Shoppers are now considering/and buying online/while actually they are physically in store. /So when you look at/what consumers are doing/with their smart phone/in store/and this comes/from another GfK survey/ "Future Buy", /from last year, /with around about 2,000 consumers/over the age of 18/in the UK, /25% of consumers/compare prices on their smart phones/while physically in the store. /19% of consumers/search for information/about the product/while physically in a shop. /17% check online reviews/and 14% check the availability/of a product or item. /That is a huge shift/in the way that consumers are purchasing products. /

就像我提到过的，/消费者的购物方式/已经发生了巨大改变。/消费者现在都在考虑/和网上购物，/而实际上他们人却在实体店里。/所以当您去看/消费者在做什么，/他们正拿着智能手机/在逛商店。/这是/捷孚凯公司另一项研究，/叫做"未来的购买行为"，/是去年开展的，/调查了大约2,000名消费者，/年龄18岁以上，/来自英国。/其中25%的消费者/会在手机上对比价格，/但是他们人却在实体店里。/19%的消费者/会上网查找信息/了解产品，/即使他们当时在实体店里。/17%会浏览网上的评价，/14%会查找网上是否能买到/某款产品。/这体现了极大的转变，/消费者的购物方式发生了巨变。/

27:55—28:45
So what does the future hold? /And in particular, /how does smart home play a big part in this? /So what we need to do is/look beyond the bubble of smart appliances. /Just what explain a little bit about/how we will define it, /it's a fairly general term. /But smart home/we look at connected devices/and automated home services. /And generally/these products are controlled/by mobile device/or remotely through the cloud. /If you look at home appliances, /washing machines/are showing enormous growth/for smart technology over the years. /Now we are 77 million pounds/in the UK/and growing at 88% year-on-year. /For refrigerators, /we are around about 12 million, /so a little bit smaller, /a little bit more modest, /but still growing very positively, /30% year-on-year. /

那么未来会是怎样的呢？/尤其是，/智能家居会如何发挥重要作用？/所以我们需要做的就是/看穿智能家电市场的泡沫。/简单解释一下/我们如何定义智能家居，/这是一个非常宽泛的概念。/但是智能家居/我们在这里只谈联网设备/和自动化家居服务。/通常来说，/这些产品受控于/移动设备/或者远程云技术。/如果大家看家电，/洗衣机/正呈现出巨大的增长态势，/这得益于智能技术过去几年的进步。/现在我们已经达到7,700万英镑/的英国市场销售额，/年增长率88%。/至于冰箱，/销售额大约1,200万，/相对有点少，/有点中规中矩，/但增长势头依然良好，/年增长率30%。/

第五单元 行业介绍 Introduction to Industries

28:45—29:44

But looking beyond/the bubble of smart appliances, /smart home will probably/ grow more slowly/than the hype suggests. /There are still/significant barriers/to consumers adopting smart home technology, /not least price. /Around about 70-75% of consumers believe/smart home is gonna have a big impact/on their lives/and it's important to them. /But the fact is/that a lot of people/are put off/because they don't necessarily fully understand it. /And they don't necessarily want/to invest in it quite yet. /And effectively, /smart home technology, /most crucially, /in order to be successful, /has to address specific consumer needs. /Innovation is/in many respects/ building a better mousetrap, /but true and pure innovation is/building a product/that consumer didn't even know/that they need it. /What consumers want/from smart technology, /effectively, /is freedom. /

但是看穿了/智能家电市场的泡沫, /智能家居很可能会/增长得更慢一些, /没有炒作说的那么快。/依然会有/很大的阻碍/阻挡消费者接受智能家居技术, /尤其是价格。/大约70%至75%的消费者认为/智能家居会极大影响/他们的生活/并且对他们很重要。/但事实是/很多人/并不感兴趣, /因为他们不一定完全理解这个东西。/他们也不一定想/现在就去投资智能家居。/实际上, /智能家居技术, /最关键的, /要获得成功的话, /必须满足消费者具体的需求。/创新/在很多方面来说/就是制造一个性能更好的捕鼠夹, /但是真正的纯粹的创新是/打造一个产品, /消费者甚至都不知道/自己需要这款产品。/消费者想要/从智能技术获得的/其实是自由。/

29:44—30:17

The appeal of smart home concept, /as I mentioned, /over 78% of consumers agreed/that smart home/was an extremely, very appealing/or fairly appealing concept. /And you can see/China leads the way with this. /91% of consumers in China, /well, which we surveyed, /agreed smart home/was extremely appealing, / very appealing/or fairly appealing. /The UK also ranks/very high in this. /66%, / over two-thirds of consumers believe/that smart home is appealing/or extremely appealing. /

智能家居概念的吸引力, /正如我提到的, /超过78%的消费者都认为/智能家居/是一个极其、非常有吸引力/或者有一定吸引力的概念。/大家也可以看到, /中国是这个领域的引领者。/91%的中国消费者, /根据我们的调查, /认为智能家居/极其有吸引力、/非常有吸引力/或者有一定吸引力。/英国排名/也很靠前。/66%, /超过三分之二消费者认为/智能家居有吸引力/或者极其有吸引力。/

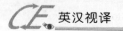

30:17—30:38

But as I said, /it has to serve specific needs. /Consumers' patience/is fading. /Over half of consumers in the UK agree/that if a new technology product/is not simple to use, /they lose interest. /Simplicity/is key to success. /And it's important/to get it right from the start/because consumers/have high expectations now. /

但就像我说过，/智能家居必须满足具体需求。/消费者的耐心/在消退。/超过一半的英国消费者认为/如果新技术产品/不容易使用，/他们就会失去兴趣。/简单/是成功的关键。/重要的是/一开始就要做好这一点，/因为消费者/现在的期望很高。/

30:38—31:17

Slowly, /we are starting to see/brands getting it right. /We are seeing/a hub created/by organization, by companies/for all things to work together seamlessly/within the hub. /We are creating/artificial intelligence/or AI/that makes the device/genuinely smart. /And finally, /we are creating/simple solutions/that are incredibly easy/for consumers to understand, /to adopt/and to interact with. /And nearly half of UK consumers feel/smart technology/is gonna have a very real impact/on their lives/over the next few years. /

渐渐地，/我们开始看到/品牌正往正确的方向努力。/我们看到了/一个中心建立起来，/由机构和公司创建，/让一切无缝对接，/内部互联。/我们正在创造/人工智能，/或者叫AI，/它能使设备/真正变得智能。/最后，/我们还在寻找/简单的解决方案，/能非常容易地/被消费者理解、接受、并与之交互。/将近一半的英国消费者觉得/智能技术/将会真真切切影响/他们的生活，/未来几年内就会到来。/

31:17—32:13

So to conclude, /Brexit may very well bring opportunity. /Despite uncertainty, /consumers are aspirational/and they will always replace/major appliances, /making these markets/highly resilient/and also highly attractive to foreign investment. /Built-in appliances/have a very bright future/in Britain. /As we've shown, /despite uncertainty, /consumers are generally aspirational/and generally, /they will always replace/major appliances, /again making these markets within built-in appliances/highly resilient. /And finally, /British consumers/are among the most connected/in Europe. /From consideration through to purchase, /the Internet/is absolutely key/to British shopping habits for appliances. /And smart home trends/cater to this need/for connectivity and convenience. /Thank you very much! /

总而言之，/英国脱欧很可能会带来机会。/尽管有不确定性，/但消费者很有追求，/也总会更换/大家电，/这使得家电市场/非常稳健，/也非常吸引外商投资。/嵌入式家电/前景很光明，/备受英国市场青睐。/就像我们展示过的，/虽然有不确定性，/但消费者通常都有高要求，/并且一般而言，/他们都想更换/大家电，/这同样使嵌入式家电市场/高度稳健。/最后，/英国消费者/是联网程度最高的/欧洲消费人群之一。/从考虑到购买，/互联网/绝对是关键，/改变了英国人购买家电的习惯。/而且智能家居趋势/迎合了人们的需要，/即对互联和便捷的需求。/谢谢大家！/

III. 实战练习二

1. 演讲背景

国际锰协 IMnI 市场分析师应邀参加"电解产品市场高峰论坛"并发表主旨演讲。他的演讲包括三部分内容：中等品位矿石产量拉动了锰矿产量的增长；中国的锰矿需求量日益增长，但去年锰矿石产量却有所下降；锂离子电池的需求快速增长，但其对锰市场的影响却微乎其微。他在演讲中引用了大量的数据，是一篇非常适合练习数字口译的演讲素材。

2. 预习词汇

manganese 锰
ore 矿石
DMTU/Dry Metric Ton Unit 干公吨
manganese alloy 锰合金
IMnI/International Manganese Institute 国际锰协
lithium-ion 锂离子
lithium-ion battery 锂离子电池
EMM/Electrolytic Manganese Metal 电解金属锰
backlog 积压的存货
carbonated ore 碳酸矿石
smelter 冶炼厂
Citibank 花旗银行
seaborne 海运的
manganese oxide 锰氧化物
manganese sulfate 硫酸锰
EMD/Electrolytic Manganese Dioxide 电解二氧化锰

nickel manganese cobalt 镍锰钴

3. 演讲文本

00:00—01:14

Good afternoon, /ladies and gentlemen. /I'm here today/to present the latest developments of the manganese market, /so that you can base your future business decisions/on accurate market information. /So to give you a bit of context, /last week the manganese ore prices, /according to Macquarie, /were around MYM8 per dmtu. / And this is more or less twice the price of exactly one year ago, /March, 2017. /So I know/this has a strong impact/on your businesses/and so today in this presentation/you will see information/that I collect directly/from manganese producers around the world. /And most of these figures/that you will see in this presentation/are an aggregate of/accurate industry company information. /They are not estimated. /So I'm going to show you today/exclusive IMnI figures/including inventory statistics/collected from major plants and mines around the world/and I'm going also to present an outlook/for the manganese ore market in the short term. /

下午好，/女士们，先生们。/我今天在这里/介绍锰市场的最新发展，/以便您可以将您未来的商业决策/建立在准确的市场信息基础上。/这里我将给您一些相关背景信息，/上周的锰矿石价格，/根据 Macquarie 给出的信息，/是大约 8 美元每干公吨。/这大约是一年前价格的两倍，/也就是 2017 年 3 月价格的两倍。/所以我知道/这极大地影响/你们的业务，/那么今天在这个展示中/你们会看到一些信息，/是我直接收集来的，/信息来自于世界各地的锰生产商。/大部分的数据，/在这次展示中你们将看到的大部分数据，/汇总了/准确的行业公司信息。/它们并不是估算得来的。/所以我要向大家展示/国际锰协会独家数据，/包括库存数据，/搜集于世界各地主要工厂和矿山，/我也将做一个预测，/与短期内锰矿市场的前景有关。/

01:14—02:43

So this is the outline of my presentation. /I'm going to start with the global manganese ore market/and I'm going to show/that the manganese ore production growth/has been driven by mid grade ore output mostly. /And then the second part of this presentation/will be dedicated to China/and I'll show that/China's rising manganese ore demand/has been coupled with declining production last year. /And finally, /the last part of this presentation/will be about demand for lithium-ion batteries/and their impact on the manganese market. /But first global manganese ore demand. /It rebounded in 2017 last year. /Manganese alloy and EMM production/increased faster than steel outputs last year/plus 12% for manganese alloy production in 2017/and this was due mostly to restocking/and 37% increase in EMM production last year/mostly because of the supply expansion by Ningxia Tianyuan. /So both manganese alloy and EMM production/increased much faster/than steel production last year. /And as a result,/manganese ore demand/increased in 2017 by around 15%/according IMnI estimates. /

这是我演讲的大纲。/我将从全球锰矿市场开始,/我将展示/锰矿产量的增长/主要是由中等品位矿石产量推动的。/然后演讲的第二部分/会着重讲中国,/我将向各位展示/中国的锰矿需求量日益增长,/去年锰矿石产量却有所下降。/最后,/演讲的最后一部分/是关于锂离子电池的需求/及其对锰市场的影响。/但首先是全球锰矿需求。/该指数在 2017 年回升。/锰合金和电解金属锰产量/增速超过去年钢铁产量的增速,/2017 年锰合金产量同比增加了 12%,/这主要是因为补货,/去年电解金属锰的产量增长 37%/主要是因为宁夏天元扩大供应。/因此锰合金和电解金属锰的产量/增速远高于/去年钢铁产量增速。/因此,/锰矿需求量/在 2017 年增加了约 15%,/这是根据国际锰协的估计。/

02:43—04:12

And this is what you see in this chart here. /So manganese ore demand/reached a little bit more than 18 million tons last year/and I'm talking about manganese contained/not gross volume. /I'm talking manganese units here. /So 18 million manganese units/and driven by this rising demand and low manganese ore stocks,/manganese ore output/boomed in 2017/and these increase in global manganese ore production last year/was mostly driven by mid-grade ore. /So we at the IMnI, /we separate manganese ore in three grades. /There's low grade/which is written in the chart here in the legend. /Low grade/is lower than 30% manganese contents. /Mid grade/is between 30 and 44% manganese contents/and high grade/is above 44% manganese. /So the global output of manganese ore total/reached 18.5 million metric tons/manganese contained. /And this is an increase of 23%/against the 2016. /So basically the backlog of material/that has, that I've been accumulated since 2013/along the supply chain/has been consumed in 2015 and 2016. /And in 2017, /we saw an excess supply in the manganese ore market, /slight excess supply. /

这就是您在这张图表中看到的。/锰矿的需求量/去年略超 1,800 万吨,/我所说的是含锰量/而不是总量。/我说的是锰单位。/1,800 万个锰单位/以及受这一不断增长的需求和低锰矿存量的驱动,/锰矿产量/在 2017 年出现爆炸性增长,/去年全球锰矿产量的增长/主要是因为中等品位锰矿产量增长。/因此国际锰协/将锰矿分为三个等级。/低品位的锰矿,/在图表的这里显示了。/低品位/是指低于 30% 锰含量。/中等品位/是指介于30%～44%之间的锰含量,/高品位/是指高于44%的锰含量。/锰矿的全球总产量/达到了1,850万吨,/指的是含锰量,/增加了23%,/这是相比于2016年而言。/所以基本上积压的原材料/据我统计/自2013年以来/在供应链上/已经在2015和2016年消耗殆尽。/2017年,/我们发现锰矿市场供应过剩,/略微过剩。/

04:12—05:39

So here in the chart/I've shown the different grades of manganese ore/produced from 2011 to 2013./As you can see/the high-grade ore production/in blue here/increased significantly by 21% from…/so in 2017/compared with 2016/and reached almost eight million tons,/manganese contained./Mid-grade ore output/increased by 41%./So that's a huge increase in mid-grade ore production./So production of manganese ore between 30 and 44% manganese./So this grade of course/includes carbonated ore from South Africa/and also ore as well./And finally low grade ore production/contracted by 12% in 2017/to 2.6 million tons/and the average grade produced in 2017/was 34% manganese./So basically the key idea here/is that mid-grade ore production/increased faster than/high grade ore output in 2017,/while low-grade ore production/dropped from 2016/and this is mostly the case in China/where the most mines/produce low-grade ore,/manganese ore./

因此,在图表中,/我展示了不同品位的锰矿/从2011到2013的产量。/如你们所看到的,/高品位矿石产量/用蓝色标出,/其产量显著增加了21%,/2017年/与2016年相比,/产量达到了800万吨,/指的是含锰量。/中等品位矿产量/增长了41%。/这是中等品位矿产量的巨大增长,/也就是含锰量在30%～44%之间的锰矿产量。/所以中等品位锰矿/包括南非碳酸矿石/和锰矿石。/最后,低品位矿石产量/在2017年下降了12%/只有260万吨,/2017生产的平均锰品位/为34%。/所以基本上这里的关键信息/是中等品位矿石产量/增速高于/2017年高品位矿石产量,/而低品位矿石产量/从2016开始下跌,/这主要是在中国,/这里大多数矿山/生产低品位矿石,/锰矿石。/

05:39—06:57

Now let's have a look at/the stock for manganese miners./The data that we collect every month/from major manganese ore producers around the world/show that/stocks of manganese ore/increased by 3% in 2017./So I just compared/the stock of major miners at the end of the year/with their stock at the beginning of the year/and saw the differences,/plus 3%./This is based on inventory figures/from miners mostly located in Africa,/South America,/Asia and Australia./And you can see here/the

第五单元 行业介绍 Introduction to Industries

comparison/between China in blue in the chart/and sorry, in green in the chart/and the rest of the world in blue. /So plus 3% for inventory/in the rest of the world/and minus 19% in inventory/in China/last year. /And this was due to mostly/rising demand from smelters in 2017 in China/and that at the end of January, 2018/manganese ore miners' stocks/were around, represented around two months' ore production on average/which is quite low. /

现在让我们来看看/锰矿矿山的库存量。/我们每月收集的数据/来源于全球主要锰矿生产商,/这些数据显示/锰矿库存量/在2017年增加了3%。/我只是比较了/主要矿山在年末的库存量/与其在年初的库存量,就发现了差别,/库存增加了3%。/这是基于库存量数据,/这些有库存的矿山大部分位于非洲、/南美洲、/亚洲和澳大利亚。/你们从这里可以看到/对比,/中国在图表中是蓝色部分的,/抱歉图中绿色部分的是中国,/世界其他地方是蓝色部分。/存货量增加3%的/是世界上其他地方,/存货量减少19%的/是中国,/这都是去年的数据。/这主要是因为/2017年中国冶炼厂需求增长,/并且在2018年1月底,/锰矿山的库存量/大约等于两个月的平均产量,/这是很低的。/

06:57—07:41

So now let's have a look at/what's happening in the China's industry. /So we see/China's rising manganese ore demand/coupled with declining production/last year. /So first/production in China, /production of manganese ore in China, /usually China's manganese ore production increases/when international ore prices are high, /because there's more incentive to mine in China/when international ore prices are high. /But not in 2017/and this was because of reducing reserves in China, /falling quality/and also safety restrictions/for mining in some mines in China. /

所以现在让我们来看看/中国锰行业发生了什么。/我们看到/中国锰矿需求量上升,/而锰矿石产量下降,/这是去年的情况。/所以首先,/中国的产量,/中国锰矿石的产量,/通常中国锰矿的产量会增加,/当国际锰矿价格上升的时候会这样,/因为这会更加刺激中国矿山锰矿石开采,/国际锰矿价格上升的时候就会这样。/但2017年并非如此,/这是因为中国锰矿石储量减少,/品位下降,/以及采取安全限制措施,/限制中国某些矿山开采。/

07:41—08:20

So the chart here/shows the manganese ore production in China/from 2011 to 2017. /And as you can see/in 2017/the production of manganese ore in China/was around 1.7 million tons manganese contained. /That's a drop of 28% compared to 2016. /China's recent weak domestic supply of ore/is likely to continue, /according to

Citibank, /and the lower domestic supply in China/increased China's demand for seaborne material/that is replacing progressively domestic ore. /

所以这里的图表, /显示的是中国的锰矿石产量, /时间是 2011 至 2017 年。/正如你们所看到的, /2017 年/中国的锰矿石产量/约为 170 万吨含锰量, /比 2016 下降了 28%。/中国近期疲软的国内铁矿石供应/可能会持续, /这是花旗银行所做的预测, /而且, 国内供应减少, /增加了中国对海外进口原材料的需求, /这将逐步取代国内生产的锰矿石。/

08:20—09:48

So this chart, /this slide here/is about manganese ore imports into China/and I want to show you/that they have continued rising last year/and they reached a new record high. /This was due obviously to/rising demand from Chinese smelters/plus 10% last year/and also due to lower domestic ore production/as I've shown in the previous slide, /minus 28%. /So here in the chart/you see the manganese ore imports into China/by origin/and in green at the bottom/you see the share of South Africa. /So China's manganese ore imports in 2017/represented 21.3 million tons. /I'm talking wet metric tons here. /So no longer manganese contained/and this includes 9.3 million metric tons from South Africa. /That's an increase of 31% in 2017 compared to 2016/ for exports from South Africa to China. /And so South Africa/at the end of 2017/ represented 44% of China's total imports. /In January this year, /China imported 2.28 million wet metric tons of ore. /So that's again a new record high for a single month/and so we see this trend of rising imports into China/continuing at the beginning of this year. /

所以这张图表, /这张幻灯片/是关于中国进口的锰矿石, /我想告诉你们的是, /锰矿石进口去年一直持续增加, /达到了历史新高。/这显然是因为/中国冶炼厂需求增长, /去年同比增长了 10%, /也因为国内锰矿产量减少, /就像我在前一张幻灯片里展示的那样, /减少了 28%。/在这张图里, /您可以看到中国锰矿进口量/是按来源地分类, /底部绿色的部分/是南非的份额。/中国 2017 年锰矿石进口/达到了 2,130 万吨。/我说的是湿公吨数, /不再是含锰量了, /其中包括 930 万吨南非进口锰矿。/2017 年相较于 2016 年增长了 31%, /这里指的是南非对中国的锰矿出口量。/所以南非/在 2017 年底/占了中国进口总额的 44%。/今年一月, /中国进口 228 万湿吨矿石。/因此, 这又是一个单月新纪录, /我们能看到中国进口量的增长趋势/从今年年初一直持续至今。/

09:48—10:34

Now a few words about stocks in China. /So we've seen/demand production in

第五单元　行业介绍 Introduction to Industries

China/and now stocks, /manganese ore prices/are supported by strong demand/and supply tightness in China's. /That's the main reason/for the supported prices/that we see at the moment in the manganese ore markets. /There were low stock levels estimate/ at the end of 2017/that triggered a restocking of manganese alloys/and these forced smelters in China/to buy aggressively during the last few months, /to buy ore aggressively during the last few months/and these supported prices/and reduce the inventory of manganese ore in China. /

现在来谈谈中国的库存量。/我们已经看到/中国的生产需求,/现在的库存、锰矿石的价格/得益于强劲的需求/以及中国锰矿供应的收缩。/这就是为什么/会有这种价格/出现在目前的锰矿市场上的原因。/低库存预期/出现在2017年底,/这引发了锰合金的补货,/也促使中国冶炼厂/在最后几个月大量买入,/在最后几个月大量购买锰矿石,/这抬高了价格,/也降低了中国锰矿石的库存量。/

10:34—11:42

So on this chart here/you see the correlation between the price, /that's the yellow curve, /price of manganese ore/and the total port stock in China. /As you can see, / as soon the stock increases in China, /the price drops. /So this was the case. /You can see/my two arrows here. /That was the case at the beginning of 2017. /There was a huge increase in manganese ore stocks/and a huge drop in manganese ore prices/and then the contrary happened/at the end of, /during most of 2017. /We saw a significant reduction in stocks in China/due to smelters buying aggressively ore/and an increase in manganese ore prices. /And recently you can see this/at the, on the right-hand side of the chart. /We've seen an increase in manganese ore stocks in China, /but prices so far continue to increase. /

在这张图表上/您能看到价格之间的相关性,/是这条黄色的曲线,/锰矿价格/还有中国港口总库存量。/正如您所看到的,/中国库存一增加,/价格就会下跌。/情况就是这样。/您可以看到/我画的两个箭头。/这是2017年初的情况。/锰矿库存大幅增加,/锰矿价格大幅下跌,/相反的情况则出现/在年末,/［2017年］全年大部分时间都是相反情况。/我们看到大幅度下跌的中国锰矿库存量,/这是因为冶炼厂大量购买锰矿石/以及锰矿石价格上升。/最近你们能看到这个,/在这个图表的右边。/我们已经看到锰矿库存在中国有所增加,/但价格目前还在继续上升。/

11:42—13:33

So the manganese market is now very tight/in China/and to show you this/I would like to show this next chart/and I'm going to explain/how manganese ore stocks in

China/reached a record low in February this year. /So stocks reached 1.7 million metric tons/last month in China. /This is equivalent with/0.9 months of apparent consumption/by Chinese smelters. /To calculate this, /we use imports/and the change of inventory from one month to the next/and we calculated, /moving average to get this estimate/of 0.9 months of apparent consumption. /So 1.7 million metric tons of ore is enough. /It is not enough/for one month of production for manganese alloy in China/and the average in last year/was 1.7 month of production in stocks/at China's ports. /So we see that/at the moment the stocks in China/are very very low/and this 0.9 month of apparent consumption/is the record low/that we've seen over the last few years. /And this is what you can see here on the chart/we compare the port inventory. /That's the blue curve. /And how many months of production it represents/and that's the red part of the chart. /So restocking of apparent consumption in China/has started in March. /Stocks are now rising/and we've seen almost 2.2 million metric tons, /wet metric tons/at the beginning of March at China's ports. /

锰市场目前供不应求,/这就是中国的情况。/为了说明这点,/我给大家看看下一张图表,/我将解释/中国的锰矿库存是如何/在今年二月达到历史新低。/锰矿库存达到170万吨,/就是在上个月。/这相当于/0.9个月的表观消费量,/中国冶炼厂的表观消费量。/为了进行计算,/我们使用了进口量/和库存的月度变化,/我们计算,/平均下来得出这个估值/为0.9个月的表观消费量。/所以170万公吨的矿石是足够的。/它无法满足/中国锰合金一个月的产量,/而且去年的平均值/是1.7个月的产量库存,/这是中国港口的库存量。/所以我们看到/目前中国的库存量/是非常非常低的,/而且这0.9个月的表观消费量/达到历史新低,/是几年来的历史新低。/这就是大家能在图表中看到的,/我们比较了港口库存量。/就是这条蓝色曲线。/它代表了多少个月的生产量,/产量就是图表里红色的部分。/因此,中国表观消费量的补货/从三月开始。/库存量目前正在上涨,/我们也看到了有将近220万吨,/以湿吨为单位,/这是三月初中国港口的库存量。/

13:33—17:11

So now I'm going to show/how the demand for lithium-ion batteries for manganese/will not completely change and transform/the manganese ore markets globally. /So there is booming li-ion battery production. /That is for sure/and we had interesting presentation on this/in the morning. /According to Roskill, /manganese consumption by lithium-ion batteries/will rise by 23% on average per year/between 2017 and 2027. /So in ten years/23% per year on average. /And this is what you can see here on the chart, /you can see/the share of manganese oxide and manganese sulfate. /And you can also see on the chart/the share of ore demand/that is represented by these li-ion batteries. /And as you can see, /it is in 2017/very very low. /We're talking about 0.1%, /0.11% of total manganese ore demand/currently consumed in lithium-ion batteries. /So this booming li-ion battery demand for manganese/has little impact on the manganese market/because of the volumes. /You've seen this chart already/in the morning. /It shows basically the manganese ore consumption by product/in 2017. /We have manganese alloys/representing the largest share, /87% of total manganese ore consumption last year. /While manganese metal/represents around 11% of total manganese ore consumption. /We have EMD/representing 2%/and finally other manganese chemicals/including manganese sulfates and others/representing 0.3% of total manganese ore consumption last year. /So I've written the figures/for manganese ore consumption. /So you have 15.7 million metric tons, /again manganese contained for manganese alloy. /Manganese metals/consume two million tons of manganese ore/last year, /0.27 million tons for EMD/and other chemicals represented 0.05, /so 50,000 tons manganese contained. /So nickel manganese cobalt/and lithium manganese oxide batteries/for electric vehicles/are made from high-grade EMD, /—all the manganese chemicals/and to a lesser extent EMM. /So their consumption/is mixed between EMM, /EMD and other manganese chemicals. /But basically/the key message here/is that the manganese volume consumed by lithium-ion batteries/is very low. /And even though this sector is, /this demand from lithium-ion batteries/is growing, /this manganese volume consumed by batteries/will remain a niche market/for the manganese industry globally/in the near term. /And this is contrary/to what many investors say at the moment. /So from manganese ore producers' point of view, /the demand from the lithium-ion batteries/would not transform the manganese ore prices/and completely change the trend of the industry. /That's my message here in this slide. /

因此我现在要说明的是, /为何锰系锂离子电池的需求/不会完全改变/全球锰矿市场。/锂离子电池产量大幅增长。/这是肯定的, /我们做了一个有趣的相关演讲, /就在今天早上。/根据 Roskill 的说法, /锂离子电池的锰消耗量/将保持 23%的年均增长率, /2017 到 2027 年间都是如此。/所以未来十年间, /保持 23%的年均增长率。/这就是你们在图表上看到的, /可以看到/锰氧化物和硫酸锰的份额。/也可以在图表上看到/锰矿石需求的份额, /指的是锂离子电池所需的锰矿石。/正如您所看到的, /这一需求在 2017 年/非常低, /为 0.1%, /为 0.11%的锰矿石总需求量, /这就是锂离子电池目前的消耗量。/因此, 锂离子电池对锰需求的增长/几乎影响不到锰市场, /因为需求量太少。/您已经看到过这个图表了, /早上就看过。/图表里基本展示了各种品类对锰矿石的消耗量, /这是 2017 年的情况。/锰合金/占额最大, /占去年锰矿总消耗量的 87%。/锰金属/占 11%左右的锰矿总消耗量。/电解二氧化锰/占了 2%, /其他锰化学品, /包括硫酸锰等/占了去年锰矿石总消耗量的0.3%。/所以我列举了一些数字，/这是锰矿的消耗量。/因此，共有1,570万公吨，/这是锰合金里锰的消耗量。/锰金属消耗了200万吨锰矿，/这是去年的消耗量。/电解二氧化锰消耗了27万吨，/其他化学品占了5万吨，/也就是5万吨的含锰量。/因此，镍锰钴/和锂锰氧化物电池，/电动车用的电池，/它们都是由高品位的电解二氧化锰制成，/包括所有的锰化学品/及少量的电解金属锰，/所以它们的消耗/混合了电解金属锰，/电解二氧化锰和其他锰化学品。/但基本上，/这里的关键信息/是锂离子电池的锰消耗量/非常低。/尽管这个行业是这样的，/锂离子电池的需求量/正在增长，/电池的锰消耗量/仍会是一个利基市场，/对于全球锰行业来说，/近期都是如此。/恰恰相反，/许多投资者目前所说的并非如此。/因此，从锰矿石生产商的角度来看，/锂离子电池需求/不会改变锰矿价格，/也不会彻底改变行业趋势。/这一信息就是这张幻灯片所要传达的。/

17:11—18:24

I would like to show you/a quick short-term outlook. /So this summarizes/some of the slides in this presentation/and gives you all of ideas/basically on the positive side/for manganese ore prices. /So on the left hand side of the chart, of the table, /these are factors supporting manganese ore prices. /We see China's declining domestic ore supply/and increasing dependence on imports. /This has an impact on manganese ore prices. /There's a possible short-term export constraint in South Africa/according to Citibank, /also supporting prices. /There's an improvement of global demand/expected during the first half of this year/when Chinese team restart/after the holidays and winter cuts. /There is also a seasonal manganese ore restocking/from the current very low stock levels at China ports/and we've seen in the past/that April/has often been a month of restocking in China. /So this could also support manganese ore prices/in the near term. /And finally there's the strengthening Rand/following the elections in South Africa. /So these factors should support manganese ore prices/in the near term. /

我想向大家展示一下/短期展望。/这里总结了/本次演讲中的一些幻灯片，/并给出观点，/基本都是正面因素，/可以提升锰矿石价格。/在图表的左侧，/是锰矿价格上涨的因素。/我们看到中国下降的国内矿石供应量/和越来越依赖进口。/这影响了锰矿价格。/可能短期内南非会限制出口，/据花旗银行透露，/这也会使价格上涨。/全球范围内的需求将会回升，/预计将出现在今年上半年，/中国的钢厂将会重新开始生产，/继春节和冬季减产后恢复生产。/还进行季节性锰矿库存重建，/而现在中国港口库存非常低。/以前，/四月/通常是中国重建库存的月份。/所以这也会提升锰矿的价格，/短期来说确实如此。/最后还有兰特升值，/是在南非大选后升值的。/因此，这些因素都会提升锰矿价格，/短期内会是这样。/

18:24—19:05

On the other side, /there is, on the right hand side of the table, /there is these factors waving on manganese ore prices and contracting. /So there's rising stocks for manganese ore producers/that we see at the moment in our statistics/and also an environmental restriction/on steel outputs/in Hebei province and other provinces/that could last longer than expected. /And this would obviously have an impact on/ manganese ore demand/and in turn on manganese ore prices. /So all the data used in this report/is available to IMnI members/and non-members can also inquire/on manganese.org. /

另一方面,/在表格的右边,/这些因素使锰矿价格波动和收缩。/锰矿石生产商的库存不断上升,/像我们现在在数据中看到的那样,/还有环境因素/限制了钢产量,/在河北省和其他省份都是如此,/其影响时长将超过预期。/这显然会影响/锰矿需求,/反过来也会影响锰矿石价格。/本报告中使用的所有数据,/国际锰协会员都可以获得,/非成员也可以查询,/在网站 manganese.org 上查询。/

19:05—19:51

And now I would like to very quickly show you/another view of IMnI services. / We have five core services/at the International Manganese Institute. /It's, to be part of the network of IMnI members, /to benefit from ore market research and statistics. /So we have weekly reports, /monthly reports/including the data that you've seen in this presentation. /We also have a health, safety and environment department. /We provide regulatory information to our members. /And finally we organize events and conferences/where people can network with the manganese community. /

现在我将快速地向大家展示一下/国际锰协的另一面。/我们提供五种核心服务,/国际锰协提供的。/包括成为国际锰协的会员,/获益于矿石市场调查和数据。/我们有周报、/月报,/其中涵盖了你们在这次演讲中看到的数据。/我们还有一个健康、安全和环保部门。/我们提供监管信息给会员。/最后,我们组织活动和会议,/方便人们与锰行业人士打交道。/

19:52—20:40

So I invite you today/to join the club of IMnI members. /We have more than 70 members at the moment/from based in 27 countries. /And Asia represents the biggest share of our membership. /We have 42% of our members/based in Asia. /All members are producers/of manganese ore, /manganese alloy, /manganese metal, / manganese chemical. /We are also producers and processors of manganese chemical/ and of course, traders, /shipping companies/and any other industry service providers. /And I added on the slide a few logos/of some of our major members. /

所以今天我邀请你们/加入国际锰协会员俱乐部。/[现在]我们有超过70名会员,/来自27个国家,/亚洲会员最多,/我们有42%的会员/来自亚洲。/所有会员都是生产商,/生产锰矿石、/锰合金、/锰金属、/锰化学品。/我们的会员也生产和加工锰化学品,/当然,还有从事贸易、/航运/和其他行业服务的。/我在幻灯片上添加了几个标志,/是我们几个主要成员公司的标志。/

20:41—21:46

The benefits of joining the IMnI/for Chinese companies/I think would be threefold. /There is the visibility/and networking. /You can easily connect/and be trusted by the sales managers/of the world's biggest manganese ore suppliers/by being part of the club of IMnI members. /We have an IMnI China Committee/that is chaired by Mr. Li Weijian/from CITIC Dameng/which is a dedicated platform for Chinese members/to exchange on technical issues, /statistics, /regulations. /So this is a very important part of the IMnI services/to all members in China/and IMnI members/also benefit from the best market research available on manganese. /So we have trade statistics/published on a monthly basis. /You get South Africa's manganese ore monthly production, /manganese metal/and EMD production figures. /And on the right-hand side of the chart, /of the slide, /you can see a few of our IMnI members/in China. /So obviously/there is CITIC Dameng and a few others. /And the IMnI membership fees/for Chinese members/are 7,000 Euros/and you can send an email/to my colleague Zhou Jian/if you want to inquire about the IMnI. /

加入国际锰协的好处/对中国公司来说/我认为有三个。/可见性/和关系网。/您可以很容易建立联系,/获得销售经理的信任,/他们都来自世界各大锰矿石供应商,/前提条件是您只需要成为国际锰协的会员。/我们有一个国际锰协中国委员会,/主席是李维健先生,/他来自中信大锰公司,/这是一个中国会员专用平台,/他们可以在上面交流有关技术、/数据/和规章制度问题。/所以这是国际锰协服务很重要的一部分,/对于所有中国会员尤为如此。/国际锰协的会员/也能受益于一流的锰市场研究。/我们有贸易数据,/每月都会发布。/您可以获得南非锰矿的月产量、/锰金属/和电解二氧化锰的生产数据。/在图表的右边,/幻灯片的右边,/您能看到几位国际锰协成员,/他们来自中国。/很显然,/里面有中信大锰和其他几位。/会员费/对中国会员/是收取7,000欧元,/您可以发电子邮件/给我的同事周建,/如果您想咨询国际锰协的信息就可以联系他。/

21:47—22:57

And finally/to conclude this presentation, /I would like to invite you/to our events or annual conference/which this year will take place in Kuala Lumpur, Malaysia/in June from the 18th to the 20th/and on the 21st/we will organize a technical tour/to visit the Sarawak plants. /Three manganese alloy plants/that started production over the last few months. /There is Sakura Ferroalloys, OM Sarawak and Pertama Ferroalloys/and we already have now more than 60 actually companies registered for this event, /more than 110 delegates already registered, /so we expect/more than 150 delegates in total. /And so I invite you to secure your seat now/to join us for this event. /Thank you very much for your attention. /And now you have a clear picture of the supply demand/and inventory trends for manganese ore/and an outlook of the market in the short term, /and I'm now ready to take any questions that you may have/or we will have an exchange panel/after the last presentation. /Thank you very much for your attention! /

最后，/在结束这次演讲之前，/我想邀请你们/参加我们的活动或年会，/今年将在马来西亚吉隆坡举行，/时间是6月18日至20日，/21日/我们会组织一次技术访问，/参观沙捞越的工厂。/三家锰合金工厂/在过去的几个月里才开始生产，/包括 Sakura Ferroalloys, OM Sarawak 和 Pertama Ferroalloys，/我们已经有60多家公司报名参加这项活动，/超过110名代表已经报名，/所以我们预计/总共有超过150名代表。/因此，我邀请各位现在来报名留位，/参加这次活动。/非常感谢您的关注。/现在您已经清楚地了解供应需求/和锰矿库存趋势/以及短期市场前景。/我现在准备回答你们的问题，/也可以在小组讨论时提问，/讨论会在最后一个演讲结束后进行。/谢谢大家！/

第六单元 反腐倡廉
Anti-corruption

I. 长句视译

虽然长句在各种讲话中占据的比例较小，但是长句句法相对来说比较复杂，各个部分之间存在逻辑关系，因此需要加强对长句的视译练习。笔译中会采用一些有效长句处理方法，比如顺序法、逆序法、分析法和综合法等，但在视译中，处理长句的基本技巧是"拆分顺译"。

【例1】One of the major reasons/for America's great success/as the world's first "universal nation",/for its astonishing and unmatched capacity/for assimilating immigrants,/has been the immigrants' acquisition of English./

译文1：美国是世界上第一个"有感召力的普世国家"，取得了巨大成功，在移民同化方面也表现出惊人的、无与伦比的能力，一个主要原因就是使移民学会英语。

译文2：有许多原因，/使美国取得巨大成功，/成为世界上第一个"有感召力的普世国家"，/使它具有惊人的巨大能力/同化来自世界各国的移民。/其中一个主要原因是使移民学会英语。/

译文1是笔译译文，先陈述美国的两方面成就——是世界上第一个"有感召力的普世国家"，取得了巨大成功，同时在移民同化方面也表现出惊人的、无与伦比的能力，再回过头来将原因表达与句末的原因具体内容结合起来。做了较大的语序调整，符合中文的行文顺序。译文2是视译译文，进行了合理断句，顺着语序翻。为了使译文表达流畅，增加了"主要原因之一"进行衔接。

【例2】According to 1998 market forecast by Boeing,/China's air transportation volume will continue to grow/at an average rate of 8.1%,/which is significantly higher than the projected world growth rate of 4.9%./

译文1：据波音公司1998年的市场预测，中国的航空运输将保持年均8.1%的增长率继续增长，远高于全球4.9%的增长预测。

译文2：据波音公司1998年的市场预测，/中国的航空运输将继续增长，/保持年均8.1%的增长率，/远高于全球4.9%的增长预测。/

例2的长句中包含一个定语从句，笔译和视译的译文都没有调整定语从句的位置，但是对于介词短语 at an average rate of 8.1%，译文1将其调整到前面，译文2则进行合理断句，保持了原句的语序。

II. 实战练习一

1. 演讲背景

英国《2010反腐败法案》立法者应邀参加"大成（深圳）法学名家大讲坛暨蓝海法律沙龙"并发表主旨演讲。他在演讲的第一部分提到了该法案是最严苛的法律，侧重解释了法案的管辖范围、犯罪构成要件、处罚、商业机构贿赂罪和抗辩理由。

2. 预习词汇

International Bribery and Corruption Law 国际贿赂和腐败法
bribery 贿赂
offence 犯罪；罪行
confession 坦白
freehand 徒手
discretion 自由裁量权
jurisdiction 管辖区；管辖权
prosecution 起诉
public sector 公共部门
private sector 私营企业
public official 公职人员
Chinese Criminal Code《中国刑法》
Foreign Corrupt Practices Act《反海外腐败法》
inchoate 刚刚发生的
trading permit 交易许可
residency permit 居住权
statute 法令
conviction 判决；定罪
corporate offence 商业机构贿赂罪
partner company 合作公司
quasi 类似的
Section Seven offense 第七节规定的罪行

defense/dcfence 抗辩理由

Harbor Master 港务局长

exemption 豁免

administrative payment 行政给付

provision 规定

ship owner 船东

public money 公款

prosecution service 检察部门

established practice 公认的做法

prosecutor 检察官

disproportionate 不相称的

subsidiary company 子公司

joint venture partner 合资企业合伙人

subcontractor 分包商

3. 演讲文本

00:00—01:24

您好！/早上好！/It is a great privilege, /a great honor/to be invited here today/to speak to you about my special, my specialist subject, /International Bribery and Corruption Law. /I have to admit to you/before I begin a confession/which is that, /before I worked for the government/advising on law reform, /I knew very little about corruption law or bribery, /very little indeed. /In fact, /very few lawyers in Britain/knew anything about corruption law, /because/it was thought/corruption is rare. /You don't come across it very often, /there is no real need/to understand the law within the United Kingdom. /Well, /we know very differently now. /There have been a number of scandals, /a number of cases/and suddenly, /everyone wants to become/an expert on anti-corruption. /Suddenly, /it is an extremely popular/and important subject. /

您好，/早上好！/今天非常荣幸、非常有幸/能受邀来这里，/和大家分享我的专业学科/——国际贿赂和腐败法。/不得不承认，/我想和大家坦白，/那就是/我为政府工作、/成为法律改革顾问前，/关于腐败法或贿赂我知道得很少，/真的非常少。/其实，/英国很少律师/知道腐败法，/因为/他们认为/腐败很少见，/并不常见，/所以不需要/了解英国的腐败法。/当然，/现在情况不一样了。/现在有很多丑闻，/和案例，/突然之间，/人人都想成为/反腐专家。/突然之间，/反腐也成为极其热门/和重要的学科。/

第六单元　反腐倡廉 Anti-corruption

01:24—03:24

And so in 2008, /10 years ago, /the government asked me/to reform the law in the United Kingdom, /which had not been reformed/for over 100 years, /and we had a complete freehand, /complete discretion/to reform the law/in any way that we wanted. /And what we did/encouraged by a number of anti-corruption groups/and experts. /We created a set of laws/which many people say/are the most strict, /the most stringent, /the harshest in many ways/of any laws in any jurisdiction. /Of course, /a law is only as good/as the extent to which it is enforced. /It is no good/to have a law in the book/if the law is not enforced in a court. /And as I will show you/ we are beginning now to see/some prosecutions/in particular of companies/who have engaged in corrupt activity/and that in the United Kingdom/is a relatively new phenomenon. /In the past/it was very rare/for a company to be charged with corruption/in the United Kingdom. /Now/not only does UK law govern UK, /United Kingdom companies, /it also applies to overseas companies/including of course Chinese companies/operating in and through the United Kingdom. /

所以在2008年，/也就是10年前，/政府委托我/改革英国的法律，/一直都没有改革过，/100多年都是如此，/我们完全是徒手做的，/完全具有自由裁量权/改革法律，/用任何我们想要的方式。/同时我们也/得到了许多反腐团队的鼓励/和专家的支持。/我们制定了一系列法律，/很多人说/这是最严格、最严苛、/在很多方面都是最严格的法律，/比其他管辖区的任何法律都要严格。/当然，/好的法律/要看它强制执行到什么程度。/最糟糕的是/法律只是一纸空文，/除非它在法庭上执行。/就像大家看到的，/我们开始看一些/起诉案件/特别是针对公司的，/这些公司有腐败行为，/而这在英国/算是比较新的现象了。/过去，/很少有/在公司被指控犯了腐败罪，/英国这种情况很少见。/现在，/英国的法律不仅管辖英国/和英国的公司，/还适用于海外公司，/当然包括中国公司，/如果它们在英国开展业务的话。/

03:31—06:21

Now/let me say a little bit about the new law. /It is difficult to strike a balance/when speaking between too much detail about the law/and too little detail. /However, /I will try to give you/an overview of what the law, /of the most important part of the law. /In the United Kingdom, /bribery is an offence, /not only when a public sector official is involved, /but also in the private sector. /In other words, /if one company tries to bribe another company/or an individual, /that is also an offence, /equally an offence. /Similarly, /the law has a very broad and wide reach/under heading number two there, /the law applies to anyone/who is ordinarily resident

129

in the United Kingdom. /In other words, /any Chinese national/who is living in the United Kingdom/as their ordinary place of residence, /the law will apply to them, /even though they are not a UK national. /Similarly, /any foreign company, /such as a Chinese company/which is doing business in the United Kingdom, /will be covered by the legislation, /even though it may not/in fact/be based in the United Kingdom/or have a subsidiary operating there. /The new legislation/includes a special offense/on the heading three/of bribing a foreign public official, /but I don't want to say too much about that today. /This is a very common offense. /It is also, /I believe, /an offense under the *Chinese Criminal Code*. /I want to focus more/on the offense under heading four. /This is an offense that applies only to companies/and it is the offense/of failing to prevent bribery by an employee or agent. /This was the most controversial/and the most far-reaching offense in the legislation/and this is the offense/that has created most debate/and discussion. /

现在/我想讲讲新法的一些内容。/很难找到一个平衡点,/既不会讲太多的法律细节,/又不会讲得太少。/但是,/我会给大家/介绍一下这部法律的概况/及其最重要的部分。/在英国,/贿赂是犯罪行为,/不仅涉及到公共部门官员,/还发生在私营企业中。/换言之,/如果一家公司想贿赂另一家公司/或者个人,/这也构成犯罪,/等同于犯罪。/同样地,/这部法律管辖权非常宽泛,/也就是在第二个标题下面,/它适用于任何人,/只要他们平时居住在英国都适用。/也就是说,/任何中国公民,/只要居住在英国,/把英国作为居住地,/这部法律对他们就是适用的,/哪怕他们不是英国公民。/同样地,/任何外国公司,/如中国公司,/在英国开展业务的,/也会受法律的约束,/就算它们的总部/实际上/不在英国,/或者在这里只有一家子公司。/新法/包括一项特殊的罪行,/也就是标题三下的内容:/贿赂外国公职人员罪,/但是今天我不想说太多这方面的内容。/这是个非常常见的罪行,/也是,/我相信是/《中国刑法》中的一项罪行。/我想侧重讲/标题四中的罪行。/这项罪行/只有公司会犯,/是指/未能预防雇员或者代理人贿赂。/这是最有争议、/最广泛的罪行,/这项罪行/引发了最多的争议/和讨论。/

06:23—08:57

But before I do that, /let me just briefly explain/how the legislation defines bribery. /In the United States, /under the *Foreign Corrupt Practices Act*, /the legislation uses the word "corruptly" /or "acting corruptly" /to express the wrong. /That was also true/under the previous British or UK legislation. /However, /in the United Kingdom/the courts gave differing views/on what the word "corrupt" means/and businesses told us that/they were unhappy/about the lack of clarity/over the meaning of the word "corrupt". /So one of the tasks/that I faced in changing the law/was to define bribery, /corruption/without using the word "corrupt" /and this is the way/in which we sought to do it. /What we said is that/when a company/or an individual/deals with another company/or with a government, /there is an expectation that/they will abide by/certain ethical standards. /Depending on the context, /there may be an expectation that/a person will act impartially, /heading little one, /that they will act in good faith, /heading two/or that they will act/in accordance with a position of trust, /that they will abide by/a position of trust. /And bribery happens/when an advantage/or something/is promised, /which leads the person/to break that expectation, /that they will act impartially, /in good faith/or in accordance with a position of trust. /In other words, /when you expect someone/with whom you're doing business/to behave in a certain way/and because/they have received a payment, /they break that expectation. /That is regarded as corruption/or bribery/in English law. /

在我开始之前,/我想简要解释一下/法律是如何定义贿赂罪的。/在美国,/《反海外腐败法》/用"腐败"/或者"腐败行为"/来表示犯罪行为。/同样,/英国之前的法律中也是这样描述的。/然而,/在英国,/法院给出了不同的观点,/来界定"腐败"一词的意思,/企业告诉我们/他们很不满,/因为法律没有厘清/"腐败"一词的意思。/所以任务之一/就是我在进行法律改革时/要定义什么是贿赂、/腐败,/但不使用"腐败"一词,/这也是/我们改革的方式。/我们的意思是/当公司/或者个人/和另一家公司/或政府打交道时,/法律希望他们/能遵守/一定的道德标准。/依据具体情况,/法律可能希望/人们公正行事,/看小标题一,/希望他们可以善意行事,/看标题二,/或者他们行事/可以遵照被信任职位的要求,/遵从/职位给予的信任。/贿赂发生在/好处/或别的东西/得到允诺的时候,/这会导致人们/违背期望,/违背公正行事、/善意行事/或者根据被信任的职位行事的期望。/换句话说,/当您希望某人、/您的生意伙伴/按特定的方式行事,/但是因为/他们收了钱财,/他们就违背了期待,/这就构成了腐败行为/或者贿赂罪,/违反了英国法律。/

08:57—10:34

And bribery is, /if I can use a technical term, /bribery is defined in the inchoate/ or incomplete mode. /That is to say/bribery is committed/whenever an offer is made/or a request is made for a payment. /It is not necessary/for the offer to be accepted/in order for bribery to be committed, /so simply to offer money/or some other advantage/ in exchange for something, /such as a trading permit/or a residency permit, /that is, / a criminal offence/even if the offer is rejected. /It is also important to note/as I say at the end there that/bribery includes/not only promising money, /but also any other kind of favor/or advantage/to use the language of the statute. /And advantages include/

offers of holidays/or any other kind of excessive hospitality. /I will come back to that point/because/corporate hospitality/is an extremely important issue/for many companies/ and it's a cause of some controversy/in this area of the law. /

贿赂是，/如果我可以用术语的话，/贿赂是刚刚发生的罪行，/处于不完全的状态。/也就是说，/贿赂罪发生/在任何只要提供了好处，/或者提出了支付请求的时候。/不一定/非得接受了/才构成贿赂罪，/因此只要提供金钱/或者其他好处/来做交易，/比如为了获取交易许可/或居住权，/那么，/就构成了刑事犯罪，/哪怕该好处被拒绝了。/要注意的重点是/我刚刚最后在这里讲到的：/贿赂包括/允诺钱财，/也包括其他形式的帮助/或好处，/这是法令的规定。/好处包括/提供假期机会/或者其他形式的过度盛情款待。/我会回到刚才那一点，/因为/公司款待/是非常重要的问题，/对许多公司而言都是如此，/这导致了争议，/这方面的法律存在争议。/

10:38—12:37

Now I have already said, /I don't need to repeat that/there is no distinction between public and private sector bribery. /I should add that/the penalty for conviction for bribery/by UK standards/is quite severe, /in other words, /the maximum penalty/ is 10 years imprisonment, /which by American standards/is hardly anything, /but by UK standards/is a very long period of time indeed. /And a company may be subject to/ an unlimited fine. /Now I've said earlier on that/the most important offense/created by the new legislation/was what is referred to/as the corporate offence. /Now perhaps just before I say more about this, /I should say that/a great deal of the reform that we introduced/did not extend the law very much/beyond what it had covered previously. / What we did was to/get rid of old language/like the word "corruptly" and so on, / introduce new language, /clearer language, /abolish the distinction/between public and private sector bribery/and also extend the jurisdiction of the law/to cover activity overseas. /I'm going to come on to that. /That's very important. /

刚刚已经提到过，/不需要我再重复说了，/公共部门和私营企业的贿赂罪是没有区别的。/我要补充的是，/贿赂罪的处罚/用英国标准来衡量的话/是非常严厉的，/也就是说，/最高处罚/是10年监禁，/但是用美国的标准来看/就不算什么了，/但是用英国标准来衡量/监禁的时间确实很长。/公司可能会被处以/无上限的罚金。/先前我已经提到，/最重大的犯罪，/根据新法规定，/就是我们所说的/商业机构贿赂罪。/在我讲得更深入之前，/我想说/我们进行的改革很大一部分/并没有丰富这部法律的内容，/没有比之前涵盖的内容要多。/我们做的就是/换掉旧的语言，/比如"腐败"等词，/采用新的、更加清楚的语言，/消除区别，/废除公共和私营部门贿赂罪的区别，/将这部法律的管辖范围/拓展到海外行为。/我即将

第六单元 反腐倡廉 Anti-corruption

要讲到这一点。/这非常重要。/

12:37—15:41

But one very big change we made/was the one on the slide/that you're looking at now. /And this is the offense/of failing to prevent bribery. /It applies only to companies. /Only a company/or organization/can commit this offense. /And the company commits a criminal offense/contrary to Section Seven, /if it fails to prevent bribery/being committed anywhere in the world/and the company will be liable/for failing to prevent bribery/if the bribery is committed/by someone associated with the company, /including not only employees/but agents/or indeed other companies, /be they subsidiaries/or partner companies/or whoever it may be. /And as we will see/when we look at the cases/that have arisen under this legislation, /that is an important aspect. /We spent, /I remember/myself spending many, many hours/with the professional drafters of legislation, /trying to work out what the right language was/to express this relationship. /Because a company/that is operating overseas/may use many different means/through which to do business. /They may use an individual. /They may use a subsidiary company. /They may use a partner company. /They may use some kind of quasi/or governmental entity that is set up/to facilitate business in that country. /We have to find language/that captures all of those entities. /So bribery, /when a company fails to prevent bribery, /what matters is/whether it fails to prevent it/by a body associated with that company. /However, /although the company will commit bribery, /sorry, /the company will commit the Section Seven offense, /if it fails to prevent bribery. /Nonetheless, /it is a defense to the crime, /you can escape conviction, /if you can show that/the company had adequate procedures in place. /That's the fifth heading there. /The company can show that/it had adequate procedures, /yes, /to prevent the bribery occurring. /And finally, /this corporate offense under Section Seven/applies to any company/carrying on a business/or a part of a business/in the United Kingdom. /

我们做了非常重大的改变,/已经呈现在幻灯片上了,/就是您看到的这一页。/这个罪行是/未能预防贿赂,/它只适用于公司。/只有公司/或组织/会犯下这项罪行。/公司会犯刑事罪行,/触犯了第七节的规定,/如果公司未能预防贿赂,/不管发生在世界哪个地方,/公司都要负法律责任,/被指控未能预防贿赂,/只要犯罪主体/是与公司有关的人,/不仅包括雇员,/还包括代理人/或其他相关公司,/不管是子公司、/合作公司/还是其他什么公司。/当我们看到/这些案件/都是触犯这部法律而导致的时候,/那是非常重要的一个方面。/我们花了,/我记得/我花了很多时间/与专业的法律起草人交流,/只为想出最合适的语言/来表达这种关系。/因为公司/进行海外经营的话,/可能会使用不同的方法/开展业务,/他们可能会以个人、子公司、合作公司等方式来进行,/也有可能借助类似的机构/或成立政府实体/来促进在该国的业务发展。/我们必须找到语言/涵盖所有这些实体的。/所以贿赂,/当公司未能预防贿赂,/重点是/公司是否未能预防贿赂,/未能利用与公司有关的机制来预防。/然而,/就算公司犯了贿赂罪,/不好意思。/公司会犯下第七节规定的罪行,/一旦它未能预防贿赂就会构成犯罪。/尽管如此,/该罪行有一种抗辩理由。/您可以不被定罪,/前提是您可以证明/公司采取了适当的程序。/这就是第五个标题的内容。/公司可以证明/自己采取了适当程序,/没错,/来防止贿赂的发生。/最后,/第七节的商业机构贿赂罪/适用于任何公司,/只要这家公司的业务/或者部分业务/是在英国开展的。/

15:48—18:45

What are the kinds of procedures/which a company must adopt/in order to avoid being convicted/of failing to prevent bribery under Section Seven? /Well, all employees/or agents/must have a policy/of no tolerance towards bribery. /Now/this is in one sense/a straightforward/or a simple thing/to suggest no tolerance. /However, /everybody knows that/this is a very difficult policy/to follow in practice. /Let me give you a simple example. /When I was drafting the law, legislation, /we consulted with many businesses/on the right way to reform. /And one owner of a shipping firm/said to me, / "Well, /you know, /I have many ships/calling at ports in countries all over the world/and it is very, very important that/when my ship arrives in the harbor, /that it is possible/to offload the goods quickly/because/they may be vegetables/or fruit/or something that will perish/or deteriorate quite rapidly. /And in order for that to happen, /it may be that the man in charge of the harbor, /the harbor master, /will say, 'Well, /if you want me to do this quickly, /I will need you to provide me/with a bottle of whiskey/or some cigarettes/or something. /I mean not nothing/or maybe you know a thousand yuan/or something. ," /Now he said, / "Are you telling me that/I can no longer give a bottle of whiskey/or a packet of cigarettes/or a thousand yuan or/something? /Because if I don't, /then my ship will stay in the harbor/and my fruit/and my vegetables/will rot/and my business will be gone. " /Well, the answer to that/is a complicated one. /The answer to that is that/it is against the law/to provide any kind of bribe. /It is against the law. /All right. /We were not prepared/to create a special exception/for small bribes. /

有哪几种程序/是公司必须采用的呢?/从而避免被定罪/即使被指控犯下了第七节规定的贿赂罪。/所有员工/或代理/必须遵循政策/对贿赂零容忍的政策。/现在,/这在某种意义上讲/是最直接、/最简单的方式/来表明零容忍的态度。/但

第六单元 反腐倡廉 Anti-corruption

是,/人人都知道/这个原则是非常难遵循的/在实际中的确如此。/举一个简单的例子。/起草这项法案时,/我们咨询了很多公司,/问他们正确的改革方式。/一家船运公司的老板/告诉我:/"嗯,/您知道吗?/我有很多船/停靠在世界各国的港口,/很重要的就是,/当我的船到达海港时/可以/尽快卸货,/因为/这些货物可能是蔬菜、/水果、/等会腐烂/或很快就坏掉的东西。/为了能够尽快卸货,/负责海港的人,/港务局长/可能会说:/'如果你想我尽快卸货,/你得给我/买瓶威士忌/或香烟/等等,/我并不是说什么都不给,/你也可以给1000块/什么的。'/这个时候那个老板问我了:/"现在您是不是要告诉我/不能给他们威士忌、/香烟、/或1000元/或其他东西?/但是如果我不给,/我的船会滞留在海港,/我的水果/和蔬菜/会烂掉,/我的生意也就做不成了。"/这个问题的答案/很复杂,/答案是,/这么做是违法的,/法律不允许任何形式的贿赂。/这是违法行为。/好吧。/我们不会/格外开恩/放过小额贿赂。/

18:45—20:46

In the United States,/under the *Foreign Corrupt Practices Act*,/there is an exemption for small bribes/or administrative payments/as I believe/they are known to avoid the term "bribe"./However,/we resisted the temptation/to introduce such a provision/rightly or wrongly./However,/what you also have to consider is/whether it would be a good use of money/by the prosecutors in London/to prosecute a ship owner/on the other side of the world,/for providing a bottle of whiskey/for a harbor master./Is that a good use of public money?/And our answer to that is/that it would be disproportionate./It would be going too far/to prosecute someone in those circumstances./So although it is against the law/to provide any kind of bribe,/even a small one,/it will only rarely be the case/that there is a sufficient justification/for prosecuting in a case of that kind./However,/the prosecution service has in the United Kingdom,/has issued a statement/saying that/if a company treats it as normal/or established practice/to make small bribes,/then the prosecution services will consider/bringing a prosecution./So there is a delicate or difficult balance/to be struck./

美国/实施的《反海外贿赂法》,/豁免小额贿赂/或行政给付,/我知道这里/它们会避免用"贿赂"一词。/然而,/我们要抵制住诱惑,/不能采用这个规定,/无论是对是错都不可以。/但是,/必须要考虑的就是,/金钱使用是否恰当。/例如伦敦检察官/花钱来起诉船东,/因为这个船东在世界其他地方/把一瓶威士忌/送给了港务局长。/这样使用公款对吗?/我们的答案是:/这是不恰当的。/这样太小题大做了,/像在这种情况下起诉某个人就太夸张了。/所以尽管是犯法的/提供这类贿赂,/哪怕是很小的贿赂,/也很少会出现这类法律案件,/因为没有充分理由/来起诉这一类案件。/但是,/英国的检察部门/发表了声明,/表明/如果公司将其视为

正常、/公认的做法/而允许小额贿赂，/那么检察部门会考虑/提起诉讼。/所以要做到公平处理是很难、/且需要技巧的。/

20:47—24:48

OK, moving on to number two. /A company must have procedures in place/for reporting all incidents in which a bribe is offered. /Now this is very important, /because/as I will show later on, /it may be to a company's advantage/to admit/or confess any instance/in which they have been/or one of their employees/or agents/has been guilty of bribery. /It may be in their interest to confess that, /but in order to do so, /they need to have the information. /So a company must have proper procedures in place/for reporting incidents/in which bribes have been offered. /Thirdly, /yes, /a company must have a clear policy/for hospitality and gifts. /Now when the legislation was introduced/and it was clear/that a company must have this policy. /I then received personally a lot of inquiries/as to what this policy should involve. /For example, /I was contacted by a high-level member/of the fashion industry/and said, / "Is it alright to send a woman's handbag/to every editor of a fashion magazine, /which we do at Christmas time? /Is that acceptable?" /And the answer to that is: yes, /it is. /Because you are sending something to everybody. /You are not trying to gain favor/with one particular individual. /But the main thing is that/there must be a clear policy for employees/and what they can accept/and what they cannot/and that would apply equally to public institutions, /like this one, /a university. /So I have also been consulted by my own University/on what is the appropriate policy for hospitality and gifts/and what we have a rule/which says/that anything over the value of 500 yuan, /you, the individual/who receives the gift/must be willing to place that, /the value of that 500 yuan/into the university's charitable fund. /If they are willing to do that, /then they may keep the gift/and that is our policy. /Now for companies, /most importantly, /at the end here, /a company must ensure that/subsidiaries/and joint venture partners/also follow an anti-corruption policy. /Now/that is a difficult demand to meet, /for example, /in the area of construction, building/or indeed in the area of shipping, /there will be many interlinked contracts, /many subcontractors, /many companies/involved in a large construction project. /And it will be the obligation of the head company, /the overseeing company/to ensure that all of the subsidiary companies/from whatever jurisdiction or country they come from/abide by the policy. /So that is quite a stringent demand. /

我们看看第二点。/公司必须落实程序，/汇报所有的行贿事件。/这点现在非常重要，/因为，/我后面再向大家展示，/因为这会对公司有利，/只要它们承认/

第六单元 反腐倡廉 Anti-corruption

或者坦白任何案情，/坦白牵涉到自身的/或者某一员工/或代理/所犯的贿赂罪。/坦白对它们有利，/但要做到这样，/它们必须掌握相关信息。/因此，公司要有适当的程序，/来汇报事情，/举报行贿。/第三，/是的，/公司必须有明确的政策/管理招待和送礼。/一旦法律开始实施，/很明显，/公司必须有这项政策。/有很多人私下问我，/这项政策应该涉及哪些内容，/比如，/一个高管联系了我，/他是从事时尚行业的，/问我：/"可以送一个女款手提包/给时尚杂志的每位编辑吗？/这是我们的圣诞节活动，/这个可以接受吗？"/答案是：是的，/可以接受。/因为您给每个人送了东西，/而不是为了得到好处/只送一个特定的人。/重点是/必须有明确的员工政策，/他们可以接受什么，/不可以接受什么，/这项政策同样适用于公共部门，/比如这里，/大学。因此我供职的大学也咨询了我，/问我对于招待和送礼什么样的政策合适，/我们有一条规定，/是说/对于任何价值超过500元的礼物，/您个人，/如果收到礼物/必须自愿捐/500元/给学校的慈善基金。/如果您愿意这样做，/那么您是可以收下这个礼物的，/这就是我们的政策。/对于公司而言，/最重要的是/在后面这里，/公司必须确保/子公司/和合资企业合伙人/遵守反腐政策。/目前，/这是一个很难达到的要求，/比如/在建筑/或船运行业，/会有很多相关的合同、/许多分包商/以及公司/参与了大型建筑项目。/总公司有义务/作为监督人/确保所有的子公司，/不管这些公司来自哪个管辖区、哪个国家，/都遵守这项政策。/这是一个非常严格的要求。/

III. 实战练习二

1. 演讲背景

下文同样摘自英国《2010 反腐败法案》立法者在"大成（深圳）法学名家大讲坛暨蓝海法律沙龙"上的主旨演讲。他在演讲的第二部分中分享了具体的案例，以及企业对商业机构贿赂罪的抗辩理由：公司必须采取预防贿赂的适当程序。最后还谈到了 2013 年开始实施的一项新程序。公司如果被指控犯下了贿赂罪，可以在法官同意的前提下，签署延缓起诉协议，并同意进行改革，公司也有可能被要求支付赔偿金。

2. 预习词汇

rule of law 法治
statute 法令；法规
criminal court 刑事法庭
unlawful conduct 违法行为
United Arab Emirates/UAE 阿联酋

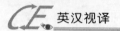

SFO/Serious Fraud Office 英国严重欺诈办公室
criminal charge 刑事指控
rolling stock（铁路上运行的）全部车辆
Rail Track 英国铁路公司
bid 竞标
joint partnership 合伙公司
The UK Stock Exchange 英国证券交易所
Saudi Arabia 沙特阿拉伯
Bribery Act 2010《2010反腐败法案》
deferred prosecution agreement 延缓起诉协议
Standard Bank PLC 标准银行公众有限公司
Rolls-Royce 劳斯莱斯
flagrant 明目张胆的；罪恶昭彰的；公然的

3. 演讲文本

00:00—03:28

Now you may be wondering/whether this new offense/has had any impact in practice. /Well, an important thing to remember is that/the law only came into force in 2010, /so eight years ago. /And in accordance with the principles of the rule of law, /you cannot apply an offense retrospectively/to conduct that occurred/before the statute came into force. /So in other words/if companies, /if wrongdoing/is uncovered by a company, /but the wrongdoing occurred before 2010, /the new legislation cannot apply to that conduct. /So inevitably, /it was going to take some time/before wrongdoing occurred after 2010, /then the wrongdoing was discovered/or came to light, /then a decision was taken/to prosecute the company/for that wrongdoing. /Inevitably, /there was going to be some considerable delay/before that happened. /But now we are eight years/after the Act came into force/and we are beginning to see some effect/that the legislation is having. /And as you can see the first conviction in the criminal courts/under Section Seven/that is failing to prevent bribery, /occurred on the 19th of February, 2016. /A UK-based construction and professional services firm/was convicted of the offense. /And in this case, /the bribery was committed/by a subsidiary company/called Cyril Sweetts/and the unlawful conduct/took place overseas in the United Arab Emirates. /And (what the serious) the SFO is the Serious Fraud Office/and they found/that a Middle-Eastern subsidiary company/had made corrupt payments/to a senior board member of a Saudi Arabian company/in order to secure a contract/to build a very, very large hotel in Dubai. /And it was determined/that the

Middle Eastern subsidiary/was an associated person of Sweetts/and that therefore/they, /Sweetts, the UK company/had failed to prevent/bribery by that subsidiary company. /

现在您可能想知道/这项新罪行/在实践中是否有影响。/要记住这个关键点, /这部法律在 2010 年才实施, /也就是 8 年前。/依照法治的原则, /法不溯及既往, /犯罪行为发生的时间/在法令实施之前就不受法令管辖。/也就是说, /如果公司/其犯罪行为/被公司揭露了, /而犯罪行为发生在 2010 年之前, /新法对此不具有溯及力。/所以无疑, /需要一段时间/2010 年后才会出现犯罪行为, /然后这些行为才会被发现、/被曝光, /接着会做出决定/来起诉这家公司/追究其犯罪行为。/无疑, /之前会有很长时间的等待/才会有罪行发生。/但是现在已经有 8 年了, /法令实施 8 年了, /我们开始看到一些影响/法令产生的影响。/您可以看到刑事法庭的第一起定罪案件/根据第七节, /这是公司未能预防贿赂的案件, /发生在 2016 年 2 月 19 日。/一家英国建筑和专业服务公司/被指控犯了贿赂罪。/在这起案件中, /犯罪主体/是一家子公司, /叫 Cyril Sweetts, /违法行为/发生在海外的阿联酋境内。/SFO, 也就是严重欺诈办公室, /发现/中东的子公司/贿赂/沙特阿拉伯公司的一个高级董事会成员, /只为拿下合同/在迪拜建一个非常非常大的酒店。/经过调查得知, /中东的子公司/是与 Sweetts 公司有关联的当事人, /因此, /他们/英国公司 Sweetts/未能预防/子公司犯下贿赂罪。/

03:35—06:30

Now/I have already spoken a little bit/about the kinds of risks/that may be involved in doing business in relation to the *Act*. /But I want to try to focus now a little bit/on some specific kinds of examples/that very commonly occur/where people may wonder/(what) how far they can go, /what the limits are of permissible conduct. /Well, /we might as well start/with the very obvious thing. /Are government officials in the United Kingdom/open to corruption? /Well, in general, /"No" is the answer to that. /There is a relatively low level of corruption/in the public sector/and it follows that/there is a relatively high risk/that the offer of a bribe/will be reported/and that will lead/at the very least/to bad publicity/and well possibly criminal charges. /However, /that just raises the question, /well, what kind of contact is it possible/to have with government officials? /What can you do? /And well it is perfectly possible/to meet government officials/in a social setting that is acceptable. /However, /the entertainment of government officials/must be modest/and restrained. /There has been a lot of controversy in recent times/over hospitality being offered, /particularly to local government officials. /Hospitality regarded as excessive, /entertainment on yachts or boats/in the South of France and so on. /And whilst there have been no prosecutions/

relating to that activity, /nonetheless/the companies have received bad publicity/and that is never good/if you are trying to establish a business foothold/in the United Kingdom. /So in general, /entertainment of government officials/should be modest/and that is all that they will normally be expecting. /I should, I mean/this is something where expert legal advice will be needed. /

现在，/我已经讲了一些/这类风险，/也就是与《英国反腐败法案》相关的开展业务方面的风险。/接下来我想多讲一些/非常具体的、/普遍的例子，/人们也想知道/哪些他们可以做，/哪些是法律允许的行为。/那么，/我们首先/看最常见的事情。/英国的政府官员/是否允许贿赂？/通常来说，/是不允许的。/相对而言，/腐败程度较低的是/公共领域，/因为/存在较高的风险，/因为行贿/会被曝光，/会导致/至少/会破坏名声，/也很可能会遭受刑事指控。/然而，/这也带来了一个问题，/有哪些接触是允许/与政府官员开展的？/您可以做什么？/毫无疑问，/与政府官员见面，/如果在社交场合那是可以接受的。/但是，/招待政府官员/必须适度、/简单。/近来存在很多争议，/与招待有关/尤其是招待当地政府官员。/比如过度盛情款待，/在游艇和船上进行招待、/去法国南部游玩等等。/尽管没有起诉/这类活动，/但是公司的名声被破坏了，/这样一点好处也没有，/因为您还想让公司开展业务/在英国立足。/总的来说，/招待政府官员/应该适度，/这也通常是他们的期待。/我的意思是，/这一点需要法律专家的建议。/

06:30—09:38

But it's important to recognize that/in the United Kingdom as elsewhere, /an official or government official/is a wide-ranging term/and it can include/somebody who is working for a government agency/and not just someone who is a member of the government itself. /Now let me, because/I think/this is most helpful, /let me try to illustrate/what I'm saying/by reference to some examples. /So let us assume that/we have a Chinese company/which wishes to sell trains/to the government agency/which is responsible for commissioning rolling stock, /as it's known, /which is called Rail Track. /It is the largest non-governmental agency in the United Kingdom. /Now the company is bidding/against other companies from other countries/for this contract/and so the company offers Rail Track officials/the opportunity to stay in a five-star hotel/where the business discussion will take place. /Is this a lawful activity? /Well, I would say that this is an activity/that is risky. /I don't say it is clearly against the law, /but I say that it is risky/that there is a risk of adverse publicity/associated with this example. /And that is because/it is not regarded as necessary/or appropriate/to offer that kind of high level of hospitality/in order to get to know officials. /It would be different, /I suspect, /if the executives of the Chinese company/were already staying in

第六单元　反腐倡廉 Anti-corruption

the hotel/and they simply say to the officials, / "Come and meet us at our hotel." / That might be acceptable. /So there are some circumstances/and that is why I say/it is not clearly contrary to the law. /However, /it would be acceptable/as I say at the end there/to ask an official to (give) come/and give a speech/or a talk about government policy/at a dinner/or a lunch/rather like this/and that will be acceptable/or more acceptable/because/it has an educational purpose/and that can make it easier/to justify what is going on. /

但重点是要意识到：/在英国就像其他地方一样，/官员或者政府官员/含义非常广，/也包括/为政府机关工作的任何人，/而不仅仅是政府成员。/现在因为/我认为/这个是最有帮助的，/所以我想解释一下/我的意思，/我引用一些例子吧。/假设/有一家中国公司，/希望将火车卖给/政府机关/该机关是负责调试铁路车辆的，/那个机构/也就是英国铁路公司。/这是英国最大的非政府机关。/现在这家中国公司参与竞标，/和其他国家的公司竞争，/只为签下这个合同，/因此这家公司让铁路公司官员/住在五星级酒店，/进行商务洽谈。/这合法吗？/我会说这个活动/有风险。/我没明确地说它是违法的，/但这种活动风险很大，/容易产生负面影响，/这个例子的风险很大。/因为/没必要/也不合适/去提供这种高规格的款待/去巴结官员。/但情况会有所不同，/我觉得/如果这家中国公司的主管/已经住在这家酒店里，/而他们只是对官员说：/"来我们住的宾馆见面吧。"/这也许是可以接受的。/所以要视情况而定，/这就是为什么我说/这样做并非显然违法。/但是，/可以接受的做法是，/PPT 最后部分有提到，/如让官员过来/演讲，/或者谈谈政府的政策，/可以安排在晚宴/或午宴，/就像我们现在这样，/这些是可以接受的，/或者接受度更高，/因为/这包含教育目的，/更容易/解释所发生的事情。/

09:39—11:32

Let me give a second slightly different example. /Now in this example, /a Chinese company/wishes to join together with an English company/to fit for a contract/and the Chinese company offers to meet... /So it's similar in this respect/to the previous example, /the Chinese company wishes/to meet senior executives from the English company/at the five-star Hotel/where they discuss their joint venture. /Is that acceptable? /Yes, /this is perfectly acceptable. /Why it is acceptable? /because/there is a greater degree of tolerance, /a higher degree of tolerance/for high levels of hospitality/between companies in the private sector. /There is a distinction, /in other words, /in practice, /not in law, /but in practice, /there is a distinction between entertaining private executives/and entertaining government officials. /Similarly, /if you are a business person/and you are invited by a British company/to attend a sporting/or cultural event/of a significant kind, /that is perfectly acceptable/as a context/in which to do business. /There is no difficulty about that. /So there is a high degree of tolerance/for hospitality within the private sector. /

我们看看第二个稍微不同的例子。/在这个例子中，/一家中国公司/希望和一家英国公司/敲定合同，/中国公司想邀约会面，/这个很相似，/和刚才那个例子一样。/中国公司希望/和英国公司的高管见面，/地点安排在五星级酒店里，/讨论合资企业的建立。/这可以接受吗？/当然，/这完全可以接受。/为什么？/因为/这里存在更高的容忍度，/更能容忍/高规格的接待/是为了私营企业之间的合作。/这种区别，/换句话说，/存在于实践中，/在法律中并不存在。/但在实践中，/需要区别接待公司行政人员/和接待政府官员。/同样地，/如果您是个商人，/您被英国公司邀请/去参加运动赛事/或文化活动/这一类重大的活动，/这完全是可以接受的，/你们可以在这种情境下/洽谈生意。/这完全没有问题。/所以法律更能容忍/私营领域的款待。/

11:32—13:56

Now/let me go back to/an important point about the law/which I mentioned earlier on. /And that is that/the legislation/applies to any company/which is carrying on a business/or part of a business/in the United Kingdom. /So English law applies to any company, /including a Chinese company/which has part of its business in the UK, /even though the Chinese company/may be based elsewhere, /they do most of its business elsewhere/and not in the United Kingdom. /Similarly, /if a joint partnership/is established with the United Kingdom company, /then the law will also apply in that circumstance. /Now that the reason why that is important is that/what it means is that/if for example, /a Chinese company tolerates/or pays a bribe overseas, /I don't know, /in the Middle East perhaps, /even though that transaction/has nothing to do with the United Kingdom, /nonetheless/it is possible that United Kingdom law/could be applied in that instance. /If there is some reason, /in other words, /for the UK prosecution services/to become involved/because of the connection that that company has/with the United Kingdom. /They have the jurisdiction to become involved. /In this respect, /UK law is now very much like the *Foreign Corrupt Practices Act of the United States*, /which gives United States prosecutors/very wide jurisdiction/to undertake bribery and corruption investigations across the globe. /

现在/我回到/这部法律的重点，/前面我提到过的。/也就是/这部法律/适用于任何公司，/只要它的业务/或者部分业务/都在英国开展。/所以英国法律适用于任何公司，/包括中国公司，/哪怕在英国只有部分业务，/即使中国公司/的总部不在英国，/就算是它的大部分业务在其他地方，/不在英国。/同样地，/如果合伙公司/是与英国公司共同建立的，/法律也同样适用于这种情况。/这点非常重要，因为，/意思是/如果/一家中国公司容忍/或者在海外行贿，/我举个例子，/比如在中东地区，/哪怕交易/与英国无关，/但是/英国的法律也有可能/适用于这种情况。/如果有理由，/换句话说/让英国检察部门/介入，/只要这家公司/与英国有关，/它们就有权介入。/就这一点，/英国法律与美国的《反海外贿赂法》非常相似，/这部法律给美国检察官/非常宽泛的管辖权，/在全球开展贿赂和腐败调查。/

13:56—15:47

So here is an example, /if a Chinese company/is listed on the United Kingdom Stock Exchange/and one of the company's agents in Saudi Arabia/arranges for the payment of a bribe/to a Saudi government official, /then Section Seven, /failure to prevent bribery, /that offence will apply, /even though the directors may be unaware of the conduct. /They may not realize what has happened. /In that example, /the Chinese company/is carrying on a business in the United Kingdom/and therefore/the *UK Bribery Act* applies. /And as I have already said/the *Act* makes it an offence for the company/to fail to prevent bribery in that example/even if the directors knew nothing of the payment. /So their only defense would be that/they had adequate procedures in place, /generally to prevent incidents of that kind occurring. /Yes, /so in that example/it is unlikely perhaps that/UK prosecutors would take action. /However, /they would be able to provide assistance/to any investigation of the company's action/by Chinese or American authorities. /And as I say/the company needs to have adequate procedures in place/to prevent bribery/in order to avoid conviction under UK law. /

举个例子，/如果一家中国公司/在英国证券交易所上市，/公司在沙特阿拉伯的一个代理/贿赂了/沙特政府官员，/该公司触犯了第七节/未能预防贿赂，/就构成了犯罪，/哪怕董事们没有意识到这个行为，/没有意识到发生了什么。/在这个例子中，/中国公司/在英国有经营业务，/因此/受英国《反腐败法案》的约束。/我说过，/《法案》将这个列为公司的罪行，/只要公司无法预防例子中的贿赂，/哪怕董事们对此毫不知情。/他们唯一的抗辩理由就是/采取适当程序，/来预防这类事情的发生。/当然，/在这个例子中，/也许不大可能/让英国的检察官采取行动，/但是，/他们可以协助/调查该公司，/协助中国或美国的主管部门开展调查。/我也提到了/公司需要采取适当的程序/来预防贿赂，/避免被英国法律定罪。/

15:47—18:29

Now I want to conclude my talk/by speaking about another development/very soon after the *Bribery Act of* 2010/and that is a new piece of procedure/introduced in 2013. /And under this procedure, /it is possible for a firm/that is suspected of bribery, /

charged with bribery/to avoid being prosecuted, /essentially if they inform prosecutors about wrongdoing. /This is similar in many ways/to procedures that exist in the United States/for dealing with financial crime. /And what this is referred to as/is a deferred prosecution agreement, /which must be approved by a judge/and under a deferred prosecution agreement, /essentially/the company admits wrongdoing, /it admits that it did something wrong, /that bribery occurred/and it agrees to reform its practices/so as to avoid bribery/or other financial crime in the future/and it may also be asked/to pay compensation. /So for example/in 2015/the Standard Bank PLC/entered into a deferred prosecution agreement/having been initially prosecuted for failing to prevent bribery. /But that prosecution was deferred/or put off/when the company admitted/using a partner company in Tanzania/to pay a very large sum of money/to a local partner to induce… /This is essentially/what's referred to as/grand corruption, /in other words, /corruption at the highest level, /in which a company/seeks to bribe government legislators themselves, /members of the government, /which is the most serious form of corruption that there can be. /And as a result, /Standard Bank/agreed to pay an extremely large sum of money, /as a financial penalty/and also compensation to the Tanzanian government/for attempting to bribe their officials. /

　　我想对今天的讲话做个总结，/分享最新发展作为总结，/也就是《2010反腐败法案》出台不久后的进展，/这是一项新程序，/于2013年开始实施。/在这个程序下，/公司/如果被怀疑、/被指控犯下了贿赂罪，/可以避免被起诉，/但关键是他们要向检察官自首。/这在很多方面类似于/美国的程序，/具体来说是处理金融犯罪的程序。/这被称为/延缓起诉协议，/必须得到法官的同意，/根据延缓起诉协议，/基本上/公司要承认罪行，/承认自己犯了错，/导致了贿赂事件，/并同意进行改革，/避免贿赂/或在未来犯下其他金融罪行，/同时它也有可能被要求/支付赔偿金。/例如，/2015年，/标准银行公众有限公司/订立了延缓起诉协议，/它刚开始因未能预防贿赂被起诉。/但是起诉被延缓/或延期了，/因为公司承认/利用在坦桑尼亚的合作公司，/用一大笔钱/引诱当地一家合作公司上钩。/这从根本上/可以看作/重大腐败事件，/也就是/最高级别的腐败，/这个指的是公司/试图贿赂政府立法人员/和政府成员，/这是最严重的腐败形式。/最终，/标准银行/同意支付巨额钱款/作为罚金，/同时也向坦桑尼亚政府支付赔偿金/作为试图贿赂政府官员的惩罚。/

18:29—21:25

Much more recently/in a very well-known case, /the internationally well-known company/Rolls-Royce/also entered into a deferred prosecution agreement. /The transaction was a complicated one/and I'm not going to try to explain it now. /But

第六单元　反腐倡廉 Anti-corruption

putting it very simply, /the company was strongly suspected/of engaging in bribery/in a number of jurisdictions, /not just one, /a number of jurisdictions. /There was a systematic practice of bribery within the company, /quite shameful really, /and the company agreed/to pay over 20 billion yuan, /an enormous sum of money/and also an extremely large financial penalty/of 20 billion. /And as you can see, /contrary to the *Bribery Act*, /the company had made corrupt payments to agents in Russia/and also failed to prevent bribery by employees/in relation to energy contracts/in Nigeria/and also in China/and Malaysia, too. /Now this is important, /because/this was a controversial case. /Because/this was a case/in which Rolls-Royce was allowed/to avoid prosecution/by paying this money, a lot of money. /But it was allowed to avoid prosecution/even though it had engaged in corruption/in what are recognized as/countries very vulnerable to corruption, /such as Nigeria. /I mean, /energy contracts in Nigeria/are a notorious source of corrupt transaction. /Any international company/should be very well aware/that is absolutely essential/to avoid bribery in this context/and yet Rolls-Royce, /in spite of the new legislation, /is flagrant. /So really this was a controversial case/that really in my personal view, /the company should have been prosecuted for/and convicted of bribery/as an example to other companies/not to engage in corruption in vulnerable countries/such as Nigeria. /However, /the company was allowed/to escape in this particular example. /

　　最近/还有一个非常知名的案件, /国际知名公司/劳斯莱斯/订立了延缓起诉协议。/这笔交易十分复杂, /我现在不会详细地讲。/简而言之, /公司被严重怀疑/涉嫌贿赂, /这发生在许多管辖区, /不只是一个地方, /许多地方都有。/公司内部存在系统性的贿赂行为, /真的非常可耻, /公司同意/支付200亿元, /非常庞大的一个数目, /非常大的一笔罚款, /高达200亿元。/可以看到, /这违背了《反腐败法案》, /公司贿赂了俄国的代理商, /也未能阻止员工行贿/去竞争能源合同, /比如尼日利亚、/中国/和马来西亚的能源合同。/这个非常重要, /因为/这是非常有争议的案件。/因为/在这起案件中, /劳斯莱斯被允许/避免起诉, /只要支付巨额罚款就可以。/它避免了被起诉, /哪怕它已经参与了腐败活动, /而且还是在公认/最容易发生腐败的国家, /例如, 尼日利亚。/我的意思是, /尼日利亚的能源合同/是臭名昭著的腐败交易来源。/任何国际公司/都应该清楚地意识到, /这一点非常重要, /有助于避免贿赂罪。/但是劳斯莱斯公司, /藐视新法律, /明目张胆地行贿。/这确实是个有争议的案件, /这只是我个人的观点, /公司本应该被起诉, /因贿赂被定罪, /以此来警示其他公司, /不要在腐败肆虐的国家参与腐败犯罪, /例如尼日利亚。/然而, /该公司却被允许/在这个案子中脱罪。/

21:25—21:56

Well, /I will stop there, /but thank you very much indeed for listening. /I appreciate it very much that/you have come here today/to spend time listening to me. /I am very enthusiastic/and enjoy my subject very much/and I look forward perhaps/to listening to questions that you may have. /Thank you very much indeed/to everyone here in Shenzhen/and to BCI/and to Dentons. /Thank you so much/for your invitation. /

好了，/我就讲到这儿，/真的非常感谢你们的聆听。/非常感谢/你们今天来到这里/听我演讲。/我充满激情，/也非常喜欢这一学科，/期待/听到你们提出的问题。/非常感谢/今天在深圳的每一个人，/感谢蓝海中心，/感谢大成律师事务所，/非常感谢/你们的邀请！/

第三部分 视译实战

第七单元 会议展览
Meetings, Incentives, Conferences, Exhibitions and Events

I. 实战练习一

1. 演讲背景

国际大会及会议协会代表应邀出席"全球会展（广州）圆桌会"并发表主旨演讲。他在演讲中简要地介绍了国际协会会议的情况，并指出如果要赢得国际协会会议的主办权，广州需要各个领域的专家学者密切合作。举办国际协会会议能为广州带来巨大的经济效益。最后他诚挚邀请广州成为国际大会及会议协会的成员。

2. 预习词汇

The Global Roundtable 全球会展圆桌会
Party Secretary General from Guangzhou 广州市委书记
Forbes《福布斯》
The Best Commercial City 最佳商业城市
neuroscience 神经学
bio-pharmaceutical 生物制药
future innovation cluster 未来创新集群
venture capital 风险投资
ICCA/International Congress and Convention Association 国际大会及会议协会
Silk Road 丝绸之路
Belt & Road Initiative "一带一路"倡议
International Symposium of Anaerobic Digestion 国际厌氧消化研讨会
The 19th International Congress of Asia Society of Vascular Surgery 第19届国际血管外科学会国际会议
Asia Pacific Academy of Ophthalmology 亚太眼科学会
The 28th Regional Congress of the ISBT 国际输血学会的第28次区域会议
ISBT/International Society of Blood Transfusion 国际输血学会

3. 演讲文本

00:00—00:22

Good afternoon to everyone, /Mr. Chen. /And I am very honored/to be here/to be part of the Global Roundtable, /and to be sit up with all the distinguished experts/in the exhibition/and the meeting industry. /So good morning once again! /My name is Noor/and I'm going to talk about/the global meeting. /

大家下午好! /陈先生下午好! /很荣幸/能来这儿/参加全球会展圆桌会, /也非常荣幸能和各位优秀的专家共聚一堂, /各位都是会展、会议行业的专业人士。/再次向大家问好! /我叫努尔, /我将谈一谈/全球会议的发展状况。/

00:23—01:05

Over the past few speakers, /what we've heard again and again, /Guangzhou is very very strong/in the exhibition market. /That is without doubt. /Even this morning, /when we had a chance/to meet the Party Secretary General from Guangzhou/and also the Mayor/and the Vice Mayor, /I've learnt/that the *Forbes*/has ranked Guangzhou as/ "The Best Commercial City" /five years in a row in China. /So well done to Guangzhou. /Guangzhou leaders/have also indicated/that the Guangzhou economy/is very resilient/and growing/despite the rural economy slowdown. /

从刚刚的几位发言人的发言中, /我们就不断听到说/广州很厉害, /在会展市场口碑很好, /这毫无疑问。/就在今天早上, /我们有机会/见到广州市委书记、/市长/和副市长, /才得知/《福布斯》/已经将广州列为/"最佳商业城市", /连续五年在中国都是如此。/广州做得不错! /广州市领导/还指出/广州经济/很有弹性, /一直保持增长, /并没有受农村经济放缓的影响。/

01:06—01:37

I also learnt this morning/that the Guangzhou city or the Guangzhou municipal/is very strong in many different areas/from the biological industrial park/which now being developed. /You have some world best top scientists/in neuroscience. /You are top/in bio-pharmaceutical. /You are going into/the future innovation cluster, /aviation, /shipping/and transportation hub, /and also you're attracting/top venture capital. /

我今天早上还得知/广州市/在很多领域都很强, /生物工业园, /目前正在开发。/你们有世界一流的科学家/从事神经学研究, /你们有顶尖的/生物制药行业, /你们正在打造/未来创新集群、/航空、/航运/和交通枢纽, /你们还吸引了/世界顶级的风险投资。/

01:52—02:05

OK. Today, /I am going to talk to you of something/that is a little bit different from/what you've already known/and expert in. /You are expert in exhibition. /I am going to talk about/the meetings industry. /

今天，/我想和你们聊聊/别的，/不同于大家熟悉/和擅长的领域。/大家都是会展业专家，/但这次我要讲讲/会议行业。/

02:06—02:29

In the west, /meeting industry/is very, very important. /I am in particular going to talk about/the international association meeting. /China and Guangzhou/have also numerous meeting, /whether it's governmental meeting/or non-governmental meeting. /And we at ICCA, /we track/about 20,000 international association meetings, /and the association builds the community. /

在西方，/会议行业/非常重要。/我想特别讲讲/国际协会会议。/中国和广州/举办过众多会议，/有政府会议，/也有非政府会议。/我们是国际大会及会议协会，/我们追踪了/大约2万个国际协会会议，/发现这些协会有助于社区建设。/

02:30—03:00

I believe/that meetings/is not invented by the western world. /Meeting is invented by China. /Meeting is invented by China/thousands of years ago. /Face-to-face meeting/has re-happened here. /And it ventured to the Silk Road. /Now/China has initiated/the Road & Belt Initiative. /

我认为/会议/不是西方国家发明的，/而是中国。/中国发明会议/是在几千年前。/面对面的会议，/就在这里重现了。/中国勇于开拓丝绸之路。/如今，/中国提出了/"一带一路"倡议。/

03:00—03:45

Can you move the slide, please? /OK, it's going backwards. /Can you move forward the slide, please? /So we need the help from the technical person. /OK. /What I am going to show here/is we have tracked/more than 20,000 meetings/since 1963. /And it has been an exponential growth/for the meetings industry, /so you can see/that more and more meetings were organized/and we track/about 12,000 over associations, /international associations around the world. /

幻灯片能翻页吗？/往前翻了。/麻烦能往后翻页吗？/需要技术人员帮忙。/好的，/我要向你们展示的/是我们已经追踪了/2万多场会议，/自1963年开始追踪，/增长很迅速，/会议行业发展很快，/因此你们可以看到/越来越多的会议。/

第七单元 会议展览 Meetings, Incentives, Conferences, Exhibitions and Events

我们还追踪了/12,000多个协会,/世界各地的国际协会。/

03:46—04:16

In 2015, /China is ranked/No. 8 in the world. /I'm showing this/not to show you/that China is doing well/or not doing well. /But more importantly, /this is as a benchmark/where China is compared with other countries in the world. /We are going to release/the 2016 figures/this May. /So please bear with me these 2015 figures. /

2015年,/中国位列/世界第八。/给大家看这个/不是要告诉你们/中国做得好/或不好。/更重要的是,/这是基准,/是中国与世界其他国家对比的情况。/我们将发布/2016年的数据,/发布时间在今年5月份,/所以大家先看看2015年的数据。/

04:17—04:57

Next slide, please. /So China is No. 8 in the world. /And how about Guangzhou? /How do you perform? /So these are the top 5 cities in China. /Beijing/in 2015/is No. 1, /followed by Shanghai, /Hangzhou. /And Guangzhou and Nanjing/shared the 4th position. /The numbers are small/as compared to all the exhibition numbers/that you have been told early on, /because we track only/international association meetings. /This is a bigger picture about how other cities also perform. /

请翻到下一页。/中国位列世界第八,/那么广州呢,/广州表现如何?/这是中国前五的城市。/北京/在2015年/排名第一,/其次是上海、杭州,/广州和南京/并列第四。/数据比较小,/相比于展会数据而言比较小,/就是大家刚刚看到的数据。/因为我们只追踪/国际协会会议。/这些是其他城市的数据。/

04:58—05:44

So how do you actually win/international association meeting? /You have to work closely/with your scholars, /with your experts/in the medical, /technology/and education, /or in your universities. /I did a little research/yesterday, /then I found out/that Guangzhou actually houses/a lot of China and world top universities. /You're expert in the Chinese medicine. /You're expert in finance and economy, /foreign studies, /agriculture, /water and electricity, /and also academy of fine arts. /So/these are the areas/that you can actually work with your local association leaders/and try to beat and host international meeting/in your city. /This is how you can move forward. /

那么,你们如何赢得/举办国际协会会议的机会呢?/你们要开展紧密合作,/需要联合学者/和专家,/他们来自医学、/技术/和教育领域,/或者高校。/我做了个小小的调查,/就在昨天,/然后我发现/广州实际上有/很多国内外一流大学。/广州擅长中医,/擅长金融、经济、外语、农业、水电/和美术。/因此,/就是这些领域,/你们可以和地方协会领导一起努力,/来赢得举办国际会议的机会,/就在广州举办。/这是你们可以采取的举措。/

05:48—06:10

Some important facts, /quick facts about Guangzhou. /You have hosted/more than 192 international associations meetings/since 1985. /In 1985, /the first international meeting held in Guangzhou, /according to our research, /is the International Symposium of Anaerobic Digestion, /which is a medical scientific meeting. /

一些重要信息,/快速浏览下这些广州的信息。/你们已经举办了/超过192个国际协会会议,/第一次是在1985年。/1985年/在广州召开的第一个国际会议,/据我们研究,/是国际厌氧消化研讨会,/是一个医学会议。/

06:11—06:35

And the most future meeting/that has been booked to come to Guangzhou/is the 19th International Congress of Asia Society of Vascular Surgery, /which will have about 800 international delegates. /And 5,370, /that is the largest international association meeting/being held in Guangzhou, /which is the Asia Pacific Academy of Ophthalmology. /

近期举办的会议,/安排是在广州举办的/是第19届国际血管外科学会国际会议,/届时有约800名国际代表参会。/有5,370名代表、/规模最大的国际协会会议/将在广州举办,/那就是亚太眼科学会会议。/

06:36—07:01

Imagine, /when you have 5,000 over delegates/coming to Guangzhou, /the economic impact/that will bring to the city/is more than 120 million RMB/over the four days' conference. /This is the above that mentioned/over four days. /Can you move the slide, please? /And it has been such a smooth organize in Guangzhou. /

想象一下,/5,000多名代表/来到广州,/其经济效益,/带给广州的/是1.2亿人民币,/会议只持续短短的四天时间。/就是这个会议,/延续四天时间。/能翻到下一页吗?/这个会议的筹备工作很顺利。/

07:02—07:23

The next case study/that I'd like to share/is the 28th Regional Congress of the

第七单元 会议展览 Meetings, Incentives, Conferences, Exhibitions and Events

ISBT, /the blood transfusion. /So now instead of talking about exhibition/and talking about all the different medical sciences meeting/that you can also host/using the expertise of the universities/and the people of Guangzhou. /

下一个案例,/我想分享的/是国际输血学会的第 28 次区域会议,/会议议题是输血。/所以现在我们不聊展会,/想聊聊各类医学会议,/你们可以办这类会议,/利用高校的专业知识,/发挥广州人民的医学专长。/

07:28—08:06

The benefit/of hosting the International Society of Blood Transfusion/in 2017, /which is coming later this year, /will be in a focus Guangzhou/as the medical excellence center, /not only just economic center. /All experts on blood transfusion/from all around the world/will be coming to Guangzhou. /Economic impact/that is anticipated/is about 55 million RMB/over the four days/with estimated about 2,400 delegates are coming. /This type of conferences/will create jobs/for the city of Guangzhou. /

有什么益处呢? /举办国际输血学会/2017 年度会议,/也就是在今年下半年,/有利于广州/成为卓越的医疗中心,/而不仅仅是经济中心。/届时输血专家/从世界各地赶来,/相聚广州。/经济效益/预计/达 5,500 万人民币,/会议为期四天,/预计有 2,400 名代表参会。/这类会议/能创造就业机会,/造福广州。/

08:07—08:19

And this is how Guangzhou has performed/over the last 10 years/in terms of number of international meetings that you have hosted. /Even though the number/is not as big as exhibition industry, /but the numbers are growing. /

这就是广州的表现,/过去 10 年/在举办国际会议上的成就。/尽管会议数量/不如展览的数量/但也在持续增长。/

08:19—08:48

ICCA, /we are a global leader/for international meeting industry, /we have about 1,000 over members/in 85 countries. /And China membership/has grown very, very huge/from 1998 with only one member. /In 2002, /we have 17 members, /and today, /we have 46 members/in 18 different cities. /

我们国际大会及会议协会/引领/国际会议行业,/我们在有 1,000 多名会员,/分布在 85 个国家。/中国的会员/增幅很大,/1998 年只有一个,/2002 年,/我们有 17 个中国会员,/今天,/我们有 46 个中国会员,/分布在 18 个不同的城市。/

153

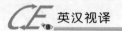

08:49—09:08

We have members/from Shanghai, /Beijing, /Xiamen, /Chongqing, /Suzhou, /Hangzhou, /Chengdu/and many others. /But we don't have a member/from Guangzhou yet. /So/we invite Guangzhou city/to be a member of ICCA. /

我们的会员/来自上海、/北京、/厦门、/重庆、/苏州、/杭州、/成都/等地,/但我们还没有会员/来自广州。/因此,/我们邀请广州/加入国际大会及会议协会。/

09:10—09:23

So this is the membership growth. /And it's very important to any association/because when you have a member, /where you have a stakeholder/from a particular city, /this will be the driving force/to bring more meetings/to the city. /

这是会员增长数据,/对任何协会来说都很重要,/因为每增加一个会员,/就有一个利益相关方/是来自某个城市的,/这将推动/更多的会议/在这个城市举办。/

09:24—09:49

So the question is, /if Guangzhou is already strong/and hosting a lot of exhibitions, /why would you want to/grow and win international association meeting? /Why international association meeting/is important? /I will leave you with this two minute-video/to show you the importance of the meeting industry. /

所以问题是,/如果广州会展业已经很强,/且举办了很多展会,/为什么广州还要/举办更多的国际协会会议呢?/为什么国际协会会议/那么重要?/我将播放一个两分钟的小视频,/让大家看看会议行业的重要性。/

09:51—10:06

In closing, /I would like to say/that exhibition/is the cradle/of your business for Guangzhou. /But if you work hard/to win international association meeting, /that will help your community. /Thank you very much. /谢谢! /

最后,/我想说/展览/孕育了/广州的商业。/如果广州努力/赢得国际协会会议举办权,/这将有助于广州的发展。/谢谢大家!/谢谢!/

II. 实战练习二

1. 演讲背景

博闻集团代表应邀出席"全球会展(广州)圆桌会"并发表主旨演讲。他在

第七单元 会议展览 Meetings, Incentives, Conferences, Exhibitions and Events

演讲中简要地介绍了博闻集团的概况，包括公司主办的活动和主营产品。此外他还谈到了影响会展目的地成功的主要因素，包括交通便利性、人力资源、会议组织、地方政府支持、安全与保障、可持续发展等。

2. 预习词汇

UBM 博闻集团

MICE/Meetings, Incentives, Conferencing/Conventions, Exhibitions/Exposition, Event 会展（业）

UBM Asia 博闻亚洲

stock-listed company 上市公司

acquisition 收购

organic growth 有机增长

trade show 贸易展会

SNECC/Shanghai National Exhibition and Convention Center 上海国家会展中心

baby maternity exhibition 孕婴展览会

cosmetics and beauty exhibition 化妆品和美容展

HOTELEX Shanghai 上海酒店用纺织品展

JIAGLE 家店装修在线

stands contracting 看台承包

freight forwarding 货运代理

tertiary institution 高等院校

PCO/professional conference organizer 专业会议组织者

Dubai 迪拜

ICCA/International Congress and Convention Association 国际大会及会议协会

3. 演讲文本

00:00—01:07

各位朋友，各位来宾，早上好。/Thank you so much for inviting me here today, /in particular, /Vice Mayor Cai. /I have been coming to Guangzhou/for many years now/and it gives me great pleasure/to be able to speak to you/on the business/very close to my heart/and to my wallet. /It pays my way. /I know I stand here between lunch/so I will try to get through it/as quickly as I can. /I am going to take you through a few areas here/in regards to UBM/and also a few points in terms of successful factors/on the MICE industry/and also just a few words/on the global exhibition industry overview. /

Dear friends, distinguished guests, good morning. /非常感谢你们今天邀请我来

155

到这里，/尤其要感谢／蔡副市长。/我到访广州,／多年来频繁到这边来,／我很高兴／能和你们谈谈／我的事业,／我很热爱我的事业／它是我的收入来源。/它支撑我的生活。/我知道快到午餐时间了,／所以我的演讲／会尽可能快地结束。/我将讲述一些领域／关于博闻集团的,／以及一些成功的因素,／决定会展业的因素,／还会简单介绍一下／全球会展业的概况。/

01:08—03:45
UBM Asia/as a subsidiary of UBM/which is a London stock-listed company/and we have been involved in Asia/for over 25 years. /Original head office/is in Hong Kong. /A very active office here/for over 20 years in Guangzhou/run by our manager here/Wendy. /Please stand up, Wendy. /She is known very well to all of the industry here in Guangzhou/particularly Guangdong. /So we have grown by acquisition/and also by organic growth/from a fairly small company to now/what is the largest commercial organizer/in China, /India/and Southeast Asia. /We have 250 events/with 1,600 staff/in 26 major cities throughout Asia/and this is between Japan to India, /which is a huge area/to be able to look after, /but our business is split into 3 areas. /One is in the Americas, /the other is in Asia, /and then the head offices, /because we are stock-listed in London, /it is in Europe. /We have 28 publications and/we have 18 online products. /Our events, /250 are exhibition trade fairs. /We are only in B2B. /We do not do any B2C. /No consumer parts. /Publications used to be very much a big part of our business/but with the advent of the Internet, /the printed world/has got reduced year on year. /However, /we are successful/in some areas for publications/because industries/still wish to have in print their research/and also in terms of being able to see themselves in print/rather than on the screen. /The online products/are things that we work with/in terms of how we interact/between our trade shows/and the Internet. /

博闻亚洲／作为博闻集团的子公司,／是一家伦敦上市公司,／我们在亚洲／已经有25多年的历史了。/原总部／在香港。/这里有一个非常繁忙的办公室／已经在广州经营了20多年了,／是由我们的经理管理运营的,／她是Wendy。/请站起来一下,Wendy。/她在广州的行业里很有知名度,／特别是广东。/所以我们的发展有赖于收购／和有机增长,／已经从一家小公司成长为／最大的商业组织者,／业务遍布中国、／印度／和东南亚。/我们主办250个活动,／有1600名员工,／在亚洲26个大城市工作。/这些城市位于日本到印度之间,／覆盖范围很广,／都是我们的业务所在地。/我们的业务分布在三个区域,／分别是美洲／和亚洲,／而总部／因为我们是在伦敦上市的,／所以第三个区域是在欧洲。/我们有28种出版物／和18种在线产品。/我们的活动／包括了250个贸易展会。/我们只做B2B,／我们不做B2C。/没有针对消费者的活动。/出版物曾经是我们业务的重要组成部分,／但随着互联网

第七单元 会议展览 Meetings, Incentives, Conferences, Exhibitions and Events

的出现,/印刷领域/逐年在缩减。/然而,/我们还是很成功的,/在一些出版领域做得很好,/因为众多行业/仍然希望它们的研究成果可以出现在印刷品上/它们的行业也可以出现在印刷品上/而不是屏幕上。/在线产品/也是我们的业务之一,/利用它们来互动,/在贸易展会/和互联网之间互动。/

03:45—04:30

Very importantly/some 10 years ago or so,/people thought/the trade fairs/and exhibitions/will go down/because/the Internet will take it over./That is certainly not true./Over the past 10 years,/we have already seen such huge increases/in the amount of trade shows/that are around the world/and we have seen a lot of evidence today/from all the speeches that you have heard/of the growths of the exhibition venues,/the hotel/and the conferences and the meetings/and also in terms of the trade shows themselves./So face to face meetings/are ever more important./

非常重要的是,/大约在10年前,/人们认为/贸易展会/和展览/会走下坡路,/因为/互联网会替代它们。/那当然不是真的。/在过去的10年里,/我们已经看到了巨大的增长/贸易展会的数量/在全球都快速增长,/我们也看到了大量的证据,/是今天的演讲嘉宾谈到的/那就是展览场馆的增加,/还有酒店、大小型会议的数量增长,/贸易展会也是一样。/所以面对面的会议/变得越来越重要。/

04:30—05:55

These are some of our major events./We have various sectors./Some of the largest ones/are in jewelry./The jewelry show in Hong Kong/is the world's largest jewelry show now./We had a huge furniture exhibition/in September/in Shanghai./China baby maternity expo,/which is in the SNECC in Shanghai/is now the largest baby maternity exhibition in the world./Cosmoprof/is Asia's largest cosmetics and beauty exhibition/which is held in Hong Kong./HOTELEX Shanghai opened this morning./That's near,/in Shanghai./And it's 417 halls./Marintech China/is the oldest/of the largest ship building,/ship marine equipment exhibition/in Asia./Not just in China,/but it is held in Shanghai./There are many others here/that you can see./I hope some of them/are familiar to them/which are also involved in food and hotels,/ingredients,/fashion etc./These are some of the publications/I was referring to earlier./

这是我们做的一些大型活动。/我们涉足各行各业。/其中一些最大型的/是珠宝。/香港的珠宝展/是世界上规模最大的珠宝展。/我们举办了一个大型的家具展/就在九月份/在上海举行的。/中国孕婴博览会/是在上海的国家会展中心举行的,/现在是世界上最大孕婴展览会。/Cosmoprof/是亚洲最大的化妆品和美容展,/在香港举行。/上海酒店用纺织品展今天上午开展,/离这里很近的/在上海举行,/启用了417个大厅,/中国国际海事技术学术会议和展览会/是历史最悠久的/规模最大的造船、/船舶设备展览会,/亚洲最大。/不仅仅在中国最大,/活动在上海举行。/这里还有很多其他的活动,/您都能看到。/我希望其中的一些活动/是你们熟悉的,/涉及食品和酒店、/原料、/时尚等方面。/这些是出版物,/我刚才有提到的。/

05:55—07:06

And online products. /Some of you may be familiar with/in the Chinese hotel and leisure site in JIAGLE. /If you haven't, /please go to them/because they are very interesting indeed. /And look at how we work/and we are searching to work with the Internet/to enhance our trade fair. /So see you there. /This is our new image positioning/in terms of showing between exhibitors and our visitors/and also ourselves as an industry. /Just a few points/in terms of success factors/for MICE destinations. /We have heard quite a lot today/about brand-new exhibitions/and brand-new venues/and conference centers. /The key thing is though/we got to look out/in terms of some accessibility, /in terms of the airport, /in terms of the airlift, /in terms of the ports, /the positioning, /in terms of the railway stations, /or hotels, /entertainment. /

还有在线产品。/你们中的一些人可能对这些产品很熟悉/在中国酒店和休闲网站家店装修在线上有展示。/如果你们不熟悉,/请去看看,/因为它确实很有趣。/然后来看看我们是如何工作的,/我们正在利用互联网,/以提升我们的贸易展会。/期待在那儿见到你们。/这是我们的新形象定位,/展示给参展商和访客,/也是我们作为一个行业的形象展示。/有几点/是关于成功因素的,/影响会展业目的地的因素。/我们今天听到了很多/关于新型展览、/新型场馆/和会议中心的信息。/关键的一点是/我们必须考虑/交通便利性,/包括机场、/空运、/港口、/定位/要考虑火车站、/酒店、/娱乐场所。/

07:07—08:16

When people come to/a lot of our trade fairs, /they also not just wish/to showcase their products/and services/but they also want to showcase themselves, /to get to know people better/and meet with either the existing clients/or the new clients. /And so they want to entertain. /So, /entertainment factors/are very important/in building relationships. /In some countries/you can build relationships/very quickly. /In others, /it takes quite a long time/but/by having the accessibility of all these things easily around, /it makes life so much easier/and the business to be that much better. /And you will always hear/people talk about/why do I like a particular place/is because I like the

第七单元 会议展览 Meetings, Incentives, Conferences, Exhibitions and Events

facility/that the trade show is in/or the conference is in/and the ease for which I am able to get, /to and from it/and also to be able to go to good restaurants/or other such things, /so be able to entertain your clients. /

当人们来到/我们不同的贸易展会时,/他们不仅仅想/展示产品/和服务,/他们也想展示自己,/更好地了解人们,/与老客户见面,/与新客户见面。/所以需要款待客户。/所以,/款待因素/非常重要,/影响了人际关系的建立。/在某些国家,/您可以建立人际关系,/速度很快。/而在其他国家,/这需要很长的时间,/但是/这些东西方便获取,/生活变得更轻松,/生意也越做越好。/您会经常听到/人们谈论/为什么喜欢某一个地方,/是因为我喜欢那里的设施,/贸易展览的设施/或是会议设施,/便利性,/交通便利,/也可以去好的餐馆/或其他诸如此类的地方,/所以我们需要很好地款待客户。/

08:16—09:31

Human resources. /This is so important/and I think it is really incumbent/upon all of us to look at two areas. /One is in terms of occasional/and this is in terms of the people/who are not at the top of running companies/but in terms of being able to ensure/that we have sufficient people around/to know how to run the venues, /who know how to do stands contracting/and also freight forwarding. /All of these are very important/to our industry. /We need people/to be able to do marketing/for our industry. /It is important also/to look at the university, /the tertiary institutions/in terms of educating people/not just in terms of engineering/or science, /or law/but also in terms of our business/because it is growing so fast. /We need people/to be able to be educated/and how to develop our business best. /So it is very important/to have extremely good human resources/and to develop them. /

人力资源。/这是非常重要的,/我认为我们义不容辞/我们所有人都要关注以下两个领域。/一个是偶然因素,/这是指一些员工,/他们并不是公司的高层,/但他们能够确保/我们有足够的人员/运营场馆,/做看台承包/和货运代理。/所有这些都非常重要/对我们的产业很重要。/我们需要人员/能够做营销/推广我们的行业。/重要的是,/关注大学/和高等教育机构,/它们培养人才/不仅仅是工程学、/科学,/或是法律专业的,/还有我们这个行业的,/因为这个行业发展得太快了。/我们需要人们/去接受教育,/知道如何来更好地发展这个行业。/所以至关重要的是/拥有优秀的人力资源/还要培养人才。/

09:32—10:58

So dynamic, /I say, PCO's here. /So professional conference organizers, /destination marketing. /Professionals involved inside your company/to be able to

159

enhance your businesses. /It is nothing worse than/going to conferences not well organized. /But look how well organized this conference is today. /Look how everything works/and look how everything is staged. /Look how we sit here today/and people are able to take part/and feel that they are learning something. /I say here, /destination attractiveness. /This is all part and parcel of something/which is important for the venues. /The image building/and branding throughout. /The MICE destination/is key/and as you heard today/Mr. Chen is also taking about things/like air quality, /how about measuring how good air qualities are. /I am sure Mr. Noor/with a lot of all of the conferences/will have a lot more new information coming about/what people/that we are looking for/and they have many good conferences/and many excellent locations/around the world. /People go to them/because they are fun/and attractive/and good to be. /

谈一谈动态的。/我说的PCO, /也就是专业会议组织者, /目的地营销。/专业人士参与到您的公司里来/提升您的业务。/最糟糕的莫过于/参加组织混乱的会议了。/但是看看今天的会议组织得多么好。/看看每件事是如何运作的, /看看一切是如何安排的。/看看我们今天坐在这里, /人人都能够参与/并且感觉到他们正在学习新的知识。/我这里说的是/目的地吸引力。/这是重要组成部分, /对场馆而言很重要。/形象塑造/和品牌建设贯穿始终。/会展业目的地/很关键, /正如您今天所听到的, /陈先生还谈到了/空气质量之类的东西, /如何测量空气质量的好坏。/我相信努尔先生/他参加过许多会议, /会给我们提供很多新的信息, /什么样的人才/是我们要寻找的, /他们有许多很好的会议/和很多很棒的场馆/分布在世界各地。/人们去参加/是因为它们很有趣, /很有吸引力, /去那里很有价值。/

10:58—11:35

So local government support. /What we see are unhindered support here in Guangdong, /Guangzhou, /particularly from the Mayor, /the Mayor ensuring the process is a success. /Very keen. /Networking/is the key to all the success of what we do/that we are all able to meet here/and have time to be able to meet also at the dinners, /the lunches, /the tea positions/as well so that we are able to build the relationships. /

地方政府的支持。/我们看到广东提供的持续的支持, /广州也是, /特别是来自市长的支持, /市长确保这一过程的成功, /他非常热心。/人脉关系/是我们所做的一切的成功关键, /我们能在这里会面, /能在晚餐、午餐、茶会上会面, /进而建立关系。/

第七单元　会议展览 Meetings, Incentives, Conferences, Exhibitions and Events

11:36—12:12

Safety and security, /key to everybody. /Positions that you do not have to think about. /You do not have to worry about/in your hotel, /or about in your conference center/or your trade show/that you are going to have any problems at all. /You go to do business, /you go to meet people/and that should be first on you mind. /You do not want to be worrying about/safety and security. /But as professionals, /as organizers, /venue managers, /we have to be very much aware of it, /we have to take all due care/and attention to it. /

安全与保障,/对每个人都很关键。/您不需要考虑地点。/您不必担心/在您的酒店,/或在您的会议中心/或您的贸易展览中/会出现任何的问题。/您去做生意,/您与人会面的时候,/这应该是您最先考虑到的。/您不想担心/安全问题。/但我们作为专业人士、/组织者、/场馆管理者,/我们必须非常清楚这一点,/我们必须对此给予应有的重视/和关注。/

12:13—14:20

Sustainable destinations. /I have been working with Ruthe, /my president, /ex-president was Chen Qiaojian. /We work very closely/on sustainable development within our organization globally/in terms of making sure that/countries and companies work/in terms of how to make the exhibitions much more sustainable/than they have to be. /How to cut out waste, /for instance, /in terms of paper or waste/from the building materials at trade shows/and also to ensure/the people are aware of the cities they come in to/and among these places you wish to go to. /We all want to go to the places/that are clean. /We want to breathe clean air. /So just a quick overview/in terms of marketplace. /Although there has been a slight slowdown globally/in 2015, /still we exhibition business/expanded by 1.7%, /so say 2%. /So this is still a huge amount which is growing. /And I do feel, /I do know from my colleagues that/last year in 2016/was also successful globally. /Although as we have seen/from Mr. Chen, /some points of concern in some countries/about easiness, /overall, /we know that there is a big growth. /We hear that/the economic growth/is still here in China, /It's not 8% as the world. /It's 6.5% or so. /In India, /it is not 9%/but it's 7%. /Still these are numbers/which are bigger/than most other areas of the world, /but it's also positive. /China also overtook Germany/as the second largest market/after the United States of America. /I will show a graph/a little bit later/about the US market/which has historically been the largest. /

目的地可持续发展。/我与 Ruthe 共事,/她是公司总裁,/前总裁是陈桥健先生。/我们紧密合作,/在全球范围内致力于组织的可持续发展。/确保国家和公司/

可以使展览更加环保,/超过强制性的标准。/如何减少废弃物,/比如说,/减少废纸或废弃物/贸易展会中建筑材料废弃物,/并确保/人们意识到要保护他们要去的城市/和那些他们希望去的地方。/我们都想去的地方/是那些干净的地方。/我们想要呼吸清新的空气。/所以快速了解一下/市场概况。/尽管全球市场略有放缓/在2015年,/但我们的展览业务/仍增长了1.7%,/所以就说是2%吧。/这仍然是一个巨大的增长。/我确实觉得,/我从同事那里得知,/去年2016年,/全球都比较成功。/虽然我们看到/陈先生刚才提到/一些国家状况不太好,/便利性不够,/但总体来说,/我们知道有很大幅度的增长。/我们听到/经济增长/在中国持续出现,/不是世界预测的8%,/而是大概6.5%左右。/印度/的经济增长不是9%,/而是7%。/这些数字依然/很大,/比世界上大多数其他地区都要大,/也是正增长。/中国超过了德国,/成为了世界第二大市场,/仅次于美国。/我将展示一个图表,/稍后再展示,/是关于美国市场的,/它一直以来都是最大的市场。/

14:21—15:05

Emerging market, /also in the gulf region/and places like Dubai, /are driving new growth/in terms of growing into businesses/which is growing into say Africa. /Africa doesn't have good venues/at this moment, /some in South Africa are OK/but central and northern Africa/which has been served by different areas. /But it will happen/and China is very much involved/in the development of Africa/which is today building railways in Africa. /So I can see that/China is gonna have a really important development for the future/in terms of how to develop also in this exhibition industries globally/not just in terms of locally. /

新兴市场,/在海湾地区/和像迪拜这样的地方,/正在驱动增长/在业务方面不断拓展,/比如把业务拓展到非洲。/非洲还没有很好的场馆,/目前没有,/南非的一些场馆还算不错,/但中非和北非/是由不同地区提供服务的。/这将会改变,/中国正在非常积极地参与/非洲的发展,/现在正在非洲铺设铁路。/所以我看到,/中国在未来会有一个非常重要的发展,/在全球发展会展行业/而不仅仅是在国内发展。/

15:06—16:00

So emerging markets. /We have seen some uncertainties/as we heard from Mr. Chen about Turkey/and some in Russia/and Brazil. /I sense that/these are gonna come back 5 years plus/because oil and gas/are still going to be needed. /Brazil is rich in commodities/and Turkey is a crossroads between Asia and Europe. /So we are going to see changes in those in the future. /But for now, /some concerns. /So trade shows account, /at the moment, /for 85% of the total exhibition market. /This is the business I am in. /I know/some of you/are also involved in B2C consumer shows/and I think it is important also for us/to be looking at education in these shows/that just how to manage these shows/and how to grow them for the future/and also for local positions. /

新兴市场。/我们看到一些不确定性, /正如我们从陈先生那里听到的土耳其的问题, /还有俄罗斯/和巴西的一些情况。/我意识到/这些问题将在5年后重现, /因为石油和天然气/仍然是必需品。/巴西商品丰富, /土耳其是亚洲和欧洲的十字路口。/所以我们将看到这些地区未来的变化。/但目前, /是有一些担忧的。/会展业/目前/占了整个展览市场的85%。/这就是我从事的业务。/我知道/某些观众/也在组织B2C的消费者展览, /我认为对于我们而言也需要关注/这些展览的教育意义, /如何管理这些展览, /以及如何在未来发展它们, /发展当地的会展业。/

16:01—17:32

Overall market size/and growth. /14 most significant markets/generated 24 billion dollars/in exhibition organizing revenues/in 2015. /The market growth, /as I said, /slowed slightly/but this is still a huge number. /Some graphs on it. /The Top 14 markets/started by USA/and China, /UK, /Germany, etc., /you can read here. / United States market/is significant by size. /It is historically/being involved in conventions, /exhibitions, /trade show markets. /So every hotel, /every airport, /every state/is linked to this business. /And the meetings industry is mature/but also still growing there. /My company reinvested a lot of millions of dollars/in the US market/over the past ten years/because it is still important. /And I can see/this happening in China/as every town, /every city/and every province, /starts to get moving/in terms of understanding the growth, /the potential, /in terms of being in the meetings industry. /So ourselves/and those of ICCA, /they will be very important here in China. /

整体市场规模/和增长。/14个最重要的市场/产生了240亿美元/展览收益, /这是2015年的数据。/市场增长/我刚才提到/略有放缓, /但这仍然是一个巨大的数字。/这是关于它的一些图表。/14个最大的市场/按顺序包括了美国、/中国、/英国、/德国等, /您可以在这里看到。/美国市场/规模很大。/多年以来, /美国是会议、/展览、/贸易展览的市场。/每家酒店、/每个机场、/每一个州/都与这项业务联系在一起。/会议行业已经很成熟, /但仍在增长。/我公司再投资了数百万美元/在美国市场/在过去的十年里, /因为它仍然是重要的市场。/我可以看到/同样的事情发生在中国, /每一个乡镇, /每个城市, /每个省, /都开始发展/人们开始理解这种增长, /这种发展潜力, /加入到会议行业中来。/这样我们自己/和那些国际大会及会议协会的同行们, /对中国的发展非常重要。/

17:33—18:03

So you've seen/the growth rates here. /In China/the percent of 8%/which is a tremendous figure. /So/in global forecast growing in 2020, /at 4.6[%] per year. /And also these are the growth markets there. /I think/you will be able/to get these slides/from the organizers afterwards. /

您已经看到/这里的增长率了。/中国/增长率达8%,/这是一个巨大的数字。/因此,/全球增长预测在2020年/的年增长率将达4.6%。/这些是增长型市场。/我想/你们可以/拿到这些幻灯片,/会议结束后主办方会给你们。/

18:04—18:56

So/the trends in industry/are looking at in terms of how political, /social/and economic uncertainties/are affecting the market. /Social media marketing. /How do we assess the utilization of elements/such as WeChat, /the technology of using WeChat, /for instance, /registration/and sustainability. /These are the key issues/in our industry here today/particularly in China. /These are some of the connecting websites/that we have for UBM Asia. /So I hope you go on to them. /I hope you partake in some of our shows/and I look forward to seeing you/in some of them in the future. /谢谢!/Thank you! /

因此,/这个行业的趋势/是基于政治、/社会/和经济的不确定性/对市场产生何种影响。/社交媒体营销。/我们如何评估下面这些要素的使用,/比如微信,/使用微信的技术/包括/注册/和可持续性。/这些是非常关键的问题,/影响当今的行业,/尤其是在中国。/这是一些网站/博闻亚洲的网站。/我希望你们能够去浏览一下。/我希望你们能参与我们的展会,/我期待看到你们/来参加我们未来的展会。/谢谢!/

第八单元　商事仲裁
Commercial Arbitration

I. 实战练习一

1. 演讲背景

英国皇家大律师 Stephen 应邀参加"国际商事仲裁交流会"并发表主旨演讲。他在演讲中首先提到了商事仲裁最早可以追溯到古希腊神话，也谈到了仲裁发展的主要推动力是国际商界，程序上的灵活性、非正式性、保密性和高效性是仲裁过程的关键属性，也是商业界偏好仲裁的核心原因。此外，他还谈到了"东方经验"，即调解和仲裁相结合，最后还谈到了仲裁与诉讼相比特有的优势，并呼吁所有国家都支持仲裁的发展。

2. 预习词汇

Poseidon 海神波塞冬
Helios 太阳神赫利俄斯
Corinth 科林斯
Briareus 百臂巨人
antiquity 古代（尤指古希腊和古罗马时期）
Athena 智慧女神雅典娜
Aegina 爱琴娜
award 判给；裁决
Zeus 天神宙斯
Hera 天后赫拉
Argolis 阿尔戈利斯
Inachus 河神伊纳科斯
pointer 线索
impartial 公正的
adjudicator 仲裁员
arbitration award 仲裁裁决
foreshadow 预示

disputant 争议者
retain 聘请
pending 未定的
litigation 诉讼
statute 成文法
effectual 有效的
seminal 影响深远的
emolument 酬金
enactment （法律）制定；颁布
judiciary 司法系统，司法机关
procedural （法律）程序上的
confidentiality 保密性
attribute 属性
repudiate 拒绝；否认
a panoply of 大量的
signatory 签署国
abiding 长久的
thereby 从而
legislature 立法机关
mediation 调解；调停
in line with 符合
empirical 实证的
autonomy 自主权
party autonomy 当事人意思自治
tribunal 仲裁法庭
envisage 设想；展望

3. 演讲文本

00:00—02:19

Distinguished guests, /ladies and gentlemen, /it is a great privilege for me/to be here today. /Thank you so much for your invitation! /The origins of international arbitration/are sometimes traced to ancient mythology. /Early instances of dispute resolution/among the Greek gods/involved between Poseidon and Helios/over ownership of the town of Corinth/which was reportedly split between them/after arbitration before a giant Briareus. /And another arbitration from antiquity/was between Poseidon and Athena/over possession of the island of Aegina, /and that was awarded to them in

第八单元 商事仲裁 Commercial Arbitration

common/by the God Zeus. /A third was between Poseidon and Hera/over ownership of Argolis. /In this case,/it was awarded entirely to Hera/by Inachus. /While apart from highlighting/Poseidon's persistent problems with his peers,/these examples provide some pointers from antiquity/about international arbitration. /The role of an impartial adjudicator,/the central role of the rule of law. /One of the enduring problems/faced by the arbitral process/is enforcement of arbitration awards. /That was foreshadowed/by Poseidon's refusal/to honor the award against him/made by Inachus. /Historically,/two different forms of arbitration/developed in parallel:/international state-to-state arbitration/and international commercial arbitrations,/and it's the latter/with which we are concerned today. /

尊敬的各位来宾,/女士们,先生们,/我很荣幸/今天来到这里。/非常感谢你们的邀请!/国际仲裁的源头/有时会追溯到古希腊神话。/早期关于解决争议的案例/发生在古希腊众神之间,/包括海神波塞冬和太阳神赫利俄斯/争夺科林斯镇的所有权/据说科林斯被分成了两半,/经过百臂巨人的仲裁之后。/另一起古代的仲裁案/发生在海神波塞冬和智慧女神雅典娜之间,/双方争夺爱琴娜岛的归属,/最终判为双方共同拥有,/仲裁员为天神宙斯。/第三个案例发生在海神波塞冬和天后赫拉之间,/他们争夺阿尔戈利斯的所有权。/在这个案例中,/阿尔戈利斯被完整地判给了天后赫拉,/仲裁员是河神伊纳科斯。/尽管放大了/海神波塞冬和他的同辈们永无休止的争议,/但这些案例提供了一些古代的线索,/指引我们关注国际仲裁这个话题。/一个公正的仲裁员扮演的角色,/是法治的核心角色。/其中一个永恒的问题/在仲裁过程都会遇到的/就是仲裁裁决的执行。/这一困难早有预示/那就是海神波塞冬拒绝/执行对他不利的裁决/也就是河神伊纳科斯作出的裁决。/历史上,/两种不同形式的仲裁/并行发展,/即国家与国家之间的仲裁/和国际商事仲裁,/后者/就是我们今天要讨论的话题。/

02:20—03:43

Some of the earliest reports/of commercial arbitration/are again from ancient Greece. /Homer describes/in 8th Century BC/resolution of a blood debt/through a public arbitral process/where the disputants appeal to a man/vested in the law of their mutual choice/who presided over the arbitration with elders/which publicly heard the parties'claims/and rendered reasons or opinions. /The reasons for resorting to arbitration/in antiquity/appeared to be remarkably modern. /Research indicates/that Greek courts suffered from congestion and backlogs;/people were afraid of their outcome/and they led, as a result, to the use of arbitrators/retained from other cities/to resolve pending disputes. /And as one commentator put it:/Arbitration was the natural and regular process of choice/for those who could not afford litigation,/were afraid of

167

its outcome/and preferred privacy,/or were manipulating the alternatives./

一些最早的案例,/关于商事仲裁的,/也是来自古希腊。/荷马形容/在公元前8世纪,/解决血债/要通过公开的仲裁过程,/争议双方向一个人求助/人选由双方共同确定,/被求助的人和长者们一同主持仲裁,/公开听取双方的陈述/并提供理据或看法。/诉诸仲裁的理据/在古代/却显得非常现代化。/研究表明,/古希腊法庭经常拥堵不堪、案件堆积成山;/人们害怕审判结果,/因此他们引进了仲裁员,/从其他城邦请过来的,/来解决悬而未决的争议。/就像一位评论家所说:/仲裁是自然的常规的选择过程,/适合那些负担不起诉讼费用、/害怕判决结果、/更看重隐私/或者操控着选择余地的人。/

03:44—05:05

Perhaps the earliest known arbitration statute/is the *English Arbitration Act of 1698*./Reflecting an objective of promoting commerce,/the *Act*'s purposes were promoting trade/and rendering awards of arbitrators/more effectual in all cases/for the final determination of controversies/referred to them by merchants and traders/or others concerning matters of account/or trade/or other matters./So, you see that trade was the primary driver/of international commercial arbitration/from the very beginning./Driven by the demands of traders,/nations encouraged arbitration/and adopted arbitration laws./Agreements to arbitrate became enforceable,/courts were empowered/to stay court proceedings/in favor of arbitration./Arbitrators were given powers/to conduct arbitration effectively,/and limited rights of appeal/given on questions of law./

或许最早已知的仲裁成文法/是1698年的《英国仲裁法案》,/反映了推动商业发展的目标。/这部法案的目的是促进贸易、/帮助仲裁员作出裁决、/使裁决在所有的案件中都能生效/以最终解决争议。/这些争议由商人和贸易者向仲裁员提出/或者是由其他涉及会计、/贸易或其他争议的人提出。/所以,大家可以看到贸易是最主要的驱动力,/推动了国际商事仲裁的发展,/一开始便是如此。/由贸易商的需求所驱动,/国家也开始鼓励仲裁/并制定仲裁法。/仲裁协议变得可以执行,/法庭被赋予了权力,/停止诉讼程序,/支持仲裁。/仲裁员也被赋予了权力,/高效进行仲裁,/同时也被赋予了有限的上诉权利,/仅对法律问题提出上诉。/

05:06—06:11

For many years/there was a nevertheless an antipathy towards arbitration/on the part of some./About 170 years ago,/Lord Campbell,/the Lord, the English Lord Chancellor/in the seminal arbitration case/of Scotland Ovary/provided a famous cynical explanation/for the court's antipathy./He said their antipathy/has its origins/in the interests of judges./There was no disguising the fact/that the emoluments of the judges'

第八单元　商事仲裁 Commercial Arbitration

depended mainly, /or almost entirely on fees, /and as they had no fixed salaries, /there was great competition/to get as many as possible of litigation/into Westminster Great Hall/and there was a great scramble in Westminster Hall/for the division of the spoils/and they had great jealousy of arbitration/whereby Westminster Hall was robbed of those cases. /So, the court did not like competition. /

很多年来, /然而, 却总存在对仲裁的反对声音, /总有某些人反对。/大概170年前, /坎贝尔大法官, /英国的大法官, /审理了一起影响深远的仲裁案, /是关于苏格兰Ovary这个地方的。/他提出了一句有名的充满讽刺意味的解释, /说明为何法院反对仲裁。/他说法院的反对/归根结底/是和法官的利益相关。/事实是无法伪装的, /法官的酬金主要依靠/或者说几乎完全依靠诉讼费, /因为他们没有固定的薪水, /激烈的竞争总是存在/为了得到尽可能多的诉讼, /进入威斯敏斯特议会大厅, /议会内部的争斗也非常激烈, /为了利益的分配/他们很嫉恨仲裁/因为议会为此被抢了很多案子。/可以看到, 法院并不喜欢竞争。/

06:12—08:18

The next significant enactment in England/was the 1889 *Arbitration Act*/which in turn/was widely adopted/throughout the British Commonwealth/and was adopted at that time in Hong Kong. /It was eventually replaced in England/by the 1950 *Act*/and it so superceded by the 1996 *Act*. /Commercial arbitrations/followed a broadly similar path/both in France and the United States/with a great deal of antipathy towards arbitration. /But in other parts of Europe, /commercial arbitrations developed/without that period of hostility from the judiciary. /Procedural flexibility, /informality, /confidentiality/and efficiency/were key attributes of the arbitral process/and central to the business communities' preference/for commercial arbitration. /And the mistrust of the arbitral process/which had arisen in some jurisdictions/and notably England in the 19th Century/was eroded/and firmly repudiated/during the 20th Century. /This was accomplished/by means of a panoply of related developments, /the adoption of international arbitration conventions, /national arbitral legislation, /institutional arbitration rules/and supportive national courts. /Perhaps most significant of all/was the adoption of the 1958 *New York Convention*. /This required courts of contracting states/to give effect to private arbitration agreements/and to recognize and enforce arbitration awards. /

下一部具有重要意义的英国法律/是1889年的《仲裁法案》。/反过来/这部法律却被广泛采用/在英联邦/并且被当时的香港所通过。/最后在英国它被替代了, /替换成1950年的《仲裁法案》, /最终被1996年的《仲裁法案》所取代。/商事仲裁/也走上了大致相同的道路, /在法国和美国都是如此, /都有大量反对仲裁的声音。/但是在欧洲其他地方, /商事仲裁发展/并没有一段被司法系统仇视的时期。/

程序上的灵活性、/非正式性、/保密性/和高效性/是仲裁程序的关键属性,/也是商业界之所以偏好的核心原因,/他们支持商事仲裁。/对仲裁程序的不信任/也曾出现在一些管辖区内/尤其是在英国19世纪。/但这种不信任被削弱/并被坚决地摒弃/是在20世纪期间。/这一切成就的取得/是通过大量相关事件的发展完成的,/包括通过国际仲裁公约、/国内仲裁法律、/机构仲裁规则/和支持性的国内法院。/或许其中最重要的/是通过了1958年的《纽约公约》。/这就要求签署国的法院/承认私人仲裁协议/并承认、执行仲裁裁决。/

08:19—09:29

China was an early signatory, /became a signatory/on the 22nd of January in 1987. /And all of these steps/evidence an abiding/and decisive commitment/to international arbitration/as a means of resolving commercial disputes/and thereby promoting international trade. /And it's important to appreciate/that the driving force/behind these developments/was the international business community, /the principal user of the arbitral process/which found ready audiences/in national legislatures and judiciaries/eager to promoting international trade, /investment, /and peace/by providing workable, /effective international dispute resolution mechanisms/and it was the combination and collaboration/between those two communities, /the public and the private/that produced the contemporary legal framework/for international commercial arbitration. /

中国是早期的签署国,/成为签署国/是在1987年1月22日。/所有这些步骤/表明一个长久的、/决定性的承诺/支持国际仲裁/作为一种解决商业纠纷的方式/从而促进国际贸易的发展。/很重要的是要意识到/驱动力/促进了发展,/来自国际商业界,/也就是主要使用仲裁程序的群体,/他们发现已经有现成的观众/在国内的立法机关和司法机关里,/商界渴望推动国际贸易、/投资/以及和平,/通过提供可操作的、/高效的国际争端解决机制。/正是联手与合作/在这两大群体之间,/公共领域和私营领域的合作/催生了当代法律框架/促进了国际商事仲裁的发展。/

09:30—10:01

Mediation in China/started long before all of this. /4,000 years ago, /the Emperor Shun, /the ancient Chinese leader, /settled the disputes for fishermen. /According to the legends, /Emperor Shun lived with groups of fishermen/for one entire year, /so he could help them/to find a reasonable and fair way/to allocate every fisherman/with an appropriate fishing spot. /

调解在中国/比这些都出现得更早。/4,000年前,/舜,/古代中国一位君王,/解决了渔民之间的纠纷。/传说/舜和一群渔夫一起生活了/整整一整年时间,/所以

第八单元　商事仲裁 Commercial Arbitration

他能帮助他们/找到一种合理又公平的方式/来给每个渔民分配/一个合适的捕鱼地点。/

10:02—11:08

In ancient China,/I understand the disputes were involved,/were resolved/within rural communities/by local nobility or scholars/who would mediate between them/over the conflicting disputes./These early mediators sought,/I understand,/to resolve disputes/efficiently and amicably/in line with Confucian thought/using the philosophical concept of "*Li*",/conflicts were resolved/through a system of rituals and manners/rather than legal argument./And the world has a lot to learn from that./This has had a significant impact/on the development of the modern Chinese legal system/and its approach to commercial dispute resolution./This early mediation also foreshadowed/and led to the modern movement/in international trade/towards a package of dispute resolution mechanisms./

在古代中国,/我知道争议是产生于、/并解决于/农村内部/由当地的乡绅或文人/在他们之间调解/以解决矛盾的争议。/这些早期的调解员一直试图,/据我理解,/解决争议/采用高效、友好的方式/符合儒家思想/运用"礼"的哲学理念,/争议能得到解决/经由礼节和习俗这套系统/而不是法律途径。/全世界都可以从中学到很多。/这也深刻影响着/现代中国法律体系的发展/以及中国商事争议的解决方法。/这种早期的调解方法也影响了/导致了现代运动的发生/国际贸易领域/试图找到一揽子解决争议的机制。/

11:09—12:39

In line with the historic Chinese practice,/what CIETAC described as oriental experience,/most trading nations/now encourage alternative dispute resolution/as the first stage/of the dispute resolution/to be followed by commercial arbitration/only where mediation fails./And in this,/it was China,/once again that led the way./Well, why have traders chosen international commercial arbitration?/Empirical evidence suggests/that those involved in international trade/have turned to international commercial arbitration/for eight specific reasons./It ensures confidentiality/and privacy of process/and this is viewed very highly/by international traders./It provides a neutral forum/for dispute resolution./Very significantly,/it respects party autonomy/and it does so in numerous ways./The parties choose the forum;/the parties choose the law;/the parties choose their tribunal/so they can choose a tribunal/with particular expertise/relevant to their dispute;/the parties choose the procedural rules/that they want to apply./

和历史上中国的做法一致，/中国国际经济贸易仲裁委员会将此描述为"东方的经验"，/大多数贸易国家/现在都鼓励使用替代性争端解决方法，/以此作为第一个阶段，/解决争议，/接下来才是选择商事仲裁，/前提是调解失败了。/在这方面，/中国，/再一次引领潮流。/那么，为什么贸易商会选择国际商事仲裁呢？/实证证据显示，/那些国际贸易从业人员/选择国际商事仲裁/有八个具体的理由。/国际商事仲裁确保了保密性/以及过程的隐私，/这一点受到了高度评价，/得到来自国际贸易从业人员的肯定。/它提供了一个中立的平台/解决争议。/很关键的是，/它尊重当事人意思自治，/在很多方面都是这么做的。/当事方自主选择仲裁院；/当事方自主选择准据法；/当事方自主选择仲裁庭；/因此他们可以选择一个仲裁庭/是具有某方面的专业经验、/与他们的争议相关的；/当事方可以选择程序规则，/双方都愿意使用的规则。/

12:40—14:07

Fourthly, /it offers internationally enforceable/dispute resolution agreements；/it offers internationally enforceable awards/depending on the chosen forum. /It very often has finality. /Seventh, /it facilities amicable settlement. /And eighth, /as compared to legislation in national courts, /if operated properly/and those words are crucial, /if operated properly, /it results in a saving of costs, speed/and avoids delays/and can avoid rigidities/and other defects in litigation in national courts. /The last group of reasons depend, /as I say, /on the arbitration being operated properly. /And here it is that you have to rely on your arbitrators. /The secret of/ensuring that arbitration operates properly/is choosing the right arbitrators/and choosing the right arbitral rules. / Evidence shows that/the arbitration institutes/which provide the greatest party autonomy, /such as your own hearing, /this area, /thereby giving flexibility of the most effective. /So, well done in going down that route. /

第四，/它提供了国际可强制执行的/解决争议的协议；/它提供了国际可强制执行的裁决，/这取决于所选的仲裁院。/它通常都具有终局性。/第七，/它促进了和解。/第八，/相比国内法院的立法，/如果操作得当，/这句话很关键，/如果操作得当，/商事仲裁可以节省支出、提高效率，/避免延迟/还能避免机械操作/和其他在国内法院诉讼的缺点。/最后一个理由取决于，/就像我说的，/取决于仲裁得到恰当的操作。/这也就是您为什么必须要依靠仲裁员。/有一个秘诀，/要确保仲裁操作得当，/就得选择正确的仲裁员/和选择正确的仲裁规则。/证据显示，/仲裁机构/如果能最大限度地保证当事人意思自治，/例如开庭审理，/在这个领域，/就能提升灵活度又确保效率最高。/所以，选择走这条道路是明智的。/

第八单元　商事仲裁 Commercial Arbitration

14:08—16:14

Let me conclude. /We've seen/that trade is the primary driver/of international commercial arbitration. /Driven by the demands of traders, /nations have encouraged arbitration. /Ultimately, /the success of international arbitration/depends upon the rule of law; /it depends upon nations/recognizing and enforcing/arbitration agreements/and arbitration awards. /You see, /in theory, /a legal system could be envisaged/which adopted an attitude/of entire indifference to arbitration, /while recognizing the rights of the parties/to agree that their disputes/should be decided by the arbitrators, /the law would do nothing/to enforce the agreement, /to reinforce the procedures/at its points of potential weakness/or to protect the parties/against the risk of procedural, /or substantive injustice, /or to enforce the award. /However, /no modern state can afford/such a detached attitude. /Arbitration is an important part/of commercial life/ and every legal system must be concerned with it. /Where the legal system differs/is in regard to the nature of the relationship/between the court and the arbitrator/and it stands to which the law regulates/and the court concerns itself/with the conduct of the reference. /Any nation that wants to participate fully in international trade, /must fully embrace international commercial arbitration. /Trade and arbitration go hand in hand. / May I wish 'One Belt, One Road' every success. /Thank you, ladies and gentlemen! /

让我做个总结。/我们讨论了/贸易是主要的驱动力/推动了国际商事仲裁的发展。/受贸易商的需求驱动,/很多国家都鼓励仲裁。/最后,/国际仲裁的成功/依靠法治;/依赖于国家/承认并执行/仲裁协议/和仲裁裁决。/大家可以看到,/理论上,/设想一个法律体系/如果采取一种态度/对仲裁完全漠视,/但同时承认当事人的权利,/他们有权决定他们的争议/应该由仲裁员来裁定,/法律袖手旁观/不执行仲裁协议,/不强化程序/来克服潜在弱势,/也不能保护当事方/免遭程序上的风险/或实体上的非正义,/也不执行裁决。/但是,/没有哪个现代国家能够采取/这种漠视的态度。/仲裁是重要的一部分,/在商业活动中,/每个法律体系都必须重视它的存在。/法律体系与之不同的是/这层关系的本质,/即法院和仲裁员的关系,/仲裁所处的环境是法律的管辖范围,/法院关心的/莫过于援引的行为。/任何国家想要全面地参与到国际贸易中,/就必须完全接受国际商事仲裁。/贸易和仲裁总是并肩齐行。/祝愿"一带一路"战略取得成功。/谢谢,女士们,先生们!/

II. 实战练习二

1. 演讲背景

瑞士仲裁员协会荣誉主席应邀参加"国际商事仲裁交流会"并发表名为"更

173

快捷、更高效的仲裁程序：机遇、陷阱及成就"的主旨演讲。他提到，大多数的仲裁案件都需要两三年才能结案，因为任何一个程序步骤都需要耗费时间，因此他比较了不同仲裁机构的加速程序，发现几乎所有的机构都倾向于在仲裁庭组成之前，采用紧急仲裁员程序加速仲裁，或者采取书面审理；仲裁庭组成后也可以根据争议金额确定该仲裁是否直接进入简易程序。最后，他分享了加速程序的弊端。

2. 预习词汇

arbitral institution 仲裁机构

arbitration 仲裁

UNCITRAL/United Nations Commission on International Trade Law 联合国国际贸易法委员会

ASA/Swiss Arbitration Association 瑞士仲裁协会

procedure 程序

International Court for Arbitration for Sports 国际体育仲裁院

Lausanne 洛桑（瑞士西部城市）

sports arbitration 体育仲裁

commodity arbitration 商品仲裁

domain name dispute 域名纠纷

WIPO/World Intellectual Property Organization 世界知识产权组织

Geneva 日内瓦

shipping arbitration 船运仲裁

party 当事人

claimant 申请人

arbitral tribunal 仲裁庭

arbitrator 仲裁员

respondent 被申请人

soft law 软法

thicket 错综复杂

arbitral proceeding 仲裁程序

ICC/International Chamber of Commerce 国际商会（仲裁院）

LCIA/London Court of International Arbitration 伦敦国际仲裁院

SCC/Stockholm Chamber of Commerce 斯德哥尔摩商会仲裁院

Stockholm 斯德哥尔摩（瑞典首都）

CIETAC/China International Economic and Trade Arbitration Commission 贸仲委；中国国际经济贸易仲裁委员会

HKIAC/Hong Kong International Arbitration Center 香港国际仲裁中心

DIS/Deutsche Institution für Schiedsgerichtsbarkeit 德国仲裁协会
SCAI/Swiss Chambers' Arbitration Institution 瑞士商会仲裁院
ICDR/International Centre for Dispute Resolution 国际争议解决中心
commence 开始
urgent arbitration 紧急仲裁
emergency arbitrator 紧急仲裁员
hearing 开庭
arbitral referee 仲裁前公断
summary reason 简明的理由
award 仲裁裁决
New York Convention《纽约公约》
interim measure 临时措施
binding 有约束力的
expedited arbitration 简易仲裁程序
financial threshold 金额门槛
opt out 排除适用

3. 演讲文本

00:00—02:02

Your excellencies,/distinguished representatives/of the arbitral institutions organizing this session,/ladies and gentlemen,/colleagues from the arbitration world,/it's a privilege for me/to appear before this distinguished audience/and a great pleasure/to have the opportunity/to visit this dynamic region. /As we have seen this morning,/we had an opportunity/of touring some of the achievements/that have been developed/and continuing developing/in this region. /When we discussed the conference/and the subject of my presentation,/I thought/the speed in arbitration/which is a subject of great concern/in Europe or in the west in general,/and which is a subject of the future work/of the United Nations Commission on International Trade Law. /We thought/that this was a subject/which would be of interest/at this conference,/and where/we could share the experience of UNCITRAL,/of the Swiss Arbitration Association,/of my law firm, Lalive. /As it turned out,/as I learnt,/it's that arbitration/and speed in arbitration/in China/is not a problem. /Arbitration is fast,/and it's so fast/that as we saw this morning,/construction is fast here,/but construction is faster/than arbitration in Europe. /So the experience/which I am talking about/may be for you far away/because/what I've seen here/is a fast activity of arbitration/and the concern with speed may be much less. /

诸位阁下，/尊敬的各位代表，/组织本次会议的仲裁机构的代表们，/女士们，先生们，/仲裁界的同仁们，/非常荣幸/能给尊贵的嘉宾们演讲，/也很高兴/有机会/访问这个富有活力的地方。/就像我们早上看到的，/我们有机会/亲眼目睹一些成就，/已经取得的/或者正在取得的成就，/这些成就发生在这个地区。/我们讨论会议/和我展示的主题时，/我认为/仲裁速度/是大家非常关心的一个主题/通常来说不管是在欧洲还是在西方，/这也是未来工作的主题，/是联合国国际贸易法委员会的工作主题。/我们认为，/这个主题/会很有趣，/适合在今天的会议上讨论，/这里/我们会分享联合国国际贸易法委员会的经验，/瑞士仲裁协会/以及我就职的律所Lalive的经验。/经验表明，/也是我学到的，/仲裁/和仲裁速度/在中国/不是一个问题。/仲裁很迅速，/非常快，/就像我们今早看到的，/这里的建设也非常快，/很快，/比欧洲的仲裁还快。/所以这个经验/是我今天想分享的，/也许没有太大的借鉴作用，/因为/我在这里看到的/是仲裁效率非常高，/对速度可能没那么担心。/

02：02—04：03

So what I would say coming back, /when I would be back in Europe, /I would say with respect to speed in arbitration, /we in the rest of the world/can learn from China. /The subject of, /now let me see where I find there, /yes, /the subject of concern in Europe/is like in the rest of the business world, /time is money. /There are some procedures in arbitration/which follow the past/which are fast/as arbitration is prays for, /and it's sports arbitration. /You may be familiar/with the arbitration at the court, /International Court for Arbitration for Sports. /In Lausanne, /they do arbitration about sports disputes/in a matter of weeks/and during the Olympic Games, /they do it overnight. /That is really in connation of fast arbitration. /You have the tradition of commodity arbitration/which also has the reputation to be fast. /In fact, /some people call it/the look and sniff arbitration/because they take the grain/or some other objects. /That is said to be half right/and say yes, you are right/or you are wrong. /Then, /there is of course the domain name disputes/on the Internet. /The World Intellectual Property Organisation/also in Geneva/has a very fast procedure, /and a procedure/at which/I have admitted here/but which is dear to the organizers here/and some of our speakers/that is shipping arbitration. /I learnt today from our colleague Mr. Hofmeyr/that he finished an arbitration/in three weeks. /This is, /for the rest of us, /a miracle. /

所以当我说我回去的时候，/也就是我回到欧洲的时候，/我会满怀敬意地讲仲裁速度，/我们其他国家/可以向中国学习。/这个主题，/我看看哪里可以找到，/在这儿，/欧洲担心的主题/就像商界担心的一样，/时间就是金钱。/仲裁包括一些

第八单元 商事仲裁 Commercial Arbitration

程序，/过去/仲裁效率很高，/和人们请求的一样快，/这是体育仲裁。/您也许熟悉/法院的仲裁，/也就是国际体育仲裁院。/在洛桑，/他们的体育仲裁/需要花几个星期，/在奥运会期间，/他们只需要一个晚上。/这确实符合快速仲裁的涵义。/你们传统的商品仲裁，/因为速度快而闻名。/事实上，/有些人把它叫做/"眼看鼻闻的仲裁"，/因为他们的争议焦点就在于粮食/或其他物品。/据说只有一半的裁决是对的，/仲裁员会说"你是对的，/或你错了"。/下面，/当然是域名纠纷，/发生在互联网上。/世界知识产权组织/是在日内瓦，/它的仲裁程序也非常快，/这个程序/这里/我很认同/但这是组织者非常看重的，/我们有些发言人也很重视的/就是船运仲裁。/我今天从 Hofmeyr 律师那里学到了很多，/他完成一个仲裁案件/只花了三个星期。/这个，/对于我们来说，/是个奇迹。/

04:03—06:43

But for most of arbitration procedures, /as we see it internationally, /they take time, /often very long time, /one year, /two years, /three years. /That is the practice/which you normally see/in international arbitration. /And that is not good. /That is not good/and the users are complaining. /So if I look at the reasons, /why there are these delays, /and why there are the complaints. /We see the various sources of the complaints. /One is the parties/and their lawyers. /They are all busy/and they take time/to assemble the case, /to build up the case, /to get everybody together, /to prepare the submissions. /All of that takes time. /I have had cases/where the claimant requested several months. /In one case/even a year to prepare the case/and of course of this one. /But similarly, /so that is one thing, /but the other thing is/that cases tend to be more and more complicated/with complicated projects, /with complicated transactions, /with the multitude of players in the game. /And then/the arbitral tribunal takes time. /One of the things/we will come to that/in a moment. /The formation of a tribunal/until you have a tribunal/takes time. /You have to set up the procedure, /you will find the arbitrators. /First of all, /the claimant has a month/to find the arbitrator. /Then/the respondent another month, /and then they have to agree on the chairman, /that can take a month/or even longer. /Sometimes/the issues of the conflicts/which may be between different companies/or the conflicts of interest/which an arbitrator may have/delayed the process. /And then in the procedure itself, /you have to find dates/that are working out for everybody, /and then the award/which the arbitrators then have to raise, /have to prepare, /also takes time. /Another point/are procedure incidents. /You have more and more counsels/in the arbitration. /Think of all kinds of procedures, /steps by which they can delay/or they create complications in the procedure. /

大多数仲裁程序，/从国际上来看，/都需要时间，/时间通常很长，/有的一年,/有的两年,/有的三年。/这就是实际情况,/您通常会看到这种情况/出现在国际仲裁中。/这样并不好。/这样不好,/用户也在抱怨。/如果找原因,/为什么存在拖延,/为什么存在抱怨。/我们会发现有各种抱怨的缘由。/一个是当事人/和他们的律师。/他们都很忙,/他们都需要时间/收集案件,/立案,/召集每个人,/准备提交书面文件。/所有这些都需要时间。/我曾经接过很多案子,/申请人都需要好几个月来准备。/有一个案子/甚至要一年来准备,/当然这也是一点。/同样地,/这是第一点,/另外一点是/案件越来越复杂,/包括复杂的项目、复杂的交易/以及一大群涉案人员。/然后/仲裁庭也需要时间。/其中一点/我们会讲到,/马上会讲到的一点。/组成法庭/在仲裁庭组成之前/也需要时间。/您需要启动程序,/选择仲裁员。/首先,/申请人有一个月的时间/选择仲裁员。/接着,/被申请人也要一个月时间,/然后他们要就首席仲裁员达成一致,/这也需要一个月,/甚至更久。/有时/争端问题/可能存在于公司之间,/或者利益冲突/仲裁员的利益冲突/会延缓程序。/然后就是程序本身,/您需要确定日期,/选择每个人都合适的日期,/仲裁裁决,/仲裁员接着要作出裁决,/这些都要准备好,/也都需要时间。/另外一点/就是程序问题。/越来越多的律师/参与仲裁。/想想所有的程序,/每个步骤都会拖延仲裁程序/或者让仲裁程序更复杂。/

06:43—08:06

Now the question is, /can this, /sorry, /can this be remedied? /What can be done about it? /There are many attempts/in different institutions/either individually by arbitrators or by parties, /by the discussions in international forum. /But there are often, /one of the things/that is becoming very frequent/are the guidelines/and other takes of soft law. /There are many takes/which you will find/and they create now some sort of a thicket of different, /not really rules, /but guidelines/which may or may not be followed/but often followed. /In fact, /I have read a paper/about the guidelines/for the preparation of guidelines. /And the one thing's/that these are being followed. /There is another document/which is very useful in this respect. /That's what we have prepared, /UNCITRAL, /the United Nations Commission for International Trade Law, /where we have provided the notes/on organizing arbitral proceedings, /which assist parties/and arbitrators/in finding the most suitable method/and the most suitable solution/to the differences. /

现在问题是,/这个,/不好意思,/这可以补救吗?/可以做些什么?/已经有了很多尝试,/不同的仲裁机构/无论是仲裁员个人还是当事人/都在国际论坛上讨论这个问题。/但是通常,/有一件事/频繁出现/也就是指南/和对软法的其他看法。/有很多看法/您会发现/它们会形成某种错综复杂的分歧,/不一定是规则,/而指南/可能会也可能不会被遵循,/但是通常还是会被遵循的。/其实,/我读过一篇论文，/讲的是指南，/如何准备指南。/有一点就是说/指南是被遵守的。/另外一篇文献/在这个方面非常有用。/就是我们已经准备的东西，/UNCITRAL，/联合国国际贸易法委员会，/我们向它提供了注释，/解释了如何组织仲裁程序，/这可以帮助当事人/和仲裁员/找到最合适的方法/和最合适的解决方案/来解决分歧。/

08:06—10:06

Now, /the subject/which I wanted to address before you today/are attempts/to solve the problem by rules, /attempts by international arbitration institutions/but to follow the problem/and find solutions. /And I have prepared a comparative analysis/of these different organizations/which you will find on the screen. /I understand/that this is being distributed/how different rules of these organizations/are set up/in order to assist the parties/in organizing the procedure/or finding solutions/to the question of speed. /You see/it is a raw range/from the International Chamber of Commerce in Paris, /from the LCIA in London, /from the SCC in Stockholm, /the CIETAC also has addressed the issue/in its rules. /Singapore has addressed it/and since we have the distinguished representatives/also from Hong Kong. /We also included in the study/the Hong Kong International Arbitration. /It's not commission, /sorry/there is a spelling mistake. /Hong Kong International Arbitration Center. /So the Deutsche Institution, /the Swiss Chambers, /and the American ICDR, /all of these, /we have looked at/and in finding the possible steps/which have been taken/in order to resolve the question. /We found/there are two stages. /One is to accelerate the process/until the arbitration tribunal is operative, /because as I explained before/it takes often a long time/until the arbitration tribunal is operative. /

现在, /主题/我今天想谈论的主题/就是做很多尝试/通过规则来解决问题的尝试, /通过国际仲裁机构的尝试, /但是会紧扣这个问题, /找到解决办法。/我准备了对比分析, /分析不同的仲裁机构/也就是你们在屏幕上看到的这些仲裁机构。/我知道/机构的排序, /根据它们不同的规则, /是如何规定来排序的, /只为帮助当事人/安排好程序/或找到解决方法/来解决耗时问题。/您看/这是原始的排序, /从巴黎的国际商会仲裁院、/伦敦国际仲裁院、/斯德哥尔摩商会仲裁院, /中国国际经济贸易仲裁委员会也解决了这个问题, /在规则中有说明。/新加坡也解决了。/因为我们也有尊敬的代表/是来自香港的, /所以我们也在这个研究中/加入了香港国际仲裁中心。/它不是委员会, /不好意思, /这里有个拼写错误。/是香港国际仲裁中心。/德国仲裁协会、/瑞士商会仲裁院/和美国国际争议解决中心, /所有这些/我们看到的, /都在寻找可能的方法, /这些方法已经采用, /只为解决这个问题。/我们发现/有两个阶段。/一是加速程序/直到仲裁庭可以运作, /因为我之前提到过/需要很长的时间/来使仲裁庭运作。/

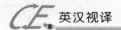

10:07—10:48

And then/how you can accelerate the arbitration/during the procedure. /Now, /with respect to the steps that can be taken before the arbitration commences, /there are two possibilities. /On the one hand, /the process of forming the tribunal can be accelerated. /We will find a few examples. /And the other/is to provide a special mechanism, /a special arbitrator/to cover the need/for urgent arbitration, /for urgent measures/during the time until the tribunal is operative. /

那么/如何加速仲裁/在仲裁过程中？/现在，/考虑到在仲裁启动之前可以采取的方法，/有两个可能性。/一方面，/组成仲裁庭的程序可以加速。/我们会举几个例子。/另一方面/是提供特殊的机制，/也就是特殊的仲裁员/来满足需求/进行紧急仲裁，/作为紧急措施/在仲裁庭运作之前使用。/

10:48—13:13

So I start with this second, /sorry there, /yes, /to start with the formation of the tribunal. /You will find/in this document/that is being distributed, /there is comparative analysis. /They are several steps/that the institutions take. /One thing is to shorten the time limits/to take away the long period/which I have described before/where you have three months/or even longer/until you have the tribunal. /So the periods can be shortened. /Often/you will find a mechanism/for shortening the formation of the tribunal, /a simpler solution. /You say, /not three arbitrators, /but one, /and then there is a discussion/in the international arbitration community/which says the simpler way/is that the tribunal should not be appointed by the parties, /but by the institution. /Now, with all respect I have/for the institution, /I think/this is a step in the wrong direction. /It's an essential element of arbitration/that the parties have the right to appoint their arbitrators/that can be modified, /that can be from a list, /or free/but then even the parties/should have a person on the tribunal/in whom they have confidence, /whom they have appointed, /so the idea of setting up, of taking the possibility of appointing arbitrators/away from the parties/is in my opinion, /not a good idea, /even the question of reducing arbitrators in complicated cases/is important, /but there are plurality of people/on the tribunal/who can look at the different aspects, /can discuss among each other/different solutions/and how best to resolve the case. /Now these are possibilities/in the acceleration of forming the tribunal. /

从第二点开始，/抱歉，是这里，/是的，/从仲裁庭的组成开始。/您会发现/在这份文件中/列举了/对比分析。/这些是措施/仲裁机构可以采取。/一是缩短时限/减少时间长度，/这我之前已经解释了，/您需要三个月/甚至更长时间/才能组成仲裁庭。/这段时间可以缩短。/通常/您可以找到机制/用来缩短组成仲裁庭的时

第八单元 商事仲裁 Commercial Arbitration

间,/这是更简单的方法。/您会说,/不用三个仲裁员,/一个就可以了,/然后就开始讨论了,/国际仲裁界一起讨论,/讨论的结果说,简单一点的方法/就是仲裁庭不应该由当事人指定,/而应该由仲裁机构指定。/我很尊重/仲裁机构,/但我认为/这一步的方向是错误的。/它是仲裁中非常重要的一部分,/当事人有权指定自己的仲裁员/也可以调整仲裁员,/可以从名册中选,/也可以自由选择,/但是至少当事人/应该在仲裁庭里有自己选定的人,/有他们信任的人,/他们指定的人。/所以将选择仲裁员的机会/从当事人那里剥夺了,/我认为/这个主意并不好,/哪怕减少仲裁员在复杂案件中的人数/很重要,/但是多一些仲裁员/组成仲裁庭/可以从不同的角度看问题,/可以彼此讨论/不同的解决方法,/讨论处理案件的最佳做法。/这些都可以/加快仲裁庭的组成。/

13:13—15:27

Sometimes/that works well/and tribunals have been formed much faster. /But still, /it doesn't resolve one of the main problems/that is conflicts of interests, /a growing problem/that arbitrators in their prior activity/or in parallel activities/have links with one/or the other parties. /And the gowns for challenging arbitrators/have continuously increased, /so/there is only limited possibility in accelerating. /In other words, /what is necessary/is the emergency arbitrator. /And in the last 10, 20 years, /many institutions have picked up this idea/of creating an arbitrator specifically/for the period/when the dispute arises/and when the arbitral tribunal/which finally will solve the dispute/has been constituted. /So/this procedure of emergency arbitrator/you will find it in the rules/of quite a number of institutions/and the procedure there is/that the appointment generally is made by the institution/and often quickly, /the ICC, for instance, /says the emergency arbitrator must be appointed/in a matter of two days. /So this is very quickly. /The procedure itself is simplified/often on documents only. /Sometimes/a party or both parties/can request a hearing, /but that is the exception. /Time limits are shortened/both for the submissions. /That is to say/parties have only a very short period/to make their submissions/for the decision of the arbitral referee, /of the emergency arbitrator. /You see/the SIAC coincidence allows them to sit there/at the end of the procedure. /A decision must be made, /and the period for this decision also often is very short. /SIAC coincidence has 14 days. /

有时/这非常有效,/仲裁庭的组成快多了。/但是/这依然没有解决其中一个主要的问题,/也就是利益冲突的问题,/这个问题越来越普遍,/仲裁员在他们先前的活动/或平行活动中/与一个/或者另一个当事人有联系。/法官质疑仲裁员的事件/不断增多,/因此/加速的可能是有限的。/换言之,/必要的/是设立紧急仲裁员。/过去一二十年里,/许多仲裁机构采用了这个方法,/设立专门的仲裁员,/这

181

个时间段是/从争端出现/到仲裁法庭/最后解决争端的仲裁法庭/组成为止。/因此,/紧急仲裁员程序/您会发现规则中有写明/相当多的仲裁机构的规则中都有,/程序规定了/仲裁员通常由仲裁机构指定,/也通常更快,/比如国际商会仲裁院/规定了紧急仲裁员指定的时间/为两天以内。/因此速度非常快。/程序本身也可以简化,/书面审理即可。/有时/一方当事人或双方当事人/可以请求开庭审理,/但这是一个例外。/时限缩短/提交书面文件的时间也缩短了。/也就是说,/当事人只有非常短的时间/来准备提交的书面文件、协助仲裁员作出决定,/帮助紧急仲裁员作决定。/您看/新加坡国际仲裁中心就刚好允许他们一直工作/到仲裁程序结束。/决定是必须要做的,/决定时间通常也非常短。/新加坡国际仲裁中心刚好有14天。/

15:27—16:53

The other element is/that the emergency arbitrator has powers/only for a limited period. /And once the tribunal itself is constituted and operative, /his powers or her powers cease. /And the decision of the emergency arbitrator/can be with summary reasons. /There is also the right of going to court in parallel. /It's preserved/like in most arbitration institutions. /Now, /the decision itself can take an order/or an award. /It's often not quite clear/what the rules make as the ground/for the distinction between order and award. /Normally, /an order should be something/that can be revisited, /whereas an award is final/and can be enforced/under the *New York Convention*/or other institutions. /The understanding generally for this decision is/that it is a decision on interim measures. /Like the arbitrators themselves/can make decisions on interim measures, /the emergency arbitrator/also can make such interim decisions. /The decision itself is binding on the parties, /so the parties must comply with it. /But the following tribunal that is then set up/can revisit the decision/and modify it. /

另外一点就是/紧急仲裁员的权力/只在有限时间内有效。/一旦仲裁庭组成并投入运作,/仲裁员的权力失效。/紧急仲裁员的决定/可以附带简明的理由。/也有权到法院提起诉讼。/该权利得到保留/大多数仲裁机构都是如此。/现在,/决定本身就是一项命令/或者是仲裁裁决。/通常不太清楚的是/规则是依据什么/来区分命令和仲裁裁决。/通常,/一项命令/应该是可以修改的,/而仲裁裁决是终局的,/可以执行的/可以依据《纽约公约》/或其他仲裁机构执行。/决定通常是这样理解的,/它只是关于临时措施的命令。/就像仲裁员一样,/他们可以就临时措施做决定,/紧急仲裁员/也可以做出临时决定。/决定本身对当事人具有约束力,/所以当事人必须遵守。/但是接下来组成的仲裁庭/可以重审决定/并作出修改。/

第八单元　商事仲裁 Commercial Arbitration

16:53—18:53

Now, /the final step in the procedure/for accelerating/is to go to the arbitration itself, /to provide expedited arbitration/as it is often called. /That is to say/to see how the arbitration can be faster. /Now, /many institutions provide a financial threshold. /That is to say/disputes below a certain amount/automatically go to the expedited procedure. /You will see/the amounts vary. /They can be for the ICC/two million US dollars, /for the ICDR, /the American institution, /it is as low as 250,000 dollars. /SIAC has six million Singapore dollars, /and Hong Kong has 12 million Hong Kong dollars. /So you see/there is a threshold/below that amount, /the mechanism automatically applies. /There's a possibility of opting out. /All the parties can agree/that they want their arbitration to be conducted in this manner. /Normally, /you have a sole arbitrator/to address the dispute. /Then/you have shorter time limits/for the procedural steps/and for the award also, /there are short periods. /Now six months in the ICC, /others three month. /Now that's what I said this morning, /what I learnt this morning, /when in China, /these periods, /six month/or three month, /even are not accelerated procedure. /I understand/that it's a normal procedure. /So/that's why I said/these procedures/or these attempts/are of limited interest here. /

现在，/程序中的最后一步/用来加速的/就是仲裁本身，/简易仲裁程序，/这是通常的叫法。/也就是说，/要看仲裁如何加速。/现在，/很多仲裁机构设下了金额门槛。/也就是说，/争议金额在一定数量之下/会自动进入简易仲裁程序。/可以看到/数额是不同的。/对国际商会仲裁院来说，/可以是200万美金，/对国际争议解决中心，/美国的这个仲裁机构来说，/可以低至25万美金。/新加坡国际仲裁中心定的是600万新加坡元，/香港定的是1,200万港币。/可以看到/这里有一个门槛，/在门槛金额以下，/这个机制自动适用。/也可以选择排除适用。/所有当事人可以一致同意/希望他们的仲裁以这种方式来进行。/通常，/由独任仲裁员/来解决争端。/然后/您有更短的时限/来走程序，/对于仲裁裁决，/作出的时间也很短。/现在，国际商会仲裁院需要6个月，/其他的要3个月。/这就是我今天上午所说的，/也是今天上午我了解到的，/在中国，/这些时长，/6个月/或3个月/根本不算是加速程序。/我了解到/这是正常程序。/因此，/这就是为什么我说/这些程序/或这些尝试/对中国的借鉴作用不大。/

18:53—20:33

Now, /there are other restrictions/on the procedure, /sometimes/documents only, /sometimes/no hearing/or hearing only when agreed, /and the reasons can often be summary. /Now, /these are the mechanical forms, /the rules/which the institutions have provided. /But basically, /they solve all the problem/only in part. /Because they

183

are more or less mechanic, /they don't really address the real problems/that have caused the delay/which I have mentioned in the beginning. /There are other means, /there are attempts/or discussions/that the parties should be limited in their budget, /how much they spend in the arbitration. /That is very disputed/because it has a relation with the parties' right to be heard, /to represent their case. /So/that is not a very much appreciated solution. /There is one thing/which is in particular the ICC applies, /that is to cut the fees of the arbitrators. /If they take more than two months, /their fees are reduced. /That is a powerful means. /But it is often unfair/depending on the circumstances. /Sometimes/there are problems/within the tribunal, /sometimes/the case is very complicated. /For the arrangement/and to find a solution/sometimes, /you have diverging views in the tribunal, /so/that is also of limited effect. /

现在, /有其他限制/出现在程序中, /有时/只采用书面审理, /有时/不开庭审理, /或者同意才开庭, /理由通常都很简洁。/现在, /这些都是呆板的形式, /这些规则/是仲裁机构设立的。/但基本上, /它们解决了所有问题/的一部分而已。/因为它们有点死板, /没有真正解决实际问题/引起延迟的问题, /这是我一开始说到的。/也有其他方法, /也有尝试/或者讨论, /当事人应该被限制预算, /限制花在仲裁上的金额。/这非常有争议, /因为它涉及到当事人申辩的权利, /阐述案情的机会。/所以/这不是个非常好的解决办法。/有一个方法, /是国际商会仲裁院运用的, /就是减少仲裁员酬金。/如果仲裁员花了两个月以上的时间, /他们的报酬就会减少。/这是一个强有力的方法。/但通常是不公平的, /因为要视情况而定。/有时/问题/也出现在仲裁庭内部, /有时/案件非常复杂。/为了安排好, /找到解决办法, /有时/仲裁庭会出现不同的观点, /因此/这个效果也是有限的。/

20:33—21:33

Another possible approach/is the efficient organization of the procedure. /And here in particular what I call/the interactive arbitrator/who discusses with the parties, /assists them in focusing on the dispute, /so that there is not a waste of time, /and documents and witnesses on all kinds of issues/but concentrated on the issues. /And I understand/that this is something that is very much practiced in China/in particular/in the relationship with the attempts of the arbitrators/to resolve the dispute/by settlement, /to bring the parties together, /lead them to a settlement. /So/my conclusion on this issue/of seeking to improve efficiency and speed in arbitration/is [to] follow the Chinese example. /Thank you! /

另一个可能的方法/是高效组织程序。/这里我特别称为/高度配合的仲裁员, /他和当事人讨论, /帮助他们关注争议的焦点, /这样就不会浪费时间, /浪费文书和证人处理各种问题, /而是关注争议焦点。/我了解到/这个在中国已经很好地实施

第八单元　商事仲裁 Commercial Arbitration

了，/尤其/与仲裁员付出的努力有关，/他们努力解决争端，/通过和解，/让当事人聚在一起，/让他们达成和解。/所以，/我对这个问题的结论，/关于如何提高仲裁效率和速度，/我的结论是：可以向中国学习。/谢谢。/

第九单元 时尚潮流
Fashion Trend

I. 实战练习一

1. 演讲背景

2014年11月1日,在线时尚潮流预测公司Fashion Snoops的亚太区总监应邀参加广交会设计潮流趋势研讨会,发布2015—2016秋冬女装时尚趋势。下文摘自其中一个主题的内容"工匠之旅",他在演讲中详细介绍了该主题产生的背景、色系、材料、印花图案、设计细节、重要单品。演讲的部分内容抽象难懂。

2. 预习词汇

Artisan Journey 工匠之旅
Bloomsbury quarter 布鲁姆伯利居住区
intellectual 知识分子
Virginia Woolf 弗吉尼亚·伍尔夫
E. M. Forster E. M. 福斯特
John Maynard Keynes 约翰·梅纳德·凯恩斯
needlepoint 刺绣
hand-drawn flower 手绘花卉
mix and match 混搭
chiffon 雪纺
ruffle 褶边;褶裥
hand-painted floral 手绘花卉
flowing midi dress 飘逸的中长裙
prints & patterns 印花图案
pine 松绿色
burgundy 暗紫红色;酒红色;勃艮第
maroon 紫褐色;栗色
burnt orange 深橙黄色
copper 古铜色

mauve 淡紫色；木槿紫
pale pink 浅粉色
mushroom 蘑菇色
look 造型
mid-calf dress 中长裙（及小腿肚）
elongated shirt 长款衬衫
shearling outerwear 羊毛外套
shearling jacket 羊毛夹克
lace 蕾丝
jacquard 提花织布
wool felt 羊毛毡
astrakhan 阿斯特拉罕羔羊皮
mohair 马海毛
Duncan Grant 邓肯·格兰特（英国画家）
Vanessa Bell 瓦内莎·贝尔（英国画家）
William Morris 威廉·莫里斯
asymmetrical/asymmetric line 不规则线条
thigh high slit 高开叉
floral embroidery 花卉刺绣
mixed media 混合拼接
styling 款式
asymmetric blanket coat 不规则毛料大衣
sheaf dress/sheath dress 紧身连衣裙
belted blanket coat 束腰毛料大衣
knit blanket coat 针织毛料大衣
outerwear 外衣
key item 重要单品
kimono sleeve 和服袖
turtleneck sweater 高领毛衣
yarn 纱；线
intarsia 嵌花
shawl collar 青果领
self belt 同料腰带
hemline 裙摆
peasant blouse 村姑衫
style guide 款式指南

3. 演讲文本

00:00—02:03

The next theme that we have for Contemporary Women's/we've called Artisan Journey, /and this is really a great story. /This is a story/that we've set in the Bloomsbury quarter of London. /It's really inspired/by the literary society of intellectuals/like authors sort of around the 20s. /The Bloomsbury set was very much dominating society in London/authors like Virginia Woolf/and E. M. Forster, /economists like John Maynard Keynes. /Immersed in a wall of books, /the Artisan Journey woman/appreciates arts and crafts/along with delicate nature, /both with surface in her humble quarters. /From needlepoint/to hand-drawn flowers, /a shabby chic interior. /That's really best represented by the main part of the furniture. /It's a very sort of shabby chic interior. /It's very sort of handmade/a bit mix and match. /This is the environment/that is ideal to craft her latest novel/with daylight pouring in, /while by night/all the mismatched elements cultivate an undeniable warm aesthetic. /Really again this is another theme/that sort of plays into that need/for us to feel safe, /warm/and cocoon in our own homes. /Though soft and romantic, /there's much more depth to this story/than chiffon and ruffles. /This really is the main theme this season/ where you can really explore the notion of romance/in your collections sort of hand-painted florals/and needlepoint progress/that sort of feminine aesthetic with a new reference point. /Always a lady in flowing midi dresses, /the Artisan Journey woman/ crafts her look with homespun elements/that appeal to her cozy nature/and her romantic femininity. /

当代女装的下个主题是/"工匠之旅", /这个主题故事超赞。/该主题/以布鲁姆斯伯利居住区为背景, /灵感源于/知识分子组成的文人社区/例如上世纪20年代的作家等。/布鲁姆伯利派是伦敦的主流社区, /作家有弗吉尼西·伍尔夫、/E. M. 福斯特, /经济学家有约翰·梅纳德·凯恩斯。/沉浸于书的海洋之中, /代表"工匠之旅"的女性/既能欣赏工艺品, /又能领会自然的精妙, /这在她的住处中也有体现。/从刺绣/到手绘花, /内饰虽显陈旧却不掩别致。/家具更能体现这一点, /陈旧而别致, /颇有手工质感/有点混搭风格。/这种环境/是理想的的小说创作环境, /日光洒进房间, /夜间/所有混搭的元素营造出一种不可否认的温暖美感。/这是另一个主题/强调需求/我们祈求安全感、/温暖/和家庭给我们的呵护。/尽管柔软和浪漫, /但这个主题的深度/不止雪纺和褶边。/这是本季的重要主题, /您可以尽情探索浪漫的概念, /应用到系列时装的手绘花/或刺绣的工艺进展中, /用新视角来探寻女性审美观。/总是穿着飘逸的中长裙/"工匠之旅"女性, /用简朴的元素来装扮自己, /这些元素契合其追求舒适的天性/和浪漫的女性主义。/

02:03—03:44

For those of you who saw my seminar last season,/you might remember/we had one theme/which was very much inspired/by the Spring14 Chanel collection/that was very bright,/very colorful,/lots of brushstrokes./This is basically that/the fall-winter continuation of that particular theme/as you saw there./So here is your colour palette for Artisan Journey./It is really a nice wide range of colors,/it's really eclectic/and it's definitely something/that we intended to be used/with prints & patterns./But what's really nice here is the Green base,/which we have at the top with Pine/as well as the on the bottom with based tone/like Burgundy/or Maroon colour./This nice combination of Burnt Orange,/Golden/and Copper towards the bottom/and that's really nice/to sort of incorporate that sort of vintage./Remember we set this theme/in 1920s London/in the Bloomsbury quarter,/so that's definitely a very retro vibe/to this particular theme./Those Burnt Oranges,/your Golds/and your Coppers/are really playing to that./Then in the middle/you have your soft colours/which are a little bit more unexpected,/but it speaks more to that sort of delicate romance/of Virginia Woolf/or E. M. Forster,/things like Mauve,/Pale Pink/and right in the middle/your Mushroom/as a really nice new base tone./

如果在上一季听过我的研讨会,/您可能会记得/我们有一个主题,/灵感源于/香奈儿2014年春装系列,/那个系列明亮、/多彩,/线条丰富。/基本上,/"工匠之旅"就是那个主题在秋冬季节的延续,/您在那边可以看到。/这是"工匠之旅"的色系。/颜色丰富,/色彩调和,/非常适合/搭配/各种印花图案。/但最美的还是绿色系,/最上方有松绿色,/最下方有基色/如酒红色/和紫褐色等。/颜色组合中包含了深橙黄色、/金色/和下方的古铜色,/动人至极,/带来复古情调。/别忘了我们的主题背景是/20世纪20年代伦敦/布鲁姆斯伯利居住区,/这绝对营造了一种复古的氛围,/非常适合这个主题。/深橙黄色、/金色/和古铜色/确实能够带来复古的感觉。/色系中间部分/展示了一些柔和色彩,/出乎人意料之外的颜色,/这恰好印证了精致浪漫/弗吉尼亚·沃尔夫/或E. M. 福斯特的浪漫,/如淡紫色/和浅粉色,/以及正中间的/蘑菇色,/一种新的基色。/

03:44—04:08

So here you have your color usage./Again the colors in this particular theme/should be used sort of/from opposite side of the color wheel./For those of you who know color theory,/it's really quite a clash of colors,/really to hide that effect/of being eclectic range of colors./

这里有各种颜色的用法。/本主题的颜色/使用的时候/可以不遵循色轮规律。/对于了解色彩理论的人而言,/这个主题体现了撞色,/隐藏了色彩效果,/色彩其

实是五颜六色的。/

04:08—04:50
So the Look for Artisan Journey, /it really is defined by that dress, /that very feminine mid-calf dress or skirt. /We're really seeing that sort of mid-calf dress/or an elongated shirt/layered look with Shearling Outerwear, /the Shearling Jacket there/ belted at the waist/for a little bit more of a composed look. /The really key thing about this/is really the Prints. /The Prints are really important here, /so we're seeing that across not just in your garment/but into your accessories as well, /whether that be on your footwear, /your bags/or on your scarf. /

这是"工匠之旅"的造型, /多为连衣裙, /或富有女人味的中长裙或短裙。/我们可以看到这种中长裙, /或者长款衬衫, /搭配羊毛外套, /或那款羊毛夹克, /配备腰带/让整个装扮更加沉稳。/更关键之处在于/印花, /印花真的非常重要。/所以我们不仅关注服装的印花, /还关注配饰上的图案, /无论是鞋袜、/包包/或是围巾。/

04:50—05:31
So looking at your materials for Artisan Journey/and this is really rooted in this notion of delicate romance, /when you look at the base materials, /romantic materials at No. 4, /you have your Chiffon; /No. 9, you have your Lace/to create that really sense of romance. /But it's sort of a novelty aspect/coming through Jacquards/or Needlepoint techniques. /The cozy notion that is so important this season. /You have in your Wool Felt at No. 1; /your Astrakhan at No. 2/and your Mohair at No. 3. /

接下来是"工匠之旅"的材料, /本主题的材料选用植根于精致浪漫的概念。/看看这些基本材料, /浪漫的材料如4号/雪纺, /9号的蕾丝/营造浪漫感。/此外还有新奇的材质, /如提花织布/和刺绣技术。/舒适的概念在本季尤为重要。/1号有羊毛毡, /2号有阿斯特拉罕羔羊皮, /3号有马海毛。/

05:31—06:32
But really this is the most important slide for this theme. /This is really the key slide/because prints and patterns/are really really essential to this theme. /It's really a print driven theme. /How you execute this particular theme really really well/is to look for prints/from around that particular time period of 1920s London. /Maybe what you see here/No. 1, Duncan Grant; /No. 3, Vanessa Bell, /No. 5, of course you see some William Morris flowers, /so you bring in the sort of English artists, /their prints from the 1920s/to really create that sense of authenticity to your look. /The interesting one that I really like/is maybe using the arts/from book covers from the 1920s, /again

第九单元 时尚潮流 Fashion Trend

elevating your prints and patterns/to something a little bit more authentic. /

这张幻灯片为本主题的重中之重, /非常关键的一页/因为印花图案/对于本主题不可或缺。/这是一个以印花为导向的主题。/想要把握好这个主题, /就要寻找印花设计/20世纪20年代伦敦流行的印花。/这里您可以看到, /1号有邓肯·格兰特, /3号有瓦内莎·贝尔, /5号有威廉·莫里斯画笔下的花。/这都是著名的英国艺术家, /他们在20世纪20年代创作的印花/让您的造型更具真实感。/我最喜欢的是/图案/20世纪20年代书皮上的图案, /能提升印花的档次, /让其更具真实感。/

06:32—07:51

Your design details are here, /keeping in mind/that sort of very fluid mid-calf silhouette/that I was talking about. /Some of your updates/could include things like No. 7, Asymmetrical Lines, /or even a thigh high slit/which you would see at No. 3, /which would be a really nice update/to your mid-calf dress silhouette. /The whole idea of romance/comes to the forefront/with things such as Floral Embroidery/which you see at No. 2; /our Ruffles which you see at No. 8, /or for a bit more a novelty piece at No. 5, /again something that's been going for a few seasons/are Mixed Media wears. /You are mixing your prints/or your materials/to really create that effect. /Looking at your shape/or your styling, /you see here, /Blanket Layers. /So you see Asymmetric Blanket Coat/dress with the Sheath Dress, /Belted Blanket Coat, /Knit Blanket. /Again noticing all these pictures, /one in two, /that mid-calf silhouette, /that's all important. /Again that sense of layering, /that sense of comfort, /that's all important this season. /

这里是设计细节, /别忘了/线条流畅的中长裙廓形/我刚才也提到过的。/如果想增添亮点, /可以考虑7号的不规则线条, /或高开叉设计, /如3号一样, /这些亮点非常迷人/让裙子的轮廓更加动人。/浪漫感/可以来自于/花卉刺绣, /如2号所示, /8号的褶边, /5号新颖的元素, /这是风靡了好几个时装季的/混合拼接。/您可以搭配印花/或材料/来打造混合拼接效果。/再看形状/和款式, /这边/比如毛料款。/这有不规则毛料大衣/搭配紧身连衣裙, /还有束腰毛料大衣/和针织毛料大衣。/我想就这些图片再次告诉大家, /简而言之, /中长廓形, /非常重要。/层次感, /舒适感, /也是本季的重点。/

07:51—08:39

So the Key Items that we're looking at here/in terms of Outerwear, /going back to the left hand side/to the Blanket Coat. /It's really essential here in this particular theme/to have the asymmetrical lines here. /Kimono sleeves that you see on that silhouette/

help to illustrate that notion of blanket outerwear. /Also can allow you for your layering options as well. /Also the Turtleneck Sweater comes in here. /It's really relevant maybe with things/such as loose yarns or Intarsia. /Quilting on the quilted jackets/again little bit like a man's smoking jacket/maybe with a shawl collar/or self-belt/to make it a little bit more feminine. /

这个主题的重要单品/是外衣,也就是左手边的/毛料大衣。本主题的关键是/添加不规则线条。/服装廓形中的和服袖/有助于体现毛料大衣的概念,/也能提供更多层次设计的选择。/接下来是高领毛衣,/与之相关的是/宽松纱线或嵌花。/绗缝夹克上的针法/有点像男士吸烟装,/加上青果领/或同料腰带/会显得更有女人味一些。/

08:39—09:08

Also more key items on this page, /we see again the middy skirt, /or the mid-calf skirt, /with more traditional layered hemline here. /It's very important to keep this trend really…very feminine. /You see that through the Peasant Blouse. /Again a great piece of Peasant Blouse for you/to play with your prints and patterns/to bring in the sense of 20s and romance. /

这页提供了更多的重要单品,/如水手裙,/还有中长裙,/多数都是传统的多层裙摆。/保持本主题的女性化是非常重要的。/我们可以从村姑衫中看出这一点。/村姑衫的美妙设计/和印花图案一道,/给您带来上世纪20年代的风味和浪漫感。/

09:08—09:36

Wrapping up our very quick walk through/for Contemporary Womenswear for Autumn/Winter 2015 - 2016, /this is the Style Guide for Artisan Journey. /Again, /we're really personifying the lives/of Virginia Woolf/and E. M. Forster/and William Morris/from the 1920s. /Bloomsbury sets are very flow, /are very romantic, /eclectic color base. /

总结一下我们快速讲解过的/2015—2016秋冬当代女装潮流趋势,/来关注一下"工匠之旅"的款式指南。/再次说明,/我们想还原那个时代的风格/弗吉尼亚·伍沃尔、/E. M. 福斯特/以及威廉·莫里斯/20世纪20年代的风格。/布鲁姆伯斯利风格既飘逸,/又浪漫,/色彩也十分调和。/

II. 实战练习二

1. 演讲背景

下文同样摘自"广交会设计潮流趋势研讨会",演讲嘉宾介绍了时尚潮流趋势

"土著领地",他介绍了该主题产生的背景、色系、造型、材料、印花图案、设计细节、重要单品。演讲的部分内容同样抽象难懂。

2. 预习词汇

young casual women's wear 年轻休闲女装
Indigenous Territory 土著领地
color palette 色系
saturated garnet 深石榴红色
deep maroon shade 深紫红眼影
golden yellow 金黄色
rust orange 暗橘红色
earthy brown 土黄色
toast 烤土司色
copper 古铜色
teal 蓝绿色;水鸭色
steel blue 钢蓝色
oyster grey 米灰色
light lavender 浅薰衣草色
mauve 淡紫色;木槿紫
earth tone 褐土色(调),土色,茶色
intarsia knit 嵌花针织
plaid 格子呢
collection 系列时装
outerwear 外衣
brushed wool 拉绒
Mongolian Lamb 蒙古羔羊毛
shearling 绵羊皮毛
fur pelt 毛皮
mohair 马海毛
cable knit 麻花针织
rugged style 粗犷风格
suede 绒面革;仿麂皮
distressed leather 仿旧皮革
embroidered floral 绣花
folkloric 民间的
patchwork 拼布

paisley 涡纹花呢
landscape 风景图案
fringe 流苏
pom-pom 绒球
soft knit faux 柔软仿针织
rounded shoulder 圆肩
key item 重要单品
blanket coat 毛料大衣
French hem 法式褶边
double faced 双面布
mixed media 混合拼接
shearling lining 剪羊毛衬里
shearling vest 羊毛马甲
anorak 带风帽的厚夹克
sweatshirt 运动衫；卫衣
paperbag waist pants 抽绳式裤子
elongated sweater 长款毛衣

3. 演讲文本

00:00—00:13

So this is now/when we are moving into your Young Casual market, /of course, /you can certainly interpret this/into your contemporary Womenswear as well. /But the focus now/turns a little bit younger. /

现在/我们看看年轻休闲女装市场, /当然, /您也可以把它解读为/当代女装。/但目前关注的是/更年轻的女性。/

00:13—01:36

This is the first theme for the Young Casual market/which we've called Indigenous Territory. /With this story/are the stories behind this/is we're following a very cool tomboy, /who's studying abroad/and is discovering/and embracing nomadic cultures from the Arctic Circle. /So think of a young woman/who's quite adventurous. /Instead of going to Europe/or Australia/or somewhere abroad/to study, /she's decided/to go into the Arctic circle, /whether it be Scandinavia/or Siberia/or Mongolia/or Alaska, /are really quite a very northern focus/to this particular theme. /So this woman/she is awaken in this unfamiliar world/and she is immersed in unknown territory/populated by ancient tribal people. /Forced to adapt, /she lives in a yurt, /travels on foot/and

第九单元 时尚潮流 Fashion Trend

learns to thrive with these nomadic people. /She learns their craft/and incorporates their native form of dress/with her own rugged style. /So this is a modern city girl/going out with nomadic tribes/and incorporating that style/with her wardrobe. /

这是关于年轻休闲女装市场的第一个主题，/我们称之为"土著领地"。/这个故事/背后的故事是，/我们一直在关注的一个非常酷的假小子，/她正在海外留学，/她发现/并热爱北极圈的游牧文化。/这样一个年轻女性，/非常具有冒险精神。/她没有去欧洲、/澳大利亚/等国外/留学，/而是决定/去北极圈，/不管是去北欧、/西伯利亚、/蒙古/还是阿拉斯加，/北方特色/就是这个主题的特点。/这位女性/在这个陌生的世界中醒来，/沉浸在这片未知领地里，/这里居住着古老的部落居民。/她逼着自己去适应，/住在一个蒙古包里，/徒步旅行，/学着和这些游牧民族一起成长。/她学习他们的手艺，/并将他们的土著风格着装/和自己的粗犷风格相结合。/所以这是一个现代城市女孩的故事，/她与游牧部落一起旅行，/将他们的风格/与她的穿衣风格融合在一起。/

01:36—01:59

Here is the trend map of Indigenous Territory. /Really, /it's talking about a girl/who is exploring, /who's adventurous, /and when she finds her way home, /her style is forever changed/and it is much more exotic/and backed by that sort of life-changing cultural experience. /

这是"土著领地"的趋势图。/实际上，/这是一个女孩的故事，/她正在探险途中，/是一个爱冒险的女孩。/当她找到回家的路时，/她的穿着风格彻底改变了，/穿着更具异国情调，/因为那段改变人生的文化之旅。/

01:59—03:16

So looking at your color palette here for Indigenous Territory, /it's really a vibrant color palette, /but it's really centered around warmth. /So you are looking here for warmth. /You are looking at your Reds/in either sort of Saturated Garnet/or darker deeper Maroon shades, /also encapsulating the sort of Sun spirit, /with Golden Yellows, /Rust Orange. /Then obviously/for something quite sort of earthy outdoor, /a theme, /you have your earthy browns/which we use Toast/or Copper. /But because this is sort of that Arctic Circle, /very frozen world, /we've mixed in a lot of unexpected blues here. /So you have your Teal, /your Steel Blue/and looking at lighter colours towards your bottom/are all balanced out/by an Oyster Grey/or your light Lavender/or your Mauve. /So very much inspired by nature, /very much inspired/by countries in that Arctic Circle region, /but also bringing in a lot of your Reds, /your Browns, /your earth tones as well/to create that sense of warmth. /

这是"土著领地"的色系，/它确实是一个鲜艳的色系，/但它是以暖色为主，/所以您能在这里寻找温暖的感觉。/现在看看红色色系，/有些深石榴红色/或暗深紫红眼影。/还会吸收太阳的热情，/如金黄色/或暗橘红色。/很明显，/还有某些户外泥土的色调，/这个主题，/可以使用土黄色、烤土司色/或古铜色。/但因为这是北极圈，/极寒世界，/我们在这里混入了许多意想不到的蓝色。/蓝绿色，/钢蓝色。/再看看底部的较浅的颜色，/取得了平衡协调的效果，/有米灰色、/浅薰衣草色/和淡紫色。/"土著领地"的色系灵感源泉是大自然，/还有/北极圈地区国家，/同时也融合了许多红色、/棕色/和土色色系，/创造那种温暖的感觉。/

03:16—04:02

So this is the classic Look/for this tomboy of ours/who is going on this particular adventure. /Keeping in mind/that this is really a heavy look, /it's taking inspiration from indigenous women/from the Arctic Circle of what they would wear, /and then really piling on all your ethnic elements/that you could think of all your Nordic prints, /all your Intarsia Knits, /your Plaids, /Layers/and Oversized Shearling as Outerwear. /So it's sort of very chunky, /warm, /sort of…/this is your destination theme. /If you have a destination theme in your collection, /this would be the destination theme/for Autumn-winter 2015–2016. /

所以这是经典造型/我们假小子的造型，/她正经历着这次独特的冒险。/记住，/这真的是一种厚重的造型，/它从土著女性那里获得灵感，/从北极圈地区居民的服饰中获得灵感，/然后将所有民族元素真正堆砌起来，/这些元素就是能想到的各种北欧印花、/嵌花针织、/格子呢、/多层服饰/和大号的皮草外衣。/所以这种风格有很强的厚重感，/温暖，/还有些……/这就是目的地主题。/如果您的系列时装中有一个目的地主题，/这个主题适用于/2015—2016年秋冬季服饰。/

04:02—04:54

So in terms of your materials conversation here, /it is obviously/a really big outerwear theme. /So you are looking at materials/No. 1, /Brushed Wools, /No. 2, /your Mongolian Lambs, /your Shearling at No. 3/as well as bringing in that sort of animal aspect/at No. 8/with your Fur Pelts. /Then knit wear is also very important here, /so you have your Mohair Knit, /you have your Cable Kinit here as well/at No. 4 and 5. /Then that sort of rugged sensibility of this nomadic indigenous woman/making use of materials available for herself, /obviously/you have a lot of leather there as well, /so you have at No. 11, /your Suede Leather/or your Distressed Leather at No. 7. /

第九单元 时尚潮流 Fashion Trend

就材料而言，/显然/这个主题主打单品是外衣。/现在看到的这些材料，/1号，/拉绒，/2号，/蒙古羔羊毛，/3号，绵羊皮毛，/另外还会加入一些动物的元素，/如8号的/毛皮。/针织服饰在这里也非常重要，/如马海毛针织，/麻花针织/如4号和5号所示。/还有游牧民族的土著女性带来的那种粗犷感受力，/她们使用自己可获得的材料，/显然/也可以使用很多皮革材质，/如11号的/绒面革/或7号的仿旧皮革。/

04:54—05:49

The prints and patterns story for this particular theme/is very very diverse/because we're really sort of encircling the world/and looking at that sort of Arctic Circle region/and bringing in every sort of ethnic print that's available,/so you have things at No. 4,/your Embroidered Florals,/No. 5,/your Folkloric prints,/Patchwork at No. 8/to give that very sort of hand-crafty feel to it. /You have your Intarsia Knits at No. 9 again/for that Scandinavian influence. /But something might be a little bit unexpected/like Paisley/or Plaids. /Then really the No. 1/and No. 10/where you bring in the Landscape aspect of the Arctic Circle/either in photoreal/or in print. /

这个主题的印花图案/非常多样，/因为我们真的像在环绕世界，/在看北极风光，/并引入各种可行的民族图案，/所以4号的/绣花，/5号的/民间印花，/8号的拼布，/给人一种手工制作的感觉。/还有9号的嵌花针织，/受到斯堪的纳维亚风格的影响。/但有些材料有点出人意料，/像涡纹花呢/和格子呢。/还有在1号/或10号中/加入北极圈的风景图案，/可以是照片/或是印花。/

05:49—06:43

Your design details,/and really again with that sort of very hand-crafty DIY aesthetic,/so you're looking at things/such as No. 2,/your Fringe,/No. 4 your Patchwork/and No. 5,/your Pom-Poms. /Also sort of included here that would be very sort of again ethnic/is your quilting techniques, /either all over a garment/or as a detail. /Certainly embroidery/or something like a soft knit Faux. /So looking at your shape,/again you can see very much a layering theme/that goes with everything else in this particular season. /Again that important,/that sort of very rounded shoulder look/that we feel is very important/for Autumn-winter 2015 – 2016. /

这些设计细节，/再次体现了那种手工制作、独立设计的美感，/您正在寻找的/就是2号的/流苏、/4号的拼布/和5号的/绒球。/此外，设计中还包括一些民族元素，/即绗缝技术，/可以用于整件服装/或是某个细节。/当然还包括刺绣/或柔软仿针织。/看服饰的形状，/再次可以看到一个层次感很强的主题，/与本季其他主题相呼应。/再次强调，/这种圆肩装扮/我们认为很重要/对2015—2016年秋冬

时装而言非常重要。/

06:43—07:37

So in terms of your key items, /really has a very nomadic vibe to it. /Ranging from your Outerwear piece/such as your Blanket Coat/which is in the center, /it really appears much more ethnic/than you've seen in the past stories. /French hems, /Double-Faced details, /mixed media constructions, /Shearling Lining/which you see on the shearling vest/to bring in that sense of warmth, /that Arctic Circle feel. /There's a great item/that sort of incorporates any form of folkloric embroidery as well/on a vest. /This sweater dress of course recurs here. /Sweaters are very very important/for Autumn-winter 2015 – 2016. /Then in terms of your outerwear, /we have a different option for fall/which is your Anorak. /

下面的重要单品，/真的很有游牧的氛围。/外衣单品款式多样，/如毛料大衣，/在中间位置，/它看上去更具民族特色，/过去的单品中体现出的民族特色比较少。/法式褶边，/双面布，/混合拼接，/还有剪羊毛衬里，/可以在羊毛马甲上看到这款衬里，/它带给人温暖的感觉，/一种北极圈地区感受到的温暖。/还有一件很棒的单品/可以融入任何形式的民俗刺绣，/那是一件马甲。/这件毛衣连衣裙在这里也再次呈现。/毛衣非常重要/对于2015—2016年秋冬季而言。/就外衣单品而言，/我们有一件别样的单品供秋季选择，/就是这件带风帽的厚夹克。/

07:37—08:24

Some other things here you could consider of your collections/are your basic modified sweatshirt, /definitely very important piece of sweatshirt/in the young women's market, /but of course/you can bring in your, /bring it into this particular theme/by adding some embroidery, /your folkloric elements, /whether it be on the collar/or elsewhere on the piece. /The paperbag waist pants, /and your knit pants/are two very very important looks for the season/as well as your again elongated sweater/which allows for layering. /So here is your Style Guide for Indigenous Territory. /

系列中的其他考虑是/打底运动衫，/这是非常重要的一件运动衫/对于年轻休闲女装市场来说。/当然/您可以引入……/在这个特别的主题中/加入一些刺绣元素，/一些民俗元素，/加在衣领上/或其他地方。/抽绳式裤子/和针织裤子/是本季两种非常重要的造型，/还有长款毛衣，/加强层次感。/接下来是"土著领地"的款式指南。/

第十单元 绿色建筑
Green Building

I. 实战练习一

1. 演讲背景

英国对华可持续城镇化事务特使应邀出席 2016 年中英建筑论坛（珠海站）并发表开幕致辞。他在致辞中指出，未来十年将是中英关系的"黄金十年"，英国将利用其在工业化和城镇化过程中积累的丰富经验帮助中国实现可持续发展的城镇化，并列举了许多英国建筑设计公司在中国参与设计的绿色地标性建筑。

2. 预习词汇

UK Envoy for Sustainable Urbanization 英国对华可持续城镇化事务特使
National New Type Urbanization Plan《国家新型城镇化规划》
National Livable Cities Program《国家宜居城市项目》
urban sprawl 城市无序扩张
Beijing Capital Airport 北京首都机场
Olympic Bird's Nest Stadium 鸟巢
Guangzhou International Financial Center 广州国际金融中心
Hong Kong-Zhuhai-Macau Bridge 港珠澳大桥
Hengqin International Financial Center 横琴国际金融中心
Guangdong-Macau Traditional Chinese Medicine Park 粤澳中医药科技产业园区
Huarong Hengqin Tower 华融横琴大厦
Bartlett School of Planning in UCL 伦敦大学学院的巴特莱特规划学院
Zhuhai Housing, Urban-Rural Planning and Development Bureau 珠海市住房和城乡规划建设局

3. 演讲文本

00:00—00:43
Thank you very much, Patrick. /Could I just say what an honor and privilege it is/ to be here today/to make the opening address, /especially in front of all you

distinguished guests, /ladies and gentlemen. /That is my first visit to Zhuhai/as the envoy, UK Envoy for Sustainable Urbanization. /Over the last year/I've made over seven visits to China, /visiting over 24 cities. /This visit to Zhuhai is, /in fact, /one of the highlights. /Thank you very much/for making me feel so welcome here. /

谢谢，Patrick！/非常荣幸/来到这里/作开幕致辞，/见到在座的嘉宾们，/各位女士们、先生们。/这是我第一次到访珠海。/我是英国对华可持续城镇化事务特使。/去年，/我来过中国7次，/访问了超过24个城市。/此番珠海之行/事实上/意义重大。/谢谢/你们的热烈欢迎！/

00:43—01:27

As you've heard/it is particular exciting time in the UK-China relationship, /with the recent visit by your President, President Xi, /to London. /I have the privilege/of meeting him at the banquet in London. /He made it quite clear that/his aspiration is for the next decade to be a golden decade, /a golden era between our relations, /the UK-China relations in business, /in culture, /in knowledge exchange. /I look forward very much/to witnessing that decade ahead of us/with such optimism being expressed at such high level. /

众所周知，/中英关系发展势头良好。/最近，/习主席/出访伦敦。/我有幸/在伦敦的宴会上与他会面。/他明确表示，/希望未来十年成为"黄金十年"，/也就是中英关系的黄金时代，/无论在商业、/文化，/还是知识交流方面。/我期待/亲眼见证未来十年。/我对此充满乐观，和两国高层一样乐观。/

01:27—02:57

Now one of China's leading economists Liu He has said that/there are two key drivers/for world growth in the next 20 years. /Firstly, /urbanization in China. /Secondly, /advanced high-tech in developed countries. /By 2050, /the number of people living in urban environment/will grow from 3.5 billion/to 7 billion. /That is quite an increase. /62% of the world economic growth/in the next ten years/will come from cities, /increasing the need for city-based services, /like transport, /energy, /infrastructure, /health, /education/and business services sector. /Therefore, /ensuring that China urbanizes in a sustainable way/is not only good for China/but good for the whole world. /I am very pleased to see and read that/China's determination in pursuing sustainable urbanization/ (that) is set out in the *National New Type Urbanization Plan*/ and the *National Livable Cities Program*/reflects exactly that. /Sustainable urbanization is an area/where the United Kingdom has world leading expertise. /We are keen to work with China/to realize your ambitious goals in this regard. /

第十单元　绿色建筑 Green Building

中国著名经济学家刘鹤表示，/两大驱动力/推动未来20年全球的发展。/第一，/中国的城镇化；/第二，/发达国家的高科技。/到2050年，/城镇居民人数/将从35亿/增长到70亿，/增幅较大。/62%的全球经济增长/在未来的10年里/将来自城市，/拉动了对城市服务的需求，/如交通、/能源、/基础设施、/医疗、/教育/和商业服务。/因此，/确保中国城镇化的可持续发展/不仅仅有利于中国，/还有利于全球。/我非常高兴得知，/中国决心实现可持续的城镇化，/制定了《国家新型城镇化规划》/和《国家宜居城市项目》，/其决心可见一斑。/在可持续城镇化方面，/英国拥有世界领先的专业技能。/我们期待与中国合作，/实现贵国的宏伟目标。/

02:57—04:53

The UK was the first country/to industrialize/and also the first country to urbanize/in the 19th century. /At that time/our city conditions were much worse/than the worst in China today. /Our pollution was probably as bad. /Our housing was low quality. /Our public services were limited. /Many of our cities/were not the most comfortable places to live in. /But we've come a long way from that time/using a lot of skills, /a lot of hard work/and a lot of investment/and we have learned many lessons. /As the first country to de-industrialize/and de-urbanize, /United Kingdom has, /in fact, /become a collector of best practice/addressing the challenges of the urbanization/and sustainable urbanization. /Today our cities cover just 9% of land, /but it accounts for 54% of our population. /Our cities account for 60% of jobs/and 63% of national output. /They are also more efficient/producing 19% more output than non-city areas/and 27% fewer carbon dioxide emissions. /We have achieved these results/by finding innovative solutions/to the problems posed by urbanization, /dealing with urban sprawl/and failing city centers, /ensuring balanced urban distribution/and dealing with urban blight/and introducing a sustainable urbanization low-carbon agenda. /

英国率先/实现工业化/以及城镇化，/这可以追溯到19世纪。/当时，/我们的城市环境恶劣，/比中国的情况糟糕得多。/污染同样严重，/住房质量低下，/公共服务有限。/大多数的英国城市/生活条件相当恶劣。/此后，我们取得了长足的发展，/应用了诸多技能，/投入了大量的精力/和资金，/吸取了很多经验教训。/英国率先实现去工业化/和去城镇化，/我们/事实上/积累了最佳方案，/应对城镇化的挑战，/实现可持续城镇化。/如今英国的城市占了9%的土地面积，/却生活着54%的人口。/创造了60%的工作机会，/产值占全国63%。/城市效率更高，/产值比农村地区高19%，/二氧化碳排放低27%。/我们的成果/得益于创新型的解决方案，/解决了城镇化的问题，/城市无序扩张/和衰败的市中心，/确保城市均衡发展，/翻新旧城，/出台可持续和低碳的城镇化政策。/

04:53—06:08

There is very much more we can achieve together/through cooperation on ideas,/policy,/expertise/and practical collaboration./Very strong building blocks are working well/with architects,/engineers/and innovators/already working in collaboration./For example,/many iconic buildings in China/have had strong UK involvement in their design and build,/such as the Beijing Capital Airport,/the Olympic Bird's Nest Stadium/and Guangzhou International Financial Center./Here in Zhuhai,/numerous UK companies have been involved/in Hengqin's development./Mark McDonalds, Arab Napkins/are all involved in designing the Hong Kong-Zhuhai-Macau Bridge./Hengqin International Financial Center/and the Guangdong-Macau Traditional Chinese Medicine Park/are both designed by Aedas./A waterfront Huarong Hengqin Tower/is designed by Atkins,/so a very large input there by our major UK companies/and many more I haven't managed to mention./

携手合作成果更为显著,/共同创新,/制定政策,/分享专业技能,/推进务实合作。/我们已经打下了坚实的合作基础,/建筑师、/工程师、/设计师密切合作。/例如,/中国许多地标性建筑/英方都积极参与设计建设,/如北京首都机场、/鸟巢、/广州国际金融中心。/在珠海这里,/许多英国公司也参与了/横琴的开发。/Mark McDonalds和Arab Napkins/都参与设计港珠澳大桥。/横琴国际金融中心/和粤澳中医药科技产业园区/都是由Aedas建筑设计事务所设计的。/滨水区的华融横琴大厦/由阿特金斯设计。/因此,英国公司积极参与横琴建设,/例子数不胜数。/

06:08—07:16

Earlier I quoted Chinese economist Liu He's statement/that only two drivers will be key to the world growth/for the next 20 years:/urbanization in China/and advanced high-tech in developed countries./Now smart cities is an area/in which these two trends come together./Smart cities represent the optimization/and use of enabling technology/to provide a more sustainable,/greener and healthier life style/for all our citizens./The UK is a leader in underpinning components/of smart and future cities/that includes the technologies,/the applications,/the standards,/experience/and thought leadership in this area./From 2012 to 2015,/China has chosen more than 300 cities or towns/to be national pilot smart cities./We can help China to achieve this ambition./We have strong support/from the highest level of the government in the UK and China./

刚才我引用了中国经济学家刘鹤的话,/只有两大驱动力推动全球增长/在未来的20年里。/那就是中国的城镇化/和发达国家的高科技。/智慧城市/见证了这两大趋势的融合。/智慧城市优化/并利用先进技术/实现可持续/绿色和健康的生活方式，/造福全体市民。/英国各方面都名列前茅，/拥有智慧和未来城市/的先进技术、/应用、/标准、/经验/和理念。/从2012年到2015年，/中国挑选了300多个城镇/为国家智慧城市试点。/英国将助力中国实现目标。/我们得到了大力的支持，/中英两国政府高层的支持。/

07:16—07:47

Now, today we will focus on architecture and design,/urban regeneration,/green building/and sustainable master planning. /I am delighted that/today we have with us seven outstanding UK companies/representing the areas where UK has a strong competitive edge. /They will explain how we use urban planning,/architecture design/and low carbon technologies/to shape a livable city/and create a destination. /

本次论坛的主题是建筑和设计、/城市复兴、/绿色建筑/和可持续的总体规划。/我非常高兴/看到七家优秀的英国公司，/他们代表了英国的优势领域。/他们将阐述如何利用城市规划、/建筑设计/和低碳技术/打造宜居城市/和未来城市。/

07:47—08:41

I am also very pleased to learn that/Lord Richard Rogers/and Professor Peter Biship/from the Bartlett School of Planning in UCL/have been appointed as the advisers/to Zhuhai International Livable City construction,/therefore tapping into some of the best brains and best practices/that we have in the United Kingdom. /The UK-Zhuhai cooperation on design and engineering/is growing every day. /My visit here today/is an offer of the UK support/for Zhuhai's livable city development. /I hope the discussions at today's seminar/will encourage you to find out more about what the UK can offer. /My colleagues from UKTI and China-Britain Business Council/who are supporting this event/will be delighted to help you with this. /

非常高兴得知，/Richard Rogers勋爵/和Peter Biship教授，/教授在伦敦大学学院的巴特莱特规划学院任职，/他们被聘为顾问，/协助珠海国际可持续城市建设，/从而利用最佳理念和方案，/和英国的优势领域。/英国和珠海在设计和工程方面的合作/日益密切。/我的到访/表明英国支持/珠海可持续城市的发展。/期待今天的讨论/有助于大家进一步了解英国的优势。/英国贸易投资总署和英中贸易协会的同事们/主办了本次论坛。/他们将非常乐意帮助大家。/

08:41—09:08

So finally/I would like to thank/the Zhuhai Housing Urban-Rural Planning and Development Bureau/for their support for today's seminar. /I very much look forward to seeing how UK capabilities/can help to contribute to/build an even more beautiful

Zhuhai in the future. /I wish this seminar all success. /Thank you very much! /

最后，/感谢/珠海市住房和城乡规划建设局/对本次论坛的支持。/期待看到英国利用自身的优势，/帮助/珠海建设得更美丽。/祝论坛圆满成功！/谢谢！/

II. 实战练习二

1. 演讲背景

比利时布鲁塞尔首都大区政府大臣乔茜乐女士 Cécile Jodogne 应邀出席"比利时中国绿色建筑经验分享会"并发表开幕致辞。她在演讲中谈到比利时政府从 2000 年开始采取措施，积极减少建筑能耗，包括 2013 年颁布了《布鲁塞尔被动式建筑 2015 年政策》，创造标签奖励示范建筑。除了公共领域的努力，私营领域的建筑师、科学家和企业都积极推广可持续发展。

2. 预习词汇

urban development 城市发展
innovative project 创新项目
energy efficiency 能源效率
green building 绿色建筑
environmental norm 环境规范
economic activity 经济活动
pilot project 试验计划
support measure 支持措施
primary energy 一次能源
eco-construction 生态建设
materials management 物料管理

3. 演讲文本

00:00—01:05
Ms. Wang Xiangyu, /distinguished guests, /ladies and gentlemen, /I am very pleased/to be among you this afternoon. /It is especially great/to see that so many of you, /representing both local and Belgian firms/ (that) could join us here in Shenzhen. /Indeed, /experience sharing is, /to me, /essential in creative fields/such as architecture/and urban development, /green building/and sustainability. /A fruitful experience sharing/requires to have experimented people/together in the conference room. /Well, /I must say we are fortunate today, /being surrounded by quite a few

第十单元 绿色建筑 Green Building

high profile professionals, /from both Belgium and China. /This variety of profiles and specialties/will no doubt lead to passionate discussions/and promising encounters. / Hopefully, /maybe will this event/initiate new collaborations! /

王湘玉女士, /尊敬的来宾, /女士们,先生们, /我很高兴/今天下午能与你们共聚一堂。/非常高兴, /与诸位嘉宾们见面, /你们代表着中国本土和比利时的企业, /与我们在深圳共聚一堂。/的确, /经验分享/对我而言, /在创意领域十分重要, /例如建筑业, /城市发展, /绿色建筑, /以及可持续发展。/举办一场卓有成效的经验分享会/需要经验丰富的人们/齐聚会议室。/那么, /我们今天十分幸运, /周围有这么多知名的专业人士, /他们来自比利时和中国。/他们的真知灼见和行业知识/无疑会带来热烈的讨论/和富有成效的思想碰撞。/但愿/此次会议/能够带来新的合作机会。/

01:05—01:55

Our delegation has the chance/this week/to discover several ambitious development projects/in Southeastern China. /Those visits and presentations/are a good way/to witness how China contemplates its development/and future. /In this framework, / Shenzhen, /of course, /appears to be at the forefront, /having known in the previous year/one of the fastest urban growth of all times. /Naturally/Brussels also has its own initiative projects, / (innovative, sorry,) /innovative projects. /Well, /allow me/to tell you a little bit/about the regional government's ideal depiction/of the future of Brussels. /

我们的代表团有机会/于本周/去了解几个规模宏大的发展项目/就在中国东南部。/那些访问和展示/有助于我们/见证中国的发展/和对未来的愿景。/在这个框架下, /深圳/当然/是排头兵, /深圳去年/是有史以来发展最快的城市之一。/自然而然, /布鲁塞尔也启动了自己的创始项目/(抱歉,是创新), /创新项目。/那么, /让我/谈一下/地方政府是如何描绘/布鲁塞尔的未来。/

01:55—04:46

Brussels is at the forefront/for the environmental matters, /regarding energy efficiency/and green building. /Our public policies/have quickly evolved to become, / in only a few years' time, /exemplary regulations/with demanding goals/regarding energetic consumption reduction. /And it makes sense, /when you know that/buildings make up for 70%/of the region's global energy consumption. /Since the year 2000, / already 16 years ago, /the Brussels Government/passed new laws/regarding new building construction/moving towards an always reduced energy consumption/of newly constructed buildings/and will-be-built buildings. /And the results are visible:/from

1990 to 2011, /the Brussels population/grew up by 16%. /Well then, /one could expect/this to have a negative impact/on energy consumption. /Well, /actually, /it didn't, /thanks to the measures implemented. /Over the same period, /energy consumption/rose by 1% only. /In 2013, /the government went further, /with the *Brussels Passive* 2015 *Policy*. /It anticipated/and outdistanced the *EU Directive on Buildings Energy Performances*. /Without getting in too much details, /you can summarize Brussels regulation/by saying that new buildings/are expected to comply with passive standard, /whereas renovations have to observe low energy standards. /I want to highlight the major role played/by the public authorities in this field/and its evolutions. /The Brussels Region/not only fixed exigent environmental norms, /it was also the driving force/in the development of a new culture of 'green buildings', /and, even more, /a new culture of sustainability/as a global attitude/which concerns also, /for example, /water, /waste, /social responsibility, /economic activities and so on. /Public authorities, /region, /municipalities/have acted as spearheads/to initiate pilot projects/and open new routes/that have boosted the development of innovative competencies/and know-how. /

布鲁塞尔高度重视/环境问题，/尤其是能源效率/和绿色建筑。/我们的公共政策/快速完善，/在短短几年之内，/成为了示范性的规章制度/制定了严格的目标/减少能耗。/这十分有道理，/当您了解到/房屋建筑使用了70%/布鲁塞尔的总能耗。/从2000年起，/迄今已经16年了，/布鲁塞尔政府/通过了新的法律，/规定新房屋建筑/应不断向减少能耗迈进，/新建建筑/和未来修建的建筑都需要遵守新规。/成果显而易见：/从1990年到2011年，/布鲁塞尔人口数量/增长了16%。/那时候，/您可能会认为/这会带来负面影响/影响能耗。/但/实际上，/并没有，/这归功于已经实施的那些举措。/同期，/能耗/仅上升1%。/2013年，/政府采取进一步措施，/颁布了《布鲁塞尔被动式建筑2015年政策》。/这一政策预期/超越《欧盟建筑能源性能指令》。/我不会说太多细节，/您可以这样总结布鲁塞尔的规定，/那就是新建建筑/需要遵守被动式标准，/而翻修建筑则需要遵循低能耗标准。/我想强调重要的作用/即政府在这一领域/及其发展中发挥的作用。/布鲁塞尔地区/不仅制定了严苛的环境规范，/而且推动了/"绿色建筑"新文化的营造，/而且，更重要的是/也营造了可持续发展新文化，/这是全球的态度，/关注/例如/水资源、/废弃物、/社会责任、/和经济活动等等。/政府部门、/地区、/市政府/是排头兵/开展试点计划、/开发新路径，/促进了创新能力发展/和专业技术的发展。/

04:46—06:08

Furthermore, /support measures for exemplary projects/have been created, /such as/facilitating services both for sustainable buildings/and neighborhoods, /teams of professionals/who are able to inform and guide architects, /contractors/and other building professionals/all along the conception and building processes. /Raising awareness/on the importance of including environmental aspects in building projects/wasn't easy. /We needed to show/it was possible, /it already scarcely-existed/and it didn't undermine/the esthetic and comfort aspects. /One of the early measures Brussels took/was creating a label for model/or exemplary buildings. /That was in 2007. /This label rewards projects/that combine the following criteria:/minimization of primary energy needs, /eco-construction measures, /waste and materials management, /affordability and reproducibility of the construction techniques, /and of course/architectural quality. /

另外,/示范项目支持措施,/已经制定出来了,/例如/提供便利性服务给可持续建筑/和社区,/专家团队/能够建议并指导建筑师、/承包商/和其他建筑专业人士,/指导服务将贯穿整个建筑方案构想和施工过程。/提高意识,/了解将环境因素纳入建筑项目的重要性,/并不容易。/我们需要展示/这是做得到的,/这在以前几乎是不存在的,/而且这并不会损害/建筑美感及舒适度。/布鲁塞尔早期采取的措施之一/是创造标签给模范/或示范建筑。/当时是 2007 年,/这一标签所奖励的项目/达到了以下标准:/一次能源需求最小化,/生态建设措施,/废弃物及物料管理,/施工技术可购性及可再现性,/当然还有/建筑质量。/

06:08—08:31

Of course, /the public sector wasn't alone/supporting this trend. /Lots of architects, /scientists/and firms/were already active in sustainability. /All these professionals/developed throughout the years/an important expertise. /You see, /"sustainable building" /and sustainability/as a whole/is quite an important field/in Brussel's economy. /And our goal is to/share the skills we've developed. /We want to promote Brussels-based companies/in their international expansion, /so that other cities/can benefit from their refined technique/and sophisticated approach. /Our efforts/to promote these experts abroad/already pays off. /A delegation of the China Real Estate Chamber of Commerce/is coming to Brussels/mid-December/to witness what is being done/and learn about sustainable building, /converted real estate and so on. /But today/you have the chance/of having real live intermediaries/who can answer your questions/and chat with you. /Mattias Debroyer, /our Economic and Commercial Counselor in China, /is also available to help you/at building bridges between China and Brussels. /Moreover, /Crystal, /our Brussels Invest & Export representative in Shenzhen, /is permanently based in this fascinating city, /for any further inquiries you might have. /She is the contact. / (Where is she? /Just in … outside to welcome maybe the latest people ...) /So she is the contact point here/to find potential partners, /to give you information/about Belgian organizations and companies. /She can also be of great help/if you are looking for practical information, /for example, /to organize a visit to Brussels. /If you plan a visit to Brussels, /please don't hesitate/to contact Mattias/or Crystal. /

当然，/公共部门并非独自/支持这一趋势的发展。/许多建筑师、科学家/和企业/都积极推广可持续发展。/这些专业人士/多年来发展了/一套重要的技术。/要知道，/"可持续建筑"/和可持续发展/作为一个整体/是重要的领域/推动了布鲁塞尔的经济发展。/我们的目标是/分享我们所开发的技术。/我们希望促进布鲁塞尔企业/走向国际，/以便其他城市/能从它们的完善技术中获益/还学习它们精巧的方法。/我们努力/促进专业人士海外交流/已经得到了回报。/中华全国工商业联合会房地产商会代表团/将赴布鲁塞尔/在十二月中旬/亲眼见证已经实施的措施，/并了解可持续建筑/和改造后的房地产等等。/但是今天/您有机会/直接与专家会面，/他们能解答您的疑问，/并与您交谈。/Mattias Debroyer 先生，/是比利时驻上海总领事馆经济及商务领事，/也会帮助您/搭建中国与布鲁塞尔之间的桥梁。/而且，/Crystal 女士/是布鲁塞尔投资与出口深圳代表/常驻这座美丽的城市，/她会为您解答任何疑问。/她是联络人。/（她在哪儿？/她在外面接待刚到场的来宾……）/她是位于深圳的联络人，/寻找潜在的合作伙伴，/为您提供信息/进一步了解比利时组织和企业。/她也能起到很大帮助，/如果您在搜集相关信息，/比如，/组织前往布鲁塞尔的访问。/如果您计划访问布鲁塞尔，/请不要犹豫，/联系 Mattias 先生/或 Crystal 女士吧。/

08:31—08:51
I think/I've covered enough ground/to feed the discussion that you are going to follow. /I am personally/very much looking forward/to talking to you/and exchanging views. /Thank you very much for your attention！/谢谢！/

我认为/我已经说的够多了，/为接下来的讨论抛砖引玉。/我个人/十分期待/能与你们交谈/和交流意见。/感谢大家的聆听！/谢谢！/

第十一单元 招商引资
Investment Promotion

I. 实战练习一

1. 演讲背景

美国俄亥俄州托莱多市商务发展组织——区域发展合作组织代表应邀参加"创建世界一流高科技园区国际论坛"并发表主旨演讲。他在演讲中分享了"产业集群"的定义、优势,并介绍了全球知名的产业集群,包括硅谷技术集群、拉斯维加斯赌场集群、好莱坞娱乐业集群、深圳 LED 集群、英格兰西北部生物医学集群、义乌小商品贸易中心。他还揭示了产业集群成功的因素,包括市场和客户、基本材料、交通运输、政府支持和资源、风险投资、人脉关系。最后,他介绍了托莱多市的玻璃制造业集群和太阳能集群,以及该市招商引资的优势。

2. 预习词汇

small-and-medium-sized enterprises/SMEs 中小企业
sectorial and geographical concentration 行业和地域集中
supporting service 配套服务
catalytic 催化的
regulatory framework 监管框架
capacity building 能力建设
interconnected company 互联公司
commercialization 商业化
Silicon Valley Technology Cluster 硅谷技术集群
semiconductor 半导体
Las Vegas Cluster Casino 拉斯维加斯赌场集群
The Entertainment Capital of the World 世界娱乐之都
Hollywood Entertainment Cluster 好莱坞娱乐业集群
theatrical performance 戏剧表演
Shenzhen LED Cluster 深圳 LED 集群
Northwest England Biomedical Cluster 英格兰西北部生物医学集群

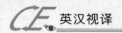

medical and health-care company 医疗保健公司
Yiwu Commodity Trade Cluster 义乌小商品贸易中心
China Commodity City/CCC 中国小商品城
World Bank 世界银行
Morgan Stanley 摩根士丹利
Largest Small Commodity Wholesale Market in the World 世界最大的小商品批发市场
Yiwu International Trade Center 义乌国际商贸城
logistics 物流
Toledo 托莱多市
intersect 交叉
Great Lakes 五大湖
Toledo Port Authority 托莱多港务局
venture capital 风险投资
production facilities 生产厂
General Motors 通用汽车
Chrysler 克莱斯勒
automotive cluster 汽车产业群
Dana Corporation 德纳公司
Solar Energy Cluster 太阳能集群
Glass Manufacturing Cluster 玻璃制造业集群
Glass Capital of the World 世界玻璃之都
Owens-Illinois 欧文斯-伊利诺伊
Owens Corning 欧文斯科宁
Libbey Glass 利比玻璃
Pilkington North America 皮尔金顿北美分公司
First Solar/FSLR 第一太阳能
thin-filmed panel 薄膜面板
spin-off 衍生的
Greater Toledo Metropolitan Detroit area 大底特律都市圈
consumer market 消费市场

3. 演讲文本

00:00—00:24

Vice Mayor Wu, /Madam Xiu, /distinguished guests, /good morning. /First, / let me say how honored I am/to be here this morning/with such a wonderful panel of

第十一单元　招商引资 Investment Promotion

experts. /I am not an expert in cluster development, /and I don't know/how much more I will be able to add/to this discussion. /But I will go through a couple of slides/ and try to add a couple of points. /

吴副市长，/修女士，/尊敬的各位来宾，/早上好。/首先，/我很荣幸/今天早上能在这里/与各位专家共聚一堂。/我不是产业集群［发展］领域的专家，/不知道/我能否提出有用的意见/供大家探讨。/但我会带大家浏览几页PPT，/试着补充几个观点。/

00:35—01:20

Industrial clusters/have increasingly been recognized/as an effective means/of industrial development/and promotion of small-and-medium-sized enterprises throughout the world. /With the sectorial and geographical concentration/of enterprises in an industrial cluster, /enterprises can better improve their competitiveness. /This is due to/the presence of specialized suppliers/of raw materials, /parts and components, /machinery, /skills and the technology/as well as other supporting services/to the entire cluster. /Also, /competitive or cooperative interactions/and linkages among the players/tend to result in/collective learning/and innovation amongst the groups. /

产业集群/已越来越被视为/一种有效方式/促进产业发展/和全球中小企业发展。/行业、地域集中化/出现在集群企业中，/有利于企业提升竞争力。这归功于/各种专业化供应商的出现，/他们供应原材料、/零部件、/机械、/技能技术/以及其他配套服务/给整个集群。/而且，/竞争或合作性互动/和各方的联系/往往能带来/群体学习/和集群内的创新。/

01:23—01:58

Cluster development/could be led better by the private sector/with government playing only a catalytic role. /However, /given the weakness of the private sector/in transition economies, /the government might initiate the process/by putting in place appropriate cluster support structures. /They include adequate regulatory frameworks, / infrastructures/and logistics, /financial facilities, /and various programs, /and capacity building/and cooperative technology development/and innovative efforts. /

集群发展/最好由私营领域牵头，/政府只发挥促进作用。/然而，/考虑到私营领域的弱点，/例如在经济转型中的弱点，/政府可能需要从中发力，/建立合适的集群配套架构，/包括充分的监管框架、/基础设施、/物流、/金融机构、/各种项目、/能力建设、/协作技术开发/和创新。/

211

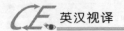

01:59—02:44

Industrial clusters/involve interconnected companies,/specialized suppliers,/service providers/and firms of related industries for the entire cluster./Industry clusters/include associated institutions./Many of us/are in the area of Toledo, Ohio./The universities/play a very very important role/in our cluster development./Industry clusters/also have geographic concentrations./Our cluster expands/and you will see some maps later/that they expand/throughout our entire region./Companies/are also very important./They compete in our clusters/but certainly/they must also cooperate,/utilizing the policies/and the proactive efforts of all/to be successful./

产业集群/涉及互联公司、/专业化供应商、/服务供应商/以及整个集群里相关产业的企业。/产业集群/包括关联机构。/很多产业集群/都在俄亥俄州的托莱多市,/大学/起到很重要的作用,/促进集群发展。/产业集群/也有地域集中性。/我们的集群在扩展,/从后面的地图你们会看到/集群扩张/覆盖了整个地区。/企业/也很重要。/企业在集群内相互竞争,/当然/也要相互合作,/利用政策/和所有人的积极努力/获得成功。/

02:45—03:07

Clustering/strengthens local economies./It can result in cost savings/for the firms in the industry cluster as a whole./Clustering/certainly permits/better focusing of our resources./Clustering/encourages network among firms/and it can facilitate commercialization/and innovation within the cluster./

集群/加强地方经济发展,/能够节约成本,/惠及整个产业集群的企业。/集群/当然也能够/更好地集中资源。/集群/促进企业联系,/能够推动商业化/和集群创新。/

03:08—03:41

A couple of clusters/that are probably well-known to most of you./Silicon Valley Technology Cluster,/the leading hub/for high-tech innovation/and development/within the US,/and also the broad set of technology-related industries,/spanning fields/such as Internet,/semiconductors,/software,/gaming/and social media./Home to/many of the world's largest technology companies/such as Google,/Microsoft,/Apple,/IBM,/Cisco/and many of thousands of/small start-up companies within the US./

有几个集群/可能大家都很熟悉。/硅谷技术集群/是一流的中心,/孕育高科技创新/与发展,/地处美国,/汇集众多技术产业,/领域涉及/互联网、半导体、/软件、/游戏/和社交媒体。/汇集/众多世界上最大的科技公司,/如谷歌、/微软、/苹果、/IBM、/思科/和数千家/美国小型初创企业。/

212

第十一单元　招商引资 Investment Promotion

03:42—04:03

Las Vegas Cluster Casino/honored as "The Entertainment Capital of the World". /It is an internationally renowned major resort city/for gambling, /shopping/as well as fine dining. /The casino industry in Las Vegas/is the largest and most dynamic of any casino industry/in the world, /also hosts nine of the top ten largest resorts in the world. /

拉斯维加斯赌场集群/被誉为"世界娱乐之都", /是世界著名的旅游城市, /在这里可以博彩、/购物/和享受美食。/拉斯维加斯博彩业/是规模最大、最具活力的, /乃世界之最, /也拥有九个全世界十大旅游胜地。/

04:04—04:30

The Hollywood Entertainment Cluster. /Hollywood is the first cluster entertainment-related industries/in film, /television, /music/as well as publishing/and is the nation's single largest export cluster. /Most globally competitive, /Hollywood is by far/the most globally recognized center/in the production of filmed entertainment in the United States, /whether for film, /television/or theatrical performance. /

好莱坞娱乐业集群。/好莱坞是第一个娱乐产业集群, /涉及电影、/电视、/音乐/以及出版业, /也是美国最大的出口集群。/好莱坞在全球极具竞争力, /是目前为止/全球认可度最高的/美国影视制作和影视娱乐中心, /涵盖电影、/电视/和戏剧表演。/

04:31—04:55

The Shenzhen LED Cluster. /Shenzhen has the largest LED cluster in China/with an industry size/of 70 billion RMB. /There are more than 1,200 enterprises/which engage in/LED lighting technology research and development, /production/and application in Shenzhen, /accounting for nearly half/of the firms throughout China. /

深圳LED集群。/深圳拥有中国最大的LED集群, /产业规模/达700亿元人民币。/有1,200多家企业/从事/LED照明技术研发、/生产/和应用, /占有将近一半的/中国LED企业。/

04:56—05:13

Northwest England Biomedical Cluster. /This is 160 biomedical/plus 120 medical and health-care companies. /Seven multinational pharmaceutical companies/are part of this biomedical cluster in Northwest England. /

英格兰西北部生物医学集群。/有160家生物医学/和120多家医疗保健公司。/7个跨国制药公司/也在这里。/

213

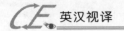

05:14—05:48

The Yiwu Commodity Trade Cluster. /I visited there/just a few short years ago. /China Commodity City, /also known as CCC, /is a large wholesale market/in Yiwu/which was honored by the UN, /the World Bank/and Morgan Stanley/among other world authorities/in 2005/as the "Largest Small Commodity Wholesale Market in the World". /Yiwu International Trade Center/has the capacity/of over 70,000 stalls, /earning huge profits/in the billions of US dollars. /

义乌小商品贸易中心。/我去过那儿,/是几年前去的。/中国小商品城,/英文简称 CCC,/是个大型批发市场,/就在义乌,/被联合国、世界银行/和摩根士丹利/等世界权威机构/在 2015 年/誉为"世界最大的小商品批发市场"。/义乌国际商贸城/能容纳/七万多个摊位,/利润丰厚,/高达数十亿美元。/

05:49—06:25

Some keys to success/certainly with our clusters/in the mid-west in the US, /and in Toledo in Ohio, /market and clients. /The clusters, /well, they need all the things/that have been talked about today. /Clusters/certainly need clients. /You need people/to sell your products/and services too. /One of the biggest advantages/that we have in Ohio, /in the mid-west of United States, /is in Toledo. /Within a one day's truck drive, /approximately 500 kilometers, /we are within 60%/of the North American population/which certainly includes/the USA and Canada. /

成功的关键,/当然对于我们的集群而言,/在美国中西部/和俄亥俄州托莱多市,/都是市场和客户。/这些集群,/都需要所有要素,/我们今天已经提到了。/集群/当然需要客户。/您需要人员/来推销产品/和服务。/最大的一个优势,/对于俄亥俄州而言,/对于美国中西部而言,/是托莱多市。/在一天的卡车行程内,/大约 500 公里路程,/我们可以辐射 60%/的北美人口,/这当然包括/美国和加拿大。/

06:26—07:02

Basic materials/are certainly very important, /and probably first and foremost/for our area's transportation and logistics. /Toledo, Ohio, /is one of the most important transportation hubs/in the United States, /for that matter throughout North America. /And the reason for that are/the modes of transportation that we have/are all intersecting in our area. /First and foremost, /the busiest road in United States, /most heavily traveled/from California to New York, /intersects/with the busiest and most heavily traveled road/from Canada to Florida. /They actually/intersect/in Toledo, Ohio. /

基本材料/当然非常重要,/很可能是最重要的,/对我们地区的交通和物流而言便是如此。/俄亥俄州托莱多市/是最重要的交通枢纽之一,/辐射美国/和整个北美。/原因是/我们的运输模式/都在托莱多市衔接。/最重要的是,/美国最繁忙的公路,/车流量最大的公路,/是从加利福尼亚到纽约路段,/与其交汇的也是/最繁忙、车流量最大的/加拿大至佛罗里达路段。/这两条公路实际上/交叉点就在/俄亥俄州托莱多市。/

07:03—07:42

So certainly/from a truck traffic and population/we get a great deal traffic/in our interstates, /also all four Class-One railroads/intersect within Toledo, Ohio, /in our region, /as well as having the most dynamic seaport/on the Great Lakes. /The Toledo Port Authority/has the largest land mass/than any ports, /any seaports on the Great Lakes. /And we also have/a phenomenal and a very dynamic airport/that has a very large cargo hub. /So certainly for clusters/needing to sell products to the clients/as well as move products in and out of the area, /our region becomes very important/for cluster development. /

因此,/从货车交通和人口方面来看,/我们有巨大交通流量/往返各州,/并且有四条一级公路/交汇在俄亥俄州托莱多市,/也就是我们所在的地区。/而且我们也有最活跃的海港,/位于五大湖。/托莱多港务局/拥有最大的占地面积,/比任何港口、/五大湖其他海港的都要大。/我们还有/一个大型的、非常有活力的机场,/那里有一个很大的货运中心。/当然,对于集群而言,/需要销售产品给客户,/也需要运输产品出入该地区。/托莱多市非常重要,/因为它有利于集群发展。/

07:43—07:52

Also, /government support and resources/is very important. /We have a very very strong government support/with very positive cluster policies/for companies in our area. /

而且,/政府支持和资源/也很重要。/我们有非常非常强大的政府支持、/非常积极的集群政策/来支持本区域的企业发展。/

07:52—08:03

Financial resources and venture capital/has already been discussed today. /We are very strong/in that area as well, /attracting capital and investment/from all around the world. /

财政资源和风险投资/我们今天已经讨论过了。/我们很强大,/在这一方面也做得很好,/吸引了资金和投资/从世界各地源源而来。/

08:03—08:35

And then, /personal connections and relationships/are probably the most important, /and certainly from the international standpoint. /Our Mayor of Toledo, /Michael Bell, /with the opening ceremony/in the Shenzhen Hi-tech Fair/yesterday, /he was on stage. /And this is our fifth trip/to China. /We have visited Shenzhen/every time. /We have made/very good connections/in the Shanghai area, /Beijing/and throughout China. /And we continue/to have very good interactions/and cooperative ventures/between China and Toledo, Ohio. /

还有，/人脉关系/可能是最重要的，/这当然是从国际角度而言。/托莱多市长/迈克尔·贝尔，/参加了开幕式，/庆祝深圳高交会开幕，/就在昨天，/他也在台上。/这是我们第五次/到访中国，/我们拜访了深圳，/每次都会来。/我们已经/建立了很好的人脉关系，/在上海、/北京、/全中国都是如此。/我们将继续/积极往来，/发展合资企业，/加强中国与俄亥俄州托莱多市的合作。/

08:36—09:03

Some of the clusters in Toledo. /Certainly/we are very strong/in the automotive industry. /Toledo is home to Jeep, /the headquarters of Jeep in Toledo, /has two production facilities. /Both General Motors and Chrysler/had facilities/in metropolitan Toledo. /And some Fortune 500 automotive-related companies/are also headquartered there/such as Dana Corporation. /Then we have/hundreds of suppliers/in the region/to support the automotive cluster. /

托莱多的一些集群/当然，/我们很有实力/的是汽车业。/托莱多是吉普之乡，/是吉普总部所在地，/有两个生产厂。/通用汽车和克莱斯勒/都有工厂/设在大都市托莱多。/而且，一些世界500强汽车行业相关公司/也将总部设在这里，/例如德纳公司。/我们还拥有/数百家供应商/在当地/支撑汽车产业集群发展。/

09:04—09:34

The Solar Energy Cluster. /It is not on here, /but I am talking/about Glass Manufacturing Cluster. /Toledo, /for many years, /is known as the Glass Capital of the World, /because of its long history of innovation/in the aspects of the glass industry. /Several large Fortune 500 companies/have their origins/in our region, /from Owens-Illinois, /Owens Corning, /Libbey Glass, /Pilkington North America/as well as many other glass manufacturers. /

太阳能集群。/不在这上面。/我要讲的是/玻璃制造业集群。/托莱多/多年来/都被誉为"世界玻璃之都"，/因为它有悠久的创新历史，/贯穿整个玻璃行业。/几家大型的世界500强企业/都起源于/托莱多，/比如：欧文斯—伊利诺伊、/欧文斯

第十一单元　招商引资 Investment Promotion

科宁、/利比玻璃、/皮尔金顿［北美分公司］/以及许多其他的玻璃制造商。/

09:35—10:16

And then out of the glass industry, /really came our Solar Cluster. /There are at least 6,000 people/work within the area's solar industry/in Toledo. /First Solar (FSLR), /which many of you know, /the world's largest producer of thin-filmed panels, /was founded in Toledo/and more than 1,000 employees/at its close to 1-million-square-foot plant. /We have more than a dozen solar-related start-up companies/in the area, /working directly with our University of Toledo/which has been recruiting some of top minds/in the solar research and development area/in the last five years, /and has produced/a great number of spin-off solar companies. /

讲完玻璃制造业之后，/接下来就是太阳能集群了。/至少有6,000人/在当地的太阳能行业工作，/就职于托莱多市。/第一太阳能（FSLR），/很多人都知道，/是世界最大的薄膜面板制造商，/创建于托莱多，/有1,000多名员工，/工厂面积接近100万平方英尺。/有十几个太阳能相关的初创企业/在本地区创立，/直接与托莱多大学合作，/托莱多大学一直在招募高端人才，/从事太阳能研发，/过去5年一直如此，/也创立了/大量太阳能衍生公司。/

10:17—10:42

Why does Toledo/attract foreign investment/and how do we/have this cluster moving? /As you can see from the map/that I have given you/a couple of figures already, /we are in the heart of the manufacturing belt/in the mid-west. /And you can see/the circle that was drawn there, /which puts us in the approximation of 60%/of the population base within North America. /So we are very close/to consumer markets/for those within our clusters. /

为什么托莱多/能吸引外资？/我们又是如何/推动集群发展的？/从地图上可以看到，/我给出了/几个数据。/我们位于制造业地带的中心，/也是中西部的中心。/你们可以看到/这里画的圈，/占据了60%的/北美总人口。/因此，我们非常靠近/消费市场，/集群企业离消费市场非常近。/

10:43—11:05

We have/a very skilled workforce, /a much lower labor cost/than certainly the coast, /whether it will be Los Angles/or New York. /And we do have/a government/that is very very supportive/not only to our cluster development, /but most importantly international investment. /As I mentioned Mayor Bell, /we will see here/a picture of his/in just a moment, /so I won't mention that yet. /

217

我们有/非常熟练的劳动力,/很低的人工成本,/当然要低于沿海城市,/如洛杉矶、/纽约。/我们也有/政府/大力支持/产业集群的发展,/尤其是国际投资。/我提到过贝尔市长,/我们会在这里看到/他的照片,/一会儿马上就能看到,/所以我就先不再就此话题赘述了。/

11:06—11:40

But for American companies, /local enterprises/in Toledo and Greater Toledo Metropolitan Detroit area, /which is only 45 minutes/from Toledo, /are encouraged to have more closed relationship with China/and explore the business possibilities/and the opportunities between Shenzhen and the rest of China and Toledo. /For China companies, /Toledo government/and local non-profit organizations/such as the Regional Growth Partnership/that I represent, /encourage investment/from China and the rest of the world/to invest in Toledo/and certainly look at some of the development opportunities/within our clusters. /

对于美国公司而言,/当地企业,/无论是在托莱多还是大底特律都市圈,/从大底特律只需45分钟车程/即可到达托莱多,/这些企业都在发展与中国的关系,/发掘商机,/发掘深圳、全中国和托莱多之间的商机。/对于中国公司而言,/托莱多政府/和当地非盈利组织,/如区域发展合作组织,/也就是我所在的机构,/都在鼓励投资,/欢迎中国和其他国家/来托莱多投资,/当然也来关注发展机遇,/到我们的集群来发展。/

11:47—12:12

Just a couple of pictures/of our Mayor, Michael Bell, /again who was at the opening ceremony yesterday, /the Hi-tech Fair. /Again we have spent many many weeks/over the last two and a half years/on our five trips here in China. /Michael/will be leaving/up to the Shanghai region/today, /continuing to develop cooperative relationships/with many partnerships that we have developed here. /

有几张照片,/是我们市长迈克尔·贝尔,/他参加了昨天的开幕式,/就在高交会。/我们在这里已经度过了好几周,/在过去的两年半时间里,/我们已经来了中国五次。/迈克尔/就要离开这里,/前往上海,/今天就出发,/继续发展合作关系,/加强与我们在中国的合作伙伴的联系。/

12:13—12:49

The future outlook. /I think/for Toledo/and for the cluster development within our region/and mid-west of the USA/is very very strong. /I would certainly encourage/those international, /certainly those of China/who wish to look into the US

第十一单元 招商引资 Investment Promotion

opportunities/and markets. /We would certainly welcome/those conversations. /We have a very strong business leadership/and a strong government leadership/that would certainly welcome those discussions/and look forward to future cooperation. /Thank you so much! 谢谢！/

展望未来。/我认为/对于托莱多，/我们地区的集群发展，/和美国中西部的发展/势头都非常强劲。/我当然鼓励/国际/和中国的企业/前来美国寻找机遇、/开拓市场，/当然我们也欢迎/交流对话。/我们有很强大的企业领袖/和政府领导层，/他们都非常欢迎磋商，/期待开展合作。/谢谢！/

II. 实战练习二

1. 演讲背景

比利时瓦隆大区代表应邀参加"创建世界一流高科技园区国际论坛"并发表主旨演讲。他在演讲伊始首先高度赞扬中国从"中国制造"转变为"中国创造"，然后详细介绍了比利时的基本情况，包括经济发展水平、人口、国际贸易、外国直接投资、便利的交通基础设施、投资优惠政策、布鲁塞尔孵化项目。最后尤其谈到了"中国迎宾办事处"提供的免费公共服务和武汉东湖国际企业孵化器即将在比利时推出的第一个国际高科技孵化器——中国—比利时技术中心。

2. 预习词汇

Belgium 比利时
Brussels 布鲁塞尔
inaugurate 开创，开幕
Excellency 阁下
Wallonia province 瓦隆大区
polyethylene 聚乙烯
pharmaceutical 药品
vegetable fiber 植物纤维
margarine 人造奶油
locomotive 火车头
Conference on Trade and Development of the United Nations 联合国贸易与发展会议
FTA/Free Trade Agreement 自由贸易协定
Cologne 科隆
curfew 宵禁
Port of Antwerp 安特卫普港

Port of Liège 列日港
Cushman & Wakefield 库什曼—韦克菲尔德
China Welcome Office 中国迎宾办事处
incubation project 孵化项目
cluster 集群
business visa 商务签证

3. 演讲文本

00:00—00:41

Good morning, /all of you. /Ms Ding, /Ms Xiu, /it is a good idea/from the organizer/of this great, impressive conference/to give me the floor/to speak about Belgium, /my country, /just after you. /Because I... /to emphasize on the topics and the links/between the scientific parks in China and in Europe, /namely in Belgium, /my country. /I would like to say to the audience/that it is the Zhongguancun Park, /as just two days ago, /inaugurate this new HQ for Europe, /in Brussels in my country. /Thank you very much! /You are welcome. /

早上好, /各位。/丁女士, /修女士, /这是一个非常好的想法, /主办方/在这个令人瞩目的会议上/给我机会/谈论比利时, /我的国家, /紧跟你们之后发言。/因为我, /想要着重讨论的主题和联系, /是有关于中国和欧洲的科技园区之间的, /我要谈的是比利时, /我的国家。/我想告诉各位的是, /中关村科技园, /就在两天前, /建立了新的欧洲总部, /就在比利时布鲁塞尔。/感谢各位, /欢迎你们前去参观。/

00:42—01:38

Dear Ms Xiu, /excellencies, /distinguished guests, /ladies and gentlemen, /thank you very much/for affording me this opportunity/to say a few words at this delightful occasion. /I'm greatly honored/by your kind and generous welcome/of a representative/of such a small country in the middle of Europe, /Belgium. /Today's visit/together with the Mrs. Governor of the Wallonia province of Belgium, /my colleagues from Brussels, /my colleagues from Wallonia, /we will be here in Shenzhen. /It is not a singular event, /but is part of a series of manifestations/that characterize the expanding economic relations/between Belgium, Europe and China. /

亲爱的修女士, /各位阁下, /尊敬的各位来宾, /女士们, 先生们, /非常感谢你们/给我这次机会/在这个令人愉快的场合发言。/非常荣幸/能受到你们的热烈欢迎, /我代表/一个中欧小国, /比利时来此参会。/今天的访问/是与比利时瓦隆大区的区长夫人, /我布鲁塞尔的同事, /瓦隆大区的同事一起的。/我们将会在深

圳。/这不是一个单独的活动,/而是一系列活动的一部分,/证明了经济合作不断扩大/比利时、欧洲和中国在深化合作。/

01:39—02:29

I came in China several times/during the last years/and let me say/what happens now in your country/is really, really unbelievable. /From a production country, /you are now, new China, /among the world economic leaders, /number one in R&D and hi-tech, /the topics of this conference, /leader in sports, /automotive industry, /electronics, /IT and so on and so on, /also as in international event organization/or also in culture. /Congratulations to China/for your Nobel Prize for the Literature! /You provide also top education in the world. /

我来过中国好几次,/过去的几年都有来。/我想说/发生在贵国的事/真的令人难以置信。/你们过去是生产大国,/你们现在是新的中国,/是世界经济的领袖之一,/在研发和高科技领域排名第一,/这两个领域也是这次会议的主题。/中国还引领着体育、/汽车业、/电子、/IT 等行业。/在国际活动的组织/和文化领域也是如此。/祝贺中国/获得了诺贝尔文学奖!/你们还提供世界一流的教育。/

02:30—02:49

Now it is your turn, /it is the China era, /to provide to the world/sophisticated products/ "Made BY China" /not only in China, /but also BY China. /and to support the world economic welfare! /It is a responsibility/that gives you respect/from me, /from all of us. /

现在轮到你们,/在这个中国的时代,/向世界提供/精良的产品。/"中国创造",/不仅仅是中国制造,/而且是由中国创造,/是你们在支持世界的经济福祉。/这种责任/让你们获得尊重,/值得我,/我们所有人尊重。/

02:49—03:38

In this frame, /I wish to the new Chinese governments/plenty of success/and commitments/in the next years, /in reaching the scientific and technological goals for China. /Guangdong here and "Technological China"/presents a multitude of opportunities and challenges/to Belgian companies/for partnerships and services/to meet the emerging needs/in terms of car and space industries, /environment, /sustainable development, /transport and management. /They are the niche markets/in which Belgian companies/have already provided and proved to the world/their know-how and expertise. /

在这个框架中,/我希望新一届中国政府/能取得巨大成功,/承担诸多责任,/

在接下来的几年里／实现中国的科学技术目标。／广东和"科技中国"／带来许多机遇和挑战，／比利时的公司／前来寻求合作与服务，／以满足新需求，／包括汽车、航天工业、／环境、可持续发展、／交通运输以及管理方面的需求。／这些是利基市场，／比利时公司／已经向世界提供并证明了／他们的专业知识与技能。／

03:39—04:13

Today, /instead of giving you dry trade figures, /I thought I would briefly talk about Belgium/and its impressive industrial history/and its impact to the world, /a real base from the new hi-tech and technology developments of today. /Because a small country in the very heart of Europe/could also be full of talents, /even if humility is also a sign of respect in our country. /

今天，／抛开枯燥的贸易数据，／我想简单谈谈比利时、／其令人印象深刻的工业史／及其对世界的影响。／它是真正的高新技术发源地。／因为一个欧洲中心的小国／也有大批的人才，／尽管比利时人是很谦虚的，但我还是要自夸一下。／

04:13—05:02

Globalization, /the word that is on every lips these days, /has long been an established fact/in life in Belgium. /While the country/represents 0.2% of the world's population, /it accounts for almost 4% of world exports. /Within the EU, /Belgium's share of population/is just around 3%, /but it generates 8% of the exports. /The ratio of Belgium's exports to GDP/is a significant 80%, /higher than UK, /than France, /and higher than Germany! /

全球化，／这个这段时间受热议的词，／已成一个既定事实，／贯穿于比利时人生活中。／比利时／占0.2%世界人口，／却有将近4%的世界出口总额。／在欧盟，／比利时人口比重／仅占约3%，／却占8%的出口。／比利时的出口与GDP的比率／高达80%，／高于英国／和法国，／也高于德国。／

05:02—05:28

Some of this tiny country's merits include:/Number one in the world/for the export of/diamonds, /polyethylene and carpets. /Number two/for the export of/pharmaceuticals, /vegetable fibers, /the famous chocolate/but also the margarine. /Number three/for the glass and so on, and so on. /

这个小国的优势包括：／世界第一大／出口／钻石、聚乙烯和地毯的国家，／第二大／出口／药品、／植物纤维、／著名的巧克力／和人造奶油的国家，／第三大／出口玻璃的国家，等等。／

第十一单元 招商引资 Investment Promotion

05:29—05:48

By the beginning of the 20th century, /Belgium/was the world's third greatest trading nation. /It exported its rails, /carriages, /locomotives, /trams/to all the corners of the world. /

20世纪初，/比利时/成为世界第三大贸易国，/出口铁轨、/车厢、/火车头、/电车/到世界各地。/

05:51—06:20

Up today, /Belgium stood up and faced it/as we try to do better/than the other countries. /We succeed in preserving employments, /foreign exchanges/and economic growth. /According to several international rankings, /we are still the sixth most attractive location in Europe/regarding foreign direct investments. /

今天，/比利时勇敢地面对现实，/因为我们想做得更好，/超过其他国家。/我们成功保持了良好的就业率，/外汇/和经济增长。/根据几项国际排名，/我们仍然是第六大最具吸引力的欧洲国家，/吸引外国直接投资。/

06:21—06:38

On the global scale, /following the statement from the Conference on Trade and Development of the United Nations, /we are even the second, /just after Hong Kong, /most performing economy/regarding foreign direct investments. /

在全球层面，/据联合国贸易与发展会议的声明，/我们甚至位列第二，/仅次于香港，/表现第二出色的经济体，/这是从外国直接投资角度而言。/

06:39—07:12

The European zone/continues today to be considered/as a market of great interests/for all international companies. /It is indeed the market/of more than 500 million consumers, /which has close ties with Russia, with Africa, /a long history with Africa, /special relationships with the United States, /and new FTAs/concluded with South Korea, /and shortly Japan. /

欧洲区/今天仍被视为/热门市场，/受所有国际公司密切关注。/这个市场/有超过5亿的消费者，/与俄罗斯和非洲保持密切联系，/与非洲有长久的关系，/与美国保持着特殊关系。/新的自由贸易协定/已与韩国签署，/不久会与日本谈判。/

07:14—07:34

From Belgium, /the Chinese companies/can reach in less than four hours trucking time, /65% of the total European market, /almost 400 million of consumers/with the highest GDP per capita in the world. /

从比利时出发，/中国公司/可以在4小时之内开卡车抵达/65%的欧洲市场。/这里有近4亿的消费者，/人均国内生产总值世界最高。/

07:35—08:59

In addition to these advantages of its geographical location, /Wallonia and Brussels in Belgium/can offer the best logistic partners, /an efficient communication network/and also a huge infrastructure/thanks to an exceptional motorway network/linking more than 130 industrial zones, /where thousands of companies/are established throughout the country. /For example, /Linked to Paris, /Cologne in Germany/and London/through the high speed trains, /European logistics center/could count on the capital city, /on Brussels International Airport, /Brussels south low cost airport, /linked with the 27 European members/and also Liège Airport, /located at the center of the Amsterdam-Paris-Frankfurt triangle, /open 24 hours a day, /7 days a week, /fully dedicated to cargo, /competing with main international airports/thanks to no imposed time slots, /no curfews/and no time losses in ground operations. /

除了这些地理位置优势以外，/比利时的瓦隆大区和布鲁塞尔/能提供最佳的物流合作伙伴、/高效的通信网络、/大型的基础设施。/这些都得益于出色的高速公路网，/它连接130多个工业区，/成千上万家公司/遍布全国。/例如/连接巴黎、/德国科隆/和伦敦/的高铁，/欧洲物流中心/还可依赖于首都，/依赖于布鲁塞尔国际机场，/布鲁塞尔南部低成本机场，/来连接27个欧洲成员国，/还有列日机场，/位于阿姆斯特丹—巴黎—法兰克福三角区的中心，/全天候营业，/每周无休，/全力开展货运，/能与主要国际机场抗衡，/这得益于它没有规定的时间段，/没有宵禁，/也没有地面操作造成的时间损失。/

09:00—09:25

The Belgium logistics/offers facilities/to transport companies specializing in combined air-rail-road transport. /We benefit of the Port of Antwerp, /fourth largest Port in the world, /second in Europe. /Its inside hub, /the Port of Liège, /the 2nd largest river port in Europe. /

比利时物流/提供便利/给从事多式联运的公司。/我们受益于安特卫普港，/它是世界第四大港，/欧洲第二大港，/其内部枢纽/列日港/是欧洲第二大河港。/

9:26—10:14

Wallonia Region in Belgium, /for example, /has been ranked as/the best region for logistics in Europe/by the company Cushman & Wakefield. /In addition to the

第十一单元　招商引资 Investment Promotion

European and federal subsidies, /also the regional authorities/have developed a whole range of instruments/to promote investments in Wallonia and in Brussels, /basic grants, /specific grants up to 30% of your investment, /great fiscal exemptions, /recruitment and training grants and facilities, /consulting benefits, /non-financial aid and support and so on. /

比利时的瓦隆大区, /比方说/已被列为/欧洲最佳物流地区, /这是库什曼—韦克菲尔德的排名。/除了欧洲和联邦的补贴, /瓦隆大区政府/也采取一系列的措施, /促进瓦隆和布鲁塞尔的投资。/这些措施包括基本补助, /具体补助可高达30%的投资额, /大型财政减免, /招聘培训的补助和服务, /咨询福利, /非金融援助和支持等。/

10:16—11:01

Many major international companies/trust us over the years. /A large number of international and multinational companies/have based their European HQs/in Brussels, /but also throughout Wallonia, /big companies/have decided to settle European distribution center/as Google, /Microsoft, /Baxter, /Caterpillar, /Johnson & Johnson, /but also Chinese companies/such as Huawei/and Datang Telecom, /also ICBC/and Bank of China, /have established European offices/in Wallonia and in Brussels. /

许多国际大公司/一直信任我们, /大量的国际和跨国公司/已将其在欧洲的总部/设立于布鲁塞尔。/而且在瓦隆, /各大公司/已经决定设立其欧洲物流中心, /这些公司包括谷歌、/微软、/百特、/卡特彼勒、/强生, /还有中国公司, /如华为、/大唐电信、/中国工商银行/和中国银行, /都已设立欧洲办事处/在瓦隆和布鲁塞尔。/

11:02—11:41

Ladies and gentlemen, /the best location and talents/are not enough. /The human behavior/is still the key point/for long-term relations/and know-how shares. /Build a personal bridge/between men and women from both regions. /To be open to the world/also means integration of world businesses, /comprehensiveness of other people, /other culture/and building our future/as economic and human crossroads. /

女士们、先生们, /最佳的地理位置和人才/还不够。/人类行为/仍很关键, /对于长期关系/和技术共享都很关键。/搭建一座联系的桥梁, /联结这两个地区的人民。/向世界开放/也意味着融入全球商界, /理解他人/和其他文化, /把我们的未来建设成/经济和人类发展的十字路口。/

11:42—12:30

That's why/for China/and for the other emerging countries,/Brussels and Wallonia/provide offices facilities,/inside, in the heart of the Europe in Brussels./The companies/could benefit of/the Brussels' special incubation projects,/to set up an office/in the heart of the Brussels,/and the European decision-making location./In my region and in my agency,/we opened also late 2009/a real China Welcome Office/to host the first international steps for Chinese companies/inside the EU markets./

因此/对中国/和其他新兴国家而言,/布鲁塞尔和瓦隆/提供办公设施,/就在欧洲布鲁塞尔的中心。/公司/可得益于/布鲁塞尔的特殊孵化项目,/将办事处设在/布鲁塞尔市中心,/也就是欧洲的决策中心。/我所在的区域和机构,/在2009年末,也开设了/一个真正的中国迎宾办事处,/帮助中国公司迈出第一步,/进入欧盟市场。/

12:30—12:53

Created just inside the Science & Technological Parks,/the China Welcome Office/is public free services/without any benefits, interests./China Welcome Office/helps the Chinese investors/to develop their business/in the real heart of Europe./

其位置就在科技园区中,/中国迎宾办事处/提供免费的公共服务,/没有任何收益。/它/帮助中国投资者们/发展业务,/进驻真正的欧洲中心。/

12:53—13:34

Very concretely,/China Welcome Office/proposes free offices/and basic furniture/for a three to six months' period,/excluding the telecommunication expenses,/but also soft services/—access to the Belgium and to the European market/in collaboration with different partners,/the business federations,/the European clusters,/the chambers of commerce./But also business lawyers' support/or invitation letters/that are required to apply for long term business visa/for businesses/and family members./

具体来说,/中国迎宾办事处/提供免费办公室/和基本的家具/长达三到六个月的时间,/不含通信费,/还提供软服务:/进入比利时和欧洲市场,/与不同伙伴合作,/包括商业联合会、欧洲集群、商会。/此外,还提供商业律师支持/或邀请函,/用来申请长期商务签证,/提供给企业/及其家人。/

13:34—14:11

This office/also gives Chinese companies the possibility/of testing the markets,/free of charge,/supported by a number of 100 trade commissioners from Belgium/all over Europe,/without getting registered./So, during that time,/the Chinese

第十一单元 招商引资 Investment Promotion

companies/can benefit all of our services/to make sure that the future investment/will be profitable. /This reduces the risks in overseas investments. /

该办事处/还让中国企业有机会/去测试市场,/无需费用。/由 100 名比利时贸易专员提供支持,/他们分布欧洲各地,/测试无需注册。/因此,在这段时间内,/中国公司/可以受益于我们所有的服务,/以确保未来的投资/有钱可赚。/这也降低了海外投资的风险。/

14:11—14:57

To conclude, /ladies and gentlemen, /（let me know,）/and let me now, /（sorry,）/introduce the last Chinese success story in Belgium. /The Wuhan East Lake International Business Incubator, /together with the network of Chinese first incubation centers all over China, /has recently confirmed its decision/to launch its first hi-tech incubator abroad, /and it is in Belgium. /The future China-Belgium Technological Center/is supported by/both governments/and the Ministry of Commerce/and the Ministry of Science & Technology of China. /

最后,/女士们先生们,/（让我知道,）/我现在,/（对不起,）/介绍最后一个中国在比利时成功的故事。/武汉东湖国际企业孵化器,/与中国第一批孵化器中心网一起,/最近证实/将推出其第一个国际高科技孵化器,/就在比利时。/未来中国—比利时技术中心/赞助方包括/两国政府,/中国商务部/和科技部。/

14:57—15:36

This first Chinese Science & Technological Park/to be built around its own shopping mall, /hotel/and general services/will count on 4 sectorial technological incubators/and one multi-sectorial/with the accommodation/and leisure facilities. /This investment of more than 200 million Euros/will lead to the creation of 1000 mixed jobs, /mixed European and Chinese/and this just at the doors of Brussels, /capital of EU. /

首个中国科技园区/会有自己的购物商场,/酒店/和通用服务,/还有 4 个产业技术孵化器/和一个多产业孵化器,/配有住宿/和休闲设施。/这项两亿多欧元的投资/会创造一千个各类就业岗位,/提供给欧洲人和中国人,/就在布鲁塞尔,/这个"欧盟首都"。/

15:36—16:14

This center/aims to attract and support/Chinese high-tech companies/in their approach of the European markets, /and to foster scientific and economic collaborations/between Belgian and Chinese companies. /But also, /as a win-win project between the two continents, /it will provide support/to European SMEs/to strengthen their Chinese

227

knowledge/before testing the Chinese market. /A real mixed center/to gain new common technologies. /

该中心/旨在吸引和支持/中国高科技企业/进军欧洲市场,/促进科技和经济合作,/即比利时与中国企业间的合作。/同时,/作为一个亚欧双赢的项目,/它将支持/欧洲中小企业,/帮助其更多地了解中国,/然后才进军中国市场。/这是一个真正的混合型中心,/能够获取新的共性技术。/

16:14—16:37

I suggest you, /I propose you/to be part of this new bridge/between Europe and China. /As a friend, /you are most than welcome/in our central region in Europe. /I thank you once again for your warm welcome/and for your support to our efforts. /Thank you very much. /谢谢! /

我建议各位,/我提议各位/积极参与,共建合作新桥梁,/促进中欧合作。/你们是我们的朋友,/非常欢迎你们/前往欧洲中部。/再次感谢你们的热情欢迎/和对我们的支持。/非常感谢!/谢谢! /

第十二单元　虚拟现实
Virtual Reality

I. 实战练习一

1. 演讲背景

利物浦大学虚拟工程中心代表应邀出席"虚拟现实产业应用国际论坛"并发表主旨演讲。他在演讲中分享了四个虚拟工程技术在工业中应用的例子，例如利用虚拟工程数字工具帮助宾利公司开发技术和汽车，利用高性能计算技术帮助小型企业实现虚拟可视化和检测产品性能，帮助小企业开发数字技术，把云平台上的虚拟分析与高性能计算连接起来用于保险风险开发和确定保费。

2. 预习词汇

Virtual Engineering Centre 虚拟工程中心
University of Liverpool 利物浦大学
simulation 模拟
automotive manufacturer 汽车制造商
Bentley Motors 宾利汽车公司
digital technique 数字技术
STRIVE/Simulation Tools for Rapid Innovation in Vehicle Engineering 车辆工程快速创新模拟工具
acronym 首字母缩略词
Volkswagen Group 大众集团
physical prototyping 物理原型制造
visual perception 视觉感知
assembly 组装
whole vehicle model 整车模型
knock-on 连锁反应
product release 产品发布
visualization 可视化
augmented reality 增强现实

internal audit 内部审计
problem capture 问题捕捉
dashboard 仪表盘
sequence 次序
external audit 外部审计
body shell 车身
physical model 物理模型
haptic 触觉的
Human Integrated Manufacturing 人体集成制造技术
issue resolution and capture 问题解决与捕捉
templet 模板
knowledge base 知识库
self-sufficient 自给自足
cyber physical system 信息物理系统
ground movement 地面活动
collision avoidance algorithms 避撞算法
real time 实时
sensory 传感的
CIVIC computing CIVIC 计算
automization 自动化
chassis 底盘
LCR4.0/Liverpool City Region Four 利物浦市地区 4.0
VR 虚拟现实
cluster 集群
Industry 4.0 工业 4.0
cyber security 网络安全
cloud computing 云计算
IoT 物联网
up-skilling 技能提升
analytics 分析
cloud platform 云平台
informatics 信息学
situation analysis 情境分析
premium 保费

3. 演讲文本

00:00—00:28

第十二单元 虚拟现实 Virtual Reality

So thank you very much/for inviting me to be here!/I am Andrew Levers/from the Virtual Engineering Centre of the University of Liverpool./The talking I am gonna give/is gonna depart a little bit/from the previous two/in that Bangla described,/how we use simulation/and virtual engineering techniques/in the industry./So I've got three examples,/four examples for you./Here we go./

谢谢/你们的邀请!/我是Andrew Levers,/来自利物浦大学虚拟工程中心。/我的演讲/不同于/前两个演讲/就像Bangla所介绍的,/我们如何将模拟/和虚拟工程技术/运用于工业中。/我将举三个例子,/四个例子说明。/那么我们开始吧。/

00:29—01:04

First,/this is a project/that we have on the tackle/for the last three years/of a very large automotive manufacturer/Bentley Motors/to show how live it up to the digital techniques./So I will talk a little bit more/about general assistance/to small-and-medium-sized companies,/and how we work with them/to develop/and implement digital technologies./So the center has been in existence/in the institute/for over 10 years,/and during that time/we developed/quite a variety or diverse range of expertise/in virtual engineering./

首先,/这个项目/我们还在进行的项目/已经持续了三年了,/是大型汽车制造商/宾利汽车公司的项目,/研究如何利用数字技术。/我会谈一谈/我们提供的帮助/给中小企业,/我们如何与他们合作/开发/和应用数字技术。/我们的中心成立/于大学里面,/已有十余年了,/在这期间,/我们开发了/多种专业技术/都是和虚拟工程有关的。/

01:04—02:33

First,/the project is called STRIVE,/which is an acronym/for Simulation Tools for Rapid Vehicle or Innovation in Vehicle Engineering/conducted for Bentley Motors,/a very famous brand/and a company/that perhaps rooted in craft disciplines,/so every vehicle is pretty much hand-made./And then with themselves,/realize that to improve their time to market,/they would need to use/the digital tools of virtual engineering./And this project was designed specifically for them./Now we go./So three main elements/in the project,/ourselves/as technology providers/and integrators,/Bentley Motors/as the owner/and the people who are actually driving the applications themselves./And then a digital supply chain development exercise as well./So three technology suppliers and providers/OPTIS,/ICONA,/and ValueChain/which develops a display technology/for Bentley./So,/as I mentioned before,/one of the key drivers for Bentley/is to reduce their time to

231

market. /Now before this project, /the typical development time for vehicle/would be, in the old roof, 54 months, /and the targets/given to them by the owner, /which is Volkswagen group, /was to reduce that/by six months, /so a very very tough target/for an automotive manufacturer. /

首先, /这个项目叫做 STRIVE, /全称是/ "车辆工程快速创新模拟工具", /项目是在宾利汽车公司进行的, /宾利是一个知名品牌, /也是一家公司, /起源于手工制作, /因此每一辆宾利汽车都是手工打造的。/宾利公司/意识到为了缩短产品上市时间, /他们需要使用/虚拟工程的数字工具。/STRIVE 项目便是为他们量身打造的。/我们进入正题。/有三大要素/包含在这个项目中：/我们/是技术供应商/和整合方；/宾利公司/是所有者；/还有那些真正推动技术应用的人。/此外还有数字供应链开发活动。/三个技术供应商, /即 OPTIS, /ICONA/和 ValueChain, /他们开发显示技术/给宾利公司。/因此, /我前面提到, /宾利的初衷就是/缩短产品上市时间, /在这个项目之前, /汽车开发时间/用传统方式开发耗时 54 个月。/而目标/是项目所有人制定的, /也就是大众集团/要求缩减/6 个月, /这是一个非常艰巨的目标, /对汽车制造商来说。/

02:33—03:17

Clearly, /because of the nature of the Bentley product, /it's a luxury product, /a lot of the up from design work/involves a lot of physical prototyping, /particularly around the look and feel of component groups, /and how they integrate with each other. /So things like gaps, /visual perceptions/are very important to them. /Previously, /that design for assembly/was only really done/by the development of whole vehicle models. /Of course, /as we are going to design/and manufacture, /the cost of chain, /if there is a problem, /becomes significant, /and has very very large knock-ons, /consequences/for product release. /And this project tries to alter some of that. /

显然, /由于宾利产品的性质, /这是豪车品牌, /包括设计在内的许多工作/都需要大量的物理原型开发, /尤其是部件的外观和感觉, /以及各部件如何组装在一起。/因此间距、/视觉感知等/对他们来说尤为重要。/此前, /组装设计/只需要/整车模型开发。/当然, /由于我们将进行设计/和生产, /生产链成本/如果有问题, /成本就会很高了, /还会产生很大的连锁反应/和后果, /影响产品发布。/这个项目旨在带来一些改变。/

03:17—04:30

So three elements, /manufacturing/and planning processes, /digital supply chain, /so it's not good enough/for the company/or a large company/to merely be able to use

第十二单元　虚拟现实 Virtual Reality

technology. /They have other routes/to develop technology/within themselves/and within their supply base, /and of course, /skills as well. /So there is a shortage of digital skills, /I think, /certainly, /the last presenter emphasized that. /And that inner venturing gap/will not be closed/unless you have digital enabled engineers. /So/three elements, /visualization, /augmented reality, /particularly useful for internal audit. /For that, /I will come on to that. /Virtual manufacture, /and virtual training of operators, /see a bit more. /And problem capture/which quite sounds strange/in a virtual/or a presentation of virtual engineering. /But problems occur/at all stages/in the product development, /so it is important/for business to capture them, /and also to be able/to format the nature of those problems, /to be able to classify them, /to be able to solve them, /and more importantly, /to be able to learn from them, /as they will follow into the future. /

　　以上是三大因素, /即制造、/规划过程、/和数字供应链。/这样还不够好, /如果公司/或者大公司/仅仅使用技术的话。/他们有其它途径/开发技术, /在公司内/或供应基地开发, /当然, /他们也有技能。/数字技术比较缺乏, /我认为, /当然, /前面的演讲嘉宾已经强调了这一点。/内在的创新鸿沟/无法弥补, /除非您有擅长数字技术的工程师。/因此, /三大要素中, /可视化/和增强现实/对于内部审计来说尤其有用。/这一点/现在我就要谈谈。/虚拟制造、/对操作员的虚拟操作培训, /我会谈一谈。/问题捕捉, /听起来有点奇怪, /在虚拟/或虚拟工程的演讲中听上去很奇怪。/但问题会发生, /出现在各个阶段/产品开发的各个阶段, /因此非常重要的是/企业要捕捉这些问题, /并且能够/总结这些问题的性质, /对问题进行分类, /解决问题, /更重要的是/能够从问题中汲取教训, /以防重蹈覆辙。/

04:30—05:34

　　So this is a bit small piece of software/called Pristine/from OPTIS, /and it's used/to evaluate the internal facts, /so it's heavily rendered/a very important feature, /and this particular product/is this gap/between the door/and the dashboard. /One of the major issues/in most of the Bentley product implementation/has been getting that gap right. /So with virtual tool, /it's possible to alter tolerancing/on different components, /or alter assembly sequence, /to understand the perception of the user/on the look and the feel of the product. /Similarly, /external audit/can be performed again, /it's involving operators/looking at gaps/between body shell components, /light, /seatings, /the general look and feel of the products. /So/it's now all on/in the virtual world/without the use of physical models. /

　　这是一个小软件, /叫做 Pristine, /是 OPTIS 公司生产的。/该软件用于/评估内部情况, /因此它有/一个重要的特征。/这个特别的产品有/间距/位于车门/和仪

233

表盘之间。/其中一个主要的问题/影响了绝大多数宾利产品的使用/就是设计一个合理的间距。/有了虚拟工具,/就可以改变公差,/不同配件之间的公差,/或改变组装次序,/可以了解使用者的认知/了解他们如何看待产品的外观和感觉。/同样地,/外部审计/也可以再次进行,/包括操作员/检查间距,/车身部件之间的间距、/灯光、/座椅、/和产品的整体外观与感觉。/所以,/这些现在都可以实现,/在虚拟世界里实现,/无需使用物理模型。/

05:38—07:01

Do we get this to play? /The video? /Yes, here we go. /OK. /So this is an example/of a virtual training. /The lady with the HTC/or the Oculus headset, /various haptic devices, /this controlling, /the man that you see/to assemble a seat model. /So the man he can also contain a representation of the stress/on the operator, /you see the red and green areas, /and she is trying to/assemble a seat/into the vehicle/with variant degree of success. /So/an automotive production/balancing the timing of each operation/is critical. /And this type of tools again, /written specifically for Bentley. /In this project, /this is called Human Integrated Manufacturing. /Again developed by OPTIS, /it's key to that, /so they can produce a virtual model, /all of the assembly, /operation at the assembly line, /to get the takt time correct. /Now we go. /Successful. /

这个视频能播放吗?/视频?/可以。/好。/这是一个例子,/展示一下虚拟培训。/这位女士戴着HTC/或Oculus耳机,/各种触觉装置,/控制设备,/您还可以看到这位男士/在组装一个座位模型。/他还可以再次施加压力/在操作员身上,/您可以看到红色和绿色区域。/她正在试着/将座位组装/到汽车上,/成功率不同。/所以,/在汽车生产中/平衡每一步操作的时间/是至关重要的。/这种工具,/也是专门为宾利开发的。/在这个项目中,/它叫做人体集成制造技术,/也是OPTIS开发的。/它非常关键,/用于生产虚拟模型、/完成组装、/在流水线上操作、/得出正确的节拍时间。/开始。/成功了。/

07:01—08:09

Issue resolution and capture. /A little piece of this software, /developed this time by ValueChain, /was eye-capture. /So you see, /every stage/through from concept design and selection, /through to virtual assessment, /virtual manufacture, /prototyping, /and then production, /will have issues. /And it's important/for any business to capture those issues/in a structured way, /so enable them to learn. /And this piece of software does that. /So you can use templets on the factory floor/to take photographs, /to classify issues. /There will be an automatic formatting/on the line side/to produce problem reports/and problem classifications,/and it can be acted upon quickly/by quality staff. /So that will then integrate into essentially a knowledge base/for the business,/not from one vehicle,/but from multiple vehicles,/to enable that capture of learning. /

　　问题解决与捕捉。/这个小软件/由 ValueChain 公司开发,/用于眼球捕捉。/您可以看到,/每个阶段/从概念设计和选择,/到虚拟评估、虚拟生产、原型制作,/再到生产,/都会产生问题。/非常重要的是/公司要捕捉这些问题,/采用结构化的方式,/并从中学习经验。/这个软件就是起这个作用的。/您可以用工厂车间地板的模板/拍照、/给问题分类、/格式自动编排/在生产线端编排/生成问题报告/和问题分类,/问题很快得以解决,/由质检员工来解决。/然后这些都会整合到知识库里,/供企业利用,/不仅是关于某一辆车的知识,/而是多种车辆的知识,/使得学习捕捉成为可能。/

08:14—09:48

　　So benefits,/really,/everybody,/I think,/will surprise in the project. /I think/the major benefit from problem resolution capture/was something in the overall 48% reduction/in the time taken previously,/using virtual tools/to capture issues/and to find a resolution to them. /You can see/the graph there/really represents that reduction in variability,/as a result of that problem capture. /More importantly,/it brings all the functions of manufacture engineering,/production operations/and sales/into a common voice/with the rest of the business/in the development of future projects. /I am sorry it will keep going back to that. /Cross-functional buying/and validation/to enable a whole company/to speak to each other/has been a key benefit from this project. /The training of the team/has been reduced substantially,/and the skills of the operators and everyone now/is in a very similar skill level. /We are with Bentley,/so able to move forward. /As I said before,/something like 48% reduction/in the time to capture/and resolve problem/as a result of/what actually is a fairly simple virtual technology. /This isn't the end/for the Bentley's journey/into the virtual world,/but what it does represent/is the end of the beginning. /So they are now self-sufficient/in their development/and their ability to specify tool sets. /

　　关于好处,/真的,/每个人/我想/都会对这个项目感到惊叹。/我想/问题解决方案捕捉的最大好处/是总体缩减了 48% 的时间,/时间比之前短,/因为运用了虚拟工具/捕捉问题/和找到解决方案。/您可以看到/那边的图表,/它说明了减少的可变因素/因为使用了问题捕捉所。/更重要的是,/它使得制造工程的所有功能、/生产操作/和销售/步调一致,/与企业的其他部门/在未来项目开发时保持一致。/很抱歉老是跳回那个页面。/跨职能部门采购/和验证/使整个公司/内部能互相对话，/这是该项目的最大好处。/团队培训/大大减少，/操作员以及其他每个人的技能/处在差不多的水准上。/我们和宾利公司/能够继续进步。/我刚才说过，/减少了48%/用于捕捉/和解决问题的时间，/这得益于/一个相当简单的虚拟技术。/这并非终点，/不是宾利公司/进军虚拟世界的终点，/但它的确代表了/这一起点的结束。/现在宾利公司能够自给自足，/开发/和规定工具箱的规格。/

09:48—10:37

So, /the other part of our work. /I mentioned/we have been sort of existence/for over ten years, /and within that time/we developed expertise/in virtually every industrial sector, /and that expertise is fundamentally important/to move learning around. /So we use an integrated system of approach/as you can see, /an example of a cyber physical system. /So you have a ground movement of an aircraft, /and a ground movement of a passenger transport vehicle/running in a virtual world/to test collision avoidance algorithms. /Again/with the virtual models of the airports, /virtual models of the buildings, /but more importantly, /the control system also running in real time/to test various sensory parts. /

那么，/关于我们的其它工作，/我刚才提过，/我们中心成立/已有十余年，/这些年来/我们积累了专业技术，/几乎各个工业领域都有，/这些专业技术至关重要，/有利于推广学习。/我们运用方法集成系统，/您可以看到，/这是信息物理系统的一个例子。/您可以让飞机地面活动/和客运交通工具的地面活动/在虚拟世界运行/来测试避撞算法。/同样地，/借助机场虚拟模型、建筑虚拟模型/但更重要的是/实时运行的控制系统，/来测试各种传感部件。/

10:37—11:19

Another example/of how we view/the virtual engineering standards/with the smaller business. /Instead of developing a digital work floor, /this company produces a single-seat, /high-performance sports vehicle. /And we use cloud technology/to develop a way/for them to access high-performance computing, /civic computing/if you like, /to produce structural automization/and analysis/on the chassis in almost real time, /and then develop acting/to a virtual visualization/of the performance of the products. /In this case/you can see, /at the bottom left, /the deflections on the various little cases. /

这是另一个例子，/用来说明我们是如何看待/虚拟工程标准/及其在小型企业的应用。/没有开发数字工作楼层，/这家公司生产了一款单座驾、性能卓越的跑车。/我们使用云技术/开发一种方式，/使他们能使用高性能计算技术，/叫做CIVIC计算/您可以这样称呼这种技术，/从而实现结构自动化/和分析，/几乎实时地分析底盘/然后开发出动作，/实现虚拟可视化，/检测产品的性能。/在这种情况

第十二单元　虚拟现实 Virtual Reality

下，/您看到/左下角/各种小案例中出现偏斜的情况。/

11:19—12:42

(It keeps going forward.) /Another large project we run, /LCR4.0, /which the acronym stands for Liverpool City Region Four, /which is an assist program/for small businesses/to develop their own digital technologies, /so they all own their own digital technologies. /Visualization, /simulation, /VR/is one technology/in a very important cluster. /Industry 4.0, /which you have heard, /also includes things/like big data, /autonomy, /and cyber security, /cloud computing, /and IoT. /People will not develop their business/unless they consider the full range of digital technologies. /So it's not really just about VR. /In this project, /it's about up-skilling, /and then enabling people to develop their own future strategy. /So the assists that we give business/aren't just technical assists. /They can also be intellectual property, /funding an investment, /planning, /skills generation, /higher skill development. /Some of the digital tools/we have already talked about. /There is a prototyping, /simulation, /and VR work, /and like goes again across all of the industry sectors, /and it's been proven successful/for smaller business. /By smaller businesses/I mean those under maybe 250 employees. /

(PPT一直往前翻页。) /我们另外一个大项目/是LCR 4.0, /全称是"利物浦市地区4.0"。/这是一个支持性项目, /帮助小企业/开发他们自己的数字技术, /使他们都能拥有属于自己的数字技术。/可视化、/模拟、/虚拟现实/是集成的技术, /应用于非常重要的集群里。/工业4.0, /你们也听到过了/也包括以下技术, /如大数据、/自动化、/网络安全、/云计算/和物联网。/人们不可能拓展业务/除非考虑各种各样的数字技术。/所以这个项目不仅仅包括虚拟现实而已。/这个项目, /还包括技能提升、/使人们能提出他们自己未来的策略。/所以我们能给企业的帮助/不仅仅是技术援助, /还有知识产权、/为投资注入资金、/规划、/技能生成、/技能提升等。/某些数字工具/我们已经提及了, /诸如原型制作、/模拟、/虚拟现实, /涉及各种产业, /事实证明这些技术很成功, /可供小企业利用。/我所说的小企业, /指的是员工人数在250人以下的企业。/

12:42—13:32

I will get it right. /To finish a couple very quick, /again tell to you the sub-regions of Algo Risk, /a local business. /It's actually a start-up of a PhD student, /using virtual analytics on a cloud platform/linked to high-performance computing/for insurance risk development. /Another one/using informatics/as a dashboard telecom/linked directly to insurance companies/and to provide situation analysis of drivers'

237

actions/and to just ensure premiums. /So that [those] are the types of projects, /in addition to the engineering projects/that you might typically find/we are now sell for. / I think that's the end of the presentation. /

我会把这个弄好。/我很快地再举两个例子。/一个是位于次区域的 Algo Risk 公司,/一家本地企业。/它实际上是一个在读博士生的初创企业,/将云平台上的虚拟分析/与高性能计算连接起来,/用于保险风险开发。/另一个/是运用信息学,/将仪表盘通讯/与保险公司直接连接起来,/提供对驾驶员行为的情境分析,/以确定保费。/以上就是项目类型,/工程以外的其他项目。/您可能发现了,/工程项目是我们的特色项目。/我的演讲到此结束。/

II. 实战练习二

1. 演讲背景

德国艺术与媒体技术中心的教授应邀参加"虚拟现实产业应用国际论坛"并发表主旨演讲。他主要谈论了如何利用虚拟现实技术拍摄电影,技术应用的挑战、解决方案和拍摄过程中为了创造接近真实的沉浸式体验需要注意的问题,其中重点强调了我们需要处理好电影戏剧拍摄中不同层次的张力和压力。

2. 预习词汇

panorama 全景图
VR/virtual reality 虚拟现实
immersive 沉浸式的
Salvador Dali 萨尔瓦多·达利(西班牙超现实主义画家)
ZKM/Zentrum für Kunst und Medientechnologie 卡尔斯鲁厄艺术与媒体中心
installation 装置
Jeffery Shaw 杰弗瑞·肖
stereoscopic 立体的
coordinates 坐标
dramaturgy 戏剧理论;戏剧作法
parallax 视差
tension 张力
Casablanca《卡萨布兰卡》
Madrid 马德里
negative parallax 负视差
Life of Pi《少年派的奇幻漂流》

Ang Lee 李安（中国台湾导演）
Robert Montgomery 罗伯特·蒙哥马利（美国导演）
Aristotle 亚里士多德
Eisenstein 爱森斯坦（苏联导演）
Einstein 爱因斯坦
Hitchcock 希区柯克（美国导演）
Achilles 阿基里斯（希腊神话人物）
Menelaus 墨涅拉俄斯（希腊神话人物）
Troy 特洛伊
Jules Verne 儒勒·凡尔纳（法国小说家）
Journey to the Moon《月球之旅》（科幻小说）
Apollo 13 阿波罗 13 号
improbability 不太可能之事

3. 演讲文本

00:00—01:20

OK. /Good morning, /and thank you very much/for this honor/of being invited here. /Where I have to put... /OK. /So I'm teaching since 22 years/at the Center of Art and Media Technology/in Germany. /And there/we have built/a new alliance/between technology, art and science. /And for showcasing it, /we created/the International Beyond Festival/and an international symposium/on future design/and future design thinking. /We did/a lot of research, /starting/with 3D film and 360-degree panorama, /following with 3D arts, /3D operas, /TV gaming and sound/and combine it with 3D laser scanning and art of visualization. /And that led us/in the last years/to research on VR learning, /virtually interactive immersive realities, /and this is/what I'm talking about today, /mostly cinematic VR. /

好的。/早上好，/非常感谢你们，/我很荣幸/能够受邀来到这里。/该放哪儿呢……/好的。/我已经教书22年了，/任职于艺术与媒体技术中心，/这个中心位于德国。/在那里，/我们建立了/一个新联盟，/一个技术、艺术和科学的联盟。/为了展示这个新联盟，/我们创办了/一个叫 International Beyond Festival 的国际活动/和一个国际研讨会/专门探讨未来的设计/和未来的设计理念。/我们做了/大量的研究，/一开始是研究/3D 电影和 360 度全景影像，/后来又研究了 3D 艺术、/3D 歌剧、/电视游戏和声音，/并将其与 3D 激光扫描以及视觉化艺术结合起来。/这也使得我们/在过去的几年里/研究了虚拟现实学习，/实际上就是交互式沉浸式现实，/这也是/我今天要讲的主题，/主要是电影中的虚拟现实。/

01:20—02:12

And this is, /we have to start/to think in artistic space-time experiences/and those space-time experiences/started with cave art. /It was not a main narrative, /it was a main experience of space and time. /It went over to the first temples, /to the churches, /to panorama paintings, /stereoscopic, /photography/and stereoscopic film making, /even painters, /like Salvador Dali, /painted two images/to create the left and the right eye/to create space illusions. /In modern times, /like in ZKM, /there were a lot of installations/like installations from Jeffery Shaw's/where you travelled into the space, /in a true virtual space. /And nowadays, /it's getting more and more normal. /We go to the VR game parks, /flight simulations. /

就是说, /我们必须开始/在艺术时空体验中思考, /那些时空体验/起源于洞穴艺术。/这个不是主要的叙述手段, /而是主要的时空体验。/这种体验出现在第一座庙宇当中, /再到教堂, /到全景画、/立体作品、/摄影/和立体电影制作, /甚至画家, /像萨尔瓦多·达利, /画了两幅图, /创造出左右眼, /营造一种空间错觉。/在当代, /像在卡尔斯鲁厄艺术与媒体中心, /就有很多装置, /比如杰弗里·肖的装置, /您穿行于他的装置空间, /置身于一个真实的虚拟空间。/现在, /这个技术变得越来越普遍了。/我们会去虚拟现实游戏公园, /体验模拟飞行。/

02:13—03:55

And the main question/when we come to cinematic VR/is: what have we learned from 3D stereoscopic film making. /So the first thing/is whenever/you work with immersive media/in space time, /you have to/start with a script, /and we have to/make a paradigm change/from frames to in 3D stages. /And when we come to VR, /we have to/think in spheres. /The space needs/and its coordinates need/some meaning, /some aesthetically, /some emotionally, /some intellectual meaning. /We need/a depth dramaturgy, /and immersive stories/have to include/a vertical, /a parallax/and a horizontal tension. /This is completely new. /So when we talk with space, /when we look at 3D films, /normally/most of the 3D films/use space/as a metaphor of space, /which is very simple. /But/you can use space as a metaphor/for emotional networks, /for relationships. /For example, /when we talk to relationship, /we said/we get closer, /we're getting apart. /So whenever/we use language/to describe relationship, /we talk about space. /So it should be easy/to translate this metaphor of relationships/into spaceful, meaningful, immersive media. /But/we can also use/the space/as a metaphor/for the internal character conflict, /for the relationship of consciousness and sub-consciousness. /So/we have the first thing/is paradigm change. /We have to stop/framing the world/like we know as film-maker. /We have

第十二单元　虚拟现实 Virtual Reality

to think/in stages/when it comes to 3D/or in spheres/when it comes to VR. /And there are a couple of/very very basic VR challenges. /

有一个主要的问题，/当我们谈起电影虚拟现实，/这个问题是：我们从 3D 立体电影制作中学到了什么？/首先，/不论何时，/当你们使用沉浸式媒体，/置身于时空之中，/你们都必须/从脚本开始，/而且我们必须/有一个范例的转变，/将框架转换成 3D 阶段。/当我们谈起虚拟现实时，/我们必须/学会从多范围思考。/空间需要、它的坐标也需要/一些意义，/一些美学上的、/一些情感上的、/一些理智上的意义。/我们需要/一种深度的戏剧作法。/且沉浸式故事/必须包括/垂直的、/视差的/和水平的张力，/这完完全全是新的。/所以当我们谈起空间时，/当我们看 3D 电影的时候，/通常/大部分 3D 电影/都利用空间/来隐喻空间，/这很好理解。/但是，/我们可以用空间来比喻/情感网络/和人际关系。/例如，/当我讲到人际关系时，/我们会说，/我们更亲近了/或者我们疏远了。/所以无论何时，/我们用语言/来描述关系时，/我们都会谈到空间。/所以应该很容易/就可以转化这种关系的比喻，/变成充满空间感的、有意义的沉浸式媒体。/但是/我们也可以用/空间/来比喻/内在的人格冲突，/比喻意识和潜意识的关系。/所以/我们做的第一件事/是范式的改变。/我们要停止/用框架去设定世界，/不能像电影制作人常见的那样做。/我们必须思考，/以阶段性方式/思考 3D, /或者分范围/思考虚拟现实。/此外还有一些/非常非常基本的虚拟现实挑战。/

03:55—04:51

The first thing. /In VR, /everything is in the frame. /What does this mean? /It means/where to put the team. /We have to hide the team. /The directors/could not be in the scene. /We have to kind of find ways/where to put the scene. /Where to put the lighting? /You see everything/in the lighting. /How to cut spheres? /This is very complicated, /because/for example, /when I look at him, /and then/I look at you, /normally/my mind/takes out in between. /So/normal film language/is very close/to our cognitive possibilities. /But we never experience/in our life/that we are here in the room, /and then in another room. /But this happens/when we cut from a sphere to a sphere. /So/how to direct the tension? /We can use of course sound. /Whenever hear the sound, /you immediately/make a movement. /So we can still direct with movements. /And our cognitive systems/always work. /When something is moving, /we have to follow it. /Of course, /we can use lighting. /

第一个挑战。/在虚拟现实中，/一切都是设定好的框架。/什么意思呢？/就是说，/把团队安排在哪里。/我们得把团队藏起来。/导演/不可以出现在这个场景中。/我们要想办法/找到地方布景。/灯光打在哪里？/您所看到的东西/都在灯光下。/如何切换空间范围？/这非常复杂。/因为/比如说，/当我看着他，/然后/再看着您，/正常来说，/我的注意力/会在两者之间转移。/所以/正常的电影语言/非常接近/我们的认知状态。但我们从未体验过/这样的生活场景：/我们身处一个房间里，/下一秒又在另一个房间里。/但这种情况会发生/当镜头从一个场景切换到另一个场景的时候。/那么，/如何引导这种张力呢？/我们当然可以使用声音。/无论什么时候听到声音，/您马上/会做一个动作。/这样我们就可以用动作来指挥。/并且我们的认知系统/总会起作用。/当有东西在动的时，/我们的注意力不得不跟随它。/当然，/我们也可以使用灯光。/

04:51—05:46

That the main thing is/that we have to relearn again/how to give spatial coordinates/emotional significance. /For example, /in the film *Casablanca*, /in this time they've thought, /that this red space/is the most sweet space/for a cinema screen. /So the object of desire/is that in this film/was always seated in this place/so that it became an emotional significance. /So even they used the effort/that when they drove through Paris, /they bought an English car, /that you were sitting on the right side/on the screen. /So another thing is/when we work/is new timing. /When you see this painting/in Madrid, /and you see the whole day, /then you go to a hotel, /you come back the next day, /because/you haven't seen it all, /so whenever we create/some very interesting and detailed visuals, /we have to/give the audience really time/to explore it. /

主要是/我们必须重新学习/如何赋予空间坐标/情感意义。/例如，/在电影《卡萨布兰卡》中，/他们认为，/这个红色区域/是最好的，/是电影屏幕上的最佳位置。/所以想要凸显的对象/在这部电影当中/总是被安排出现在这个位置，/因此被赋予了情感意义。/他们甚至努力做到这一点，/比如当他们在巴黎开车时，/他们买了一辆英国汽车，/于是演员就坐在了右边，/出现在屏幕右侧。/另一个挑战是，/当我们操作起来，/另一个挑战是新的时间把控。/当您看到这幅画时，/您人在马德里，/您欣赏了一整天，/然后回酒店，/第二天您又回来，/因为/您还没有看完，/所以每当我们创造了/一些非常有趣的和细节丰富的视觉效果，/我们必须/真的给观众时间/去探索。/

05:46—07:25

So we need to work on/depth-budgeting. /Because/the depth, /which is normally not taught/in film school, /has a very specific meaning, /and it has dramaturgical reason. /We can create contrast/and also for eye relaxation. /So we have/five depth fields. /This is very important/when you kind of consider/how close you want/to get to people. /We have an intimate space. /An intimate space/is almost is/where you kind of still can smell each other, /where you can touch each other. /When something/like a negative parallax/is coming into your intimate space, /you know/more or less/you don't like that. /We have a personal space. /This is/more or less/where we can still touch people. /We have an interactive or social space. /This is for example, /where we are. /Now we/are in an interactive space. /We can react immediately/to a feedback to each other. /We have a public space. /This is, for example, /were you guys off here behind, /I still can see you, /we still can interact, /but we normally/will have no/direct feedback. /If you make a movement, /it doesn't affect me. /And we have a surrounding space. /A surrounding space/normally/has no direct feedback/to an interaction, /but it creates/the atmosphere. /A surrounding space/only creates/a direct reaction or feedback, /when for example, /a volcano explodes/or we have a really heavy weather. /So/normally, /surrounding space, /when you use different spaces/in your VR experience, /you have to/be very careful, /because/every different space/has a very different meaning to/our cognitive possibilities, /to our emotional reaction. /So/this is/where you have to/be very careful/when you have/negative parallaxes/or pop-outs. /

　　所以我们需要做/深度预算。/因为/深度预算/一般没有教授/给电影学校的学生，/但有着非常具体的意义，/且含有戏剧理性。/我们可以创造对比，/这也是为了放松眼睛。/所以我们有/五个深度场域。/这个非常重要，/比如当您考虑/您想要多么亲近/别人的时候。/我们有一个亲密空间。/亲密空间/基本是/你们还可以闻到彼此气味的地方，/是你们可以触摸到彼此的地方。/当一些东西/比如负视差/进入你们的亲密空间时，/你们知道/或多或少/你们会不喜欢。/我们有一个私人空间，/这是/或多或少/我们仍可以接触到人的地方。/我们还有一个互动或社交空间。/例如，/我们现在所处的空间便是。/现在我们/正处于一个互动空间。/我们可以立即做出反应，/回应彼此的反馈。/我们有一个公共空间。/举个例子，/假如你们离开这里到后边去，/我还是能看到你们，/我们仍然可以互动，/但一般/我们不会有/直接的反馈。/如果你们做了一个动作，/也不会影响到我。/我们有一个周围空间。/周围空间/通常/没有直接的反馈/去回应互动。/但是它营造了/气氛。/周围空间/只会产生/直接的反应或反馈，/例如，/火山爆发，/或者我们遇上非常恶劣的天气。/所以/通常情况下，/周围空间，/当你们使用不同空间/运用到虚拟现实体验中的时候，/你们必须/非常小心，/因为/每一个不同的空间/有非常不同的意义，/对我们的认知而言意义不同，/对我们的情感反应意义也不一样。/所以/这就是/你们得/非常谨慎的地方，/当你们运用/负视差/或画面弹出时要注意这一点。/

07:25—08:32

When we made 3D films, /the first idea of 3D film/was always sticking something/into your audience. /But most of the time/the audience the first is/they didn't like it. /And the other thing, /it immediately/crashed the illusion, /because you said, / "Oh, I'm in a 3D film." /So one thing, /which is really important for me/ and which is normally/not really understood, /whenever you start writing/for a new media, /you have to/have the media in mind, /you have to/write different screenplays/for 3D films/or for VR/then to other films. /Whatever/is not in the script/ cannot be staged. /Not a single director/can add something/like only effects/if it's not meaningful in the screenplay. /And this is/one of the few possibilities/at the end of *Life of Pi*/by Ang Lee, /where you see in the screenplay, /the last scene/is in the screenplay it writes, /the depth of the whole image/is kind of vanishing, /and the color/is gone, /but the sound/goes towards the cinema. /So/when you have such ideas/already planned in the screenplay, /then it's easy/for a director/to understand/ and to direct meaningful space time. /

当我们制作3D电影时，/第一个关于3D电影的想法/就是要把一些东西/塞给观众。/但是大多数时候，/观众首先是/不喜欢这些东西的。/此外，/这些东西立刻/破坏了幻觉。/因为大家会意识到：/"哦，我是在看3D电影。"/所以有一点/对我来说真的很重要，/这一点一般/也不会被理解，/也就是无论何时你们开始写作、/为新媒体写作，/你们都必须/把媒体放在心里，/你们必须/写不同的剧本/用于3D电影/或者虚拟现实/和其他电影。/任何东西/不在脚本中的/就不能搬上舞台。/没有哪个导演/能添加东西，/比如只添加特效，/除非这些特效在剧本中有实际意义。/这是/为数不多的例外，/出现在《少年派的奇幻漂流》的片尾，/导演是李安，/你们在剧本中可以看到，/最后一个场景/剧本是这么描写的，/整个画面的深度/逐渐消失，/颜色/也消褪了，/但声音/传入电影院。/因此，/当您有了这些想法/且已经在剧本里规划好了，/那么就很容易/让导演/去理解/并指导出有意义的时空。/

08:33—10:21

So/one of the most important things/when we think of VR/is, /I call it, /our customer/is an electron observer. /It's like an electron. /We don't know/where he is/ or where she is. /We don't know/where they look at. /And we have to explain them/ why they are in the scene. /They have a first person point of view. /For example, / because/the scene/is not reacting to them, /but/they are in the scene, /so/there must be/an explanation. /There was one film/in the 1947, /from Robert Montgomery, / where the whole film/was filmed/in the first point of view, /you always were/the main character. /And it completely flopped. /People didn't like it. /So/when we now go to VR, /we have to/kind of create ideas, /or stories' ideas, /why the person/is in the scene. /The easiest thing is/when we have an active participant, /when we interact with the data/and thus the world reacts. /But this then/starts/to get more complicated. /So/when you interact with data, /you come what I called/ "data-driven narratives". /So/when we talk, /I said/that space experience, /artistic space experience/existed/since cave time. /But/what we have/since Aristotle/is a dramaturgic theory:/how to tell story, /how to tell story in time. /And now, /we have to kind of/combine the idea of dramaturgical storytelling/to space time experience. /And I call this/we have to go from story structure/to story architecture. /We have to/create a complete new visual language, /and I always said/it's something between/Eisenstein and Einstein, /something about relativity theory, /and a new language of film-making. /

所以/最重要的事情之一, /当我们想到虚拟现实时, /就是, /我是这么说的, /我们的客户/是电子观察者。/就像一个电子, /我们不知道/他在哪里/或者她在哪里, /我们不知道/他们在看哪里。/而且我们必须向他们解释/为什么他们会出现在场景里, /因为他们处于第一人称视角。/例如, /因为/场景/没有对他们做出反应, /但是/他们又在场景中, /所以/必须/有一个解释。/有一部电影, /拍摄于1947 年, /导演是罗伯特·蒙哥马利, /整部电影/拍摄/都是第一人称视角, /观众一直是/主角。/但这部电影彻底惨败了。/观众不喜欢。/所以, /当我们现在谈到虚拟现实时, /我们必须/创造想法, /或者故事的理念, /即为什么这个人/出现在场景中。/最简单的就是, /当我们有积极的参与者时, /当我们与数据互动时, /周围的世界会做出反应。/但这就/开始/变得更加复杂了。/因此, /当您与数据交互时, /就会出现我所说的/ "数据驱动的叙述"。/所以/我们说, /我说过/空间体验、艺术空间体验/一直存在, /起源于洞穴时期。/但是/我们所拥有的/自亚里士多德以来/便是戏剧理论, /即如何叙述故事, /在时间上如何讲述故事。/而现在, /我们必须/把讲故事的戏剧理论/和时空体验结合起来, /我称之为/我们必须从故事框架/走向故事体系。/我们必须/创造一种全新的视觉语言, /而且我总是说/它介于/爱森斯坦和爱因斯坦之间, /是关于相对论的东西, /是一种新的电影制作语言。/

10:21—11:08
So/the first thing is, /the whole drama theory/since Aristotle/was/how to work in time, /how to compress time. /And Hitchcock/always said, /film is life/without the boring parts. /We organize/a tension in time. /What is/completely not explored yet/but we have to/explore it/when we go to immersive media... /is? /I know. /One first thing, /every good drama, /every real drama, /has three levels of tensions/or

three levels of stress. /We have an outer plot conflict, /a relationship conflict, /and an inner character conflict. /So/when we add these/to those four possible space time tensions, /then we have/a temporal tension, /a horizontal tension, /a vertical tension/ and a parallax tension. /

所以/第一件事是, /整个戏剧理论/自亚里士多德之后/都是关于/如何处理时间, /如何压缩时间。希区柯克/常说, /电影就是生活/剔除掉无聊的那部分。/我们安排/时间的张力。/什么是/完全还未被探索的/但是我们必须/探索的、有关沉浸式媒体的, /是什么呢?/我知道。/首先, /每一场精彩的戏剧, /每一部真正的戏剧, /都有三个层次的张力/或三个层次的压力。/我们有外在的情节冲突、关系冲突/和内在的性格冲突。/所以/当我们把这些添加/到那四种可能的时空张力时, /我们就会得到/一个时间的张力、/水平的张力、/垂直的张力/和视差张力。/

11:09—12:02

And a horizontal tension, /the x-axis, /this is what I call/an erotic motivation, /but erotic motivation/not in the sense of erotic in a sexual sense, /but in the Greek sense of Aristotle. /It was everything/what is wanna-have driven, /what is greed-driven. / When we want/to have something, /we move normally horizontal/towards it. /So/ whatever we want to have/is a horizontal tension. /But/we also have/a vertical tension. /The whole evolution/is more or less/a vertical tension. /A vertical tension/is more or less/combined with another, /with an inner character conflict, /and this is/ what the old Greece Aristotle called/the Tripodic Tension. /And the Tripodic Tension/ is not the wanna-have tension, /is the wanna-become tension. /And that can explain/ very shortly, /when we look at Achilles. /

水平张力, /X轴, /这就是我所说的/欲望动机, /但欲望动机不是/指性爱层面上的, /而是希腊哲人亚里士多德认为的动机。/意思是一切/都是欲望驱动的, /贪婪驱使的。/当我们想要/得到某物时, /我们通常会水平移动/向它靠近。/所以/无论我们想要什么, /都是水平张力。/但是/我们也有/垂直张力, /整个进化过程/或多或少是/垂直张力。/垂直的张力/或多或少/与另一个张力相结合, /与内在的性格冲突结合, /这就是/古希腊的亚里士多德所称的/三脚张力, /而三脚张力/不是想要获得某物的张力, /而是想要成就自我的一种张力。/这个解释起来/很简单, /我们看看阿基里斯就知道了。/

12:02—13:19

When Achilles/was asked by Menelaus/to join him/in Troy War, /he despised this guy, /but he asked/his mother/if he should go to Troy. /And his mother said, / "If you stay here, /you become/a rich king, /you will have/a lot of wives and children. /

If you go to Troy, /you die, /but thousands of years, /people/will still sing songs/ about you." /And he immediately went to Troy. /This is a Tripodic Tension. /So/ when we create/the last tension, /I call it/it's the first dimension. /it's parallax tension, /it's how close your audience is/towards protagonists, /towards the scenes. / So this is/a drama theory/we developed/for 3D films, /where we use/all those different character conflicts, /outer conflicts, /and put them into/space time meaningful tension relationships. /And we are now working/doing dramaturgical models/for different VR cinematic VR experience. /We will look like/this is a work/where we are now a consultant/of a VR project. /We try to kind of use/all those different levels of conflict, /all these different levels of space/and all the different levels of coordinates/to create/a meaningful VR dramaturgical story. /

当阿基里斯/被墨涅拉俄斯叫去/和他一起/参加特洛伊战争时,/他鄙视这个人,/但他问/母亲/他是否应该去特洛伊。/他的母亲说:/"如果你留在这里,/你会成为/一个富有的国王,/你会有/很多妻子和孩子。/如果你去特洛伊,/你会死,/但是几千年后,/人们/仍然会唱歌/歌颂你。"/于是他马上就去了特洛伊。/这就是一种三脚张力。/所以/当我们创造/最后一种张力时,/我把它叫做/第一个维度,/就是视差张力,/它表示观众有多近,/离主角/和场景有多近。/这就是/一个戏剧理论,/我们发展出来/用于3D电影的理论,/我们使用/所有那些不同的角色冲突、/外部冲突,/并将它们放入/时空中有意义的张力关系中去。/我们现在正在/做戏剧模型,/用于不同的电影虚拟现实体验。/我们会看到,/这是一个作品,/我们在其中充当顾问,/服务于虚拟现实项目。/我们试图利用/所有那些不同层次的冲突、/所有这些不同层次的空间、/以及不同层次的坐标/来创造/一个有意义的虚拟现实戏剧理论故事。/

13:20—15:00

So it's a short time, /so I can not explain it/too much in detail, /but/I want/to describe a little bit/an overall project/what we are working in/and it's future design thinking. /And future design thinking/is normally, /we imagine/and we simulate desirable futures, /and then/we count it down/to the present. /We do not take the present/as a next step here. /We try to imagine/where we wanna go, /and from there, /we kind of count down/to the present/to find a way of/to kind of really design/ new ideas and new stories. /And one of the thing/which is for me very important:/ you, me, humans/are story-driven animals. /The morning/we wake up, we believe in/ unbelievable things. /If it's religion, /if it's culture, /if it's nation, /it's all a story. /But it becomes/an inter-subject phenomenon, /because/when so many people/ believe in/the same story, /it becomes/a reality, /and it even can become/a deadly reality/what we see/for example/in religions. /But/it's still a story. /So/even the economics/is a story. /The moment we don't believe in/the dollar anymore, /the dollar/will drop/to zero. /So/it's just a story. /As long we believe in/the dollar, /it will have/some value. /The moment we stop/believing it, /it has no value anymore. /So/we have to understand/this power of story. /So/today's ideas of narratives/are the foundations of tomorrow's history. /The stories you invent/are the foundation of tomorrow's history. /

因为时间有限, /我无法解释得/太过详细, /但是/我想要/描述一下/一个整体的项目, /也是我们正在做的一个项目, /就是未来的设计理念。/未来的设计理念/通常是, /我们想象、/我们模拟理想的未来, /然后/我们把它变成/现实。/我们不把现在/作为下一步。/我们试着想象/我们想要去往哪里, /并从那里/回到/现在, /找到一种方法/真正地去设计/新的想法和新的故事。/有一点/对我来说非常重要: /你们, 包括我自己, 所有人类/都是故事驱动的动物。/早上/我们醒来, /我们相信了/不可思议的事情。/不管是宗教, /还是文化, /还是国家, /都是一个故事。/但是它变成了/一种主观互证的现象, /因为/当那么多人/相信/同一个故事, /它就会成为/现实, /它甚至可以成为/一个铁铮铮的现实, /我们看到/例如/宗教便是如此。/但/它仍然是一个故事。/因此, /甚至经济学/也是一个故事。/当我们不相信/美元的时候, /美元/就会贬值/为零。/所以/美元只是一个故事。/只要我们相信/美元, /它就会有/价值。/当我们不再/相信它的时候, /它就不再有价值了。/所以/我们必须理解/故事的力量。/因此, /今天的叙事理念/是未来历史的基础。/您编的故事/是未来历史的基础。/

15:00—16:17

So/I came up/with this idea. /This is an image/from 1873/from the novel of Jules Verne, /*Journey to the Moon*. /And when you see this, /this rocket/already looks like Apollo 13, /only it has/a steam engine, /because/in this time, /the only energy/could be a steam engine. /So/the main question is:/has Jules Verne/looked into the future/or has he created future? /And I believe/he has created future. /By putting the story, this idea, /in the heads of thousands of young people/and then/technology/changed, /and then/those people/became/engineers and astronauts, /and then/they flew/to the moon/with a vehicle/which was kind of designed/in a novel/more than a hundred years before. /So/my desire is this:/with future design, /artists and students/create/not only new design, /but they create/a new narrative/for the future, /creating probabilities/and desirable improbabilities. /It's not about impossibilities. /Impossibilities/are impossible. /But/the moment we create/a desirable improbability/and a lot of people/believe in, /it become truth. /So/we can do that/beyond the limitation of

248

life. /

　　所以/我有了/这个想法。/这张图/创作于1873年,/来自于儒勒·凡尔纳的小说/《月球之旅》。/当你们看到这幅图,/你们会发现这个火箭/看起来就像阿波罗13号,/只不过它有/一个蒸汽引擎,/因为/在那个时候,/唯一的动力/是蒸汽机。/所以/主要问题是:/儒勒·凡尔纳/是否展望到了未来,/或者说他创造了未来?/我认为/他创造了未来。/通过把故事和这个想法/灌输给成千上万的年轻人,/然后/技术/改变了,/然后/那些人/成为了/工程师和宇航员,/然后/他们飞去了/月球,/乘坐的交通工具/被设计出来/是在小说里,/一百多年前就设计好了。/所以/我希望,/通过未来的设计,/艺术家和学生/创造的/不仅仅是新的设计,/而且他们创造的/是一种新的叙述方式,/去描述未来,/创造可能性/和看似不可能的事情。/我说的不是不可能的事情。/不可能的事情/就是不可能。/但/当我们创造了/一种看似不可能实则又值得拥有的的事物,/并且很多人/相信,/那么它就会成真。/所以/我们是可以做到的,/可以超越生活的限制。/

16:18—17:23

One last thing. /I don't like London too much, /but/whenever I'm in the subway/in London, /I get reminded/what art is all about. /Because/every time/you hear/this phrase, /"Mind the gap. Mind the gap." /And the gap/is what art is all about. /When you/stand in front of a beautiful image, /you feel/your personality, /your own feelings, /your own desire, /your own experience/into the gap to the artwork. /When you watch a movie, /you see the movie, /but/you feel/your own experience too/into the gap towards the movie, /what means/when we work with/almost real immersive media, /we have to/be very careful/to mind the gap. /If we create/a complete immersion, /we make our audience/stupid and helpless. /So/whenever you create/new media, /new immersive media, /take care of/your audience, /and mind the gap. /谢谢! /

　　最后一点。/我并不是特别喜欢伦敦,/但是/每当我在地铁站、在伦敦坐地铁的时候,/我都会想起/什么是艺术。/因为/每次/我都会听到/这句话:"请注意站台的空隙。请注意站台的空隙。"/而空隙/就是艺术的意义所在。/当你们/站在一幅美丽的画前,/你们会感觉到/自己的个性,/自己的感觉,/自己的欲望,/以及自己的体验,/掉入艺术作品空隙的体验。/当你们看电影时,/你们看着电影,/但是/你们感受到/你们自己的体验,/掉入电影空隙的体验。/这意味着,/当我们使用/近乎真实的沉浸式媒体时,/我们必须/非常小心地/注意到空隙。/如果我们创造了/一个完全沉浸的效果,/我们就会让我们的观众/看起来愚蠢又无助。/所以,/无论何时您创造了/新的媒体,/新的沉浸式媒体,/都要照顾到/观众,/并且注意这个空隙。/谢谢! /

参考文献

秦亚青,何群. 英汉视译 [M]. 北京:外语教学与研究出版社,2009.
王炎强. 视译基础 [M]. 北京:外语教学与研究出版社,2011.
仲伟合,詹成. 同声传译 [M]. 北京:外语教学与研究出版社,2009.